D1535126

# SPINOZA

# S P I N O Z A

BY

JOHN CAIRD

BOOKS FOR LIBRARIES PRESS
FREEPORT, NEW YORK

First Published 1888
Reprinted 1971

INTERNATIONAL STANDARD BOOK NUMBER:
0-8369-5877-2


LIBRARY OF CONGRESS CATALOG CARD NUMBER:
75-164593


PRINTED IN THE UNITED STATES OF AMERICA

# PREFATORY NOTE.

THE materials which the author had prepared for this book were found greatly to exceed the limits assigned to it. He has therefore, besides other parts of his plan to which special reference need not here be made, been compelled to leave out the account of Spinoza's life and letters, and to confine the work to an examination of his philosophical system. This is the less to be regretted that the life has been so fully narrated in the recent works of Mr Pollock and Dr Martineau. These works contain, also, very able and elaborate expositions of the Spinozistic philosophy, but this book attempts to deal with that philosophy from a point of view different from that of either of these writers.

# CONTENTS.

# SPINOZA.

## INTRODUCTION.

A GREAT system of philosophy is exposed to that kind
of injustice which arises from the multiplicity of its
interpreters, and from the fact that these interpreters
are apt to contemplate and criticise it, not from the
point of view of its author, but from their own. Critics
and commentators of different schools and shades of
opinion are naturally desirous to claim for their own
views the sanction of a great writer's name, and unconsciously exercise their ingenuity in forcing that sanction
when it is not spontaneously yielded. If any ambiguities or inconsistencies lurk in his doctrines, they are sure
to be brought to light and exaggerated by the tendency
of conflicting schools to fasten on what is most in accordance with their own special principles. And even
when a writer is on the whole self-consistent, it is possible for a one-sided expositor so to arrange the lights
and shadows, so to give prominence to what is incidental
and throw into the shade what is essential, as to make
him the advocate of ideas really antagonistic to his own.

More, perhaps, than most systems of philosophy, that of Spinoza has been subjected to this sort of misconstruction. Doctrines the most diversified and contradictory have been extracted from it. Pantheism and atheism, idealism and empiricism, nominalism and realism, a non-theistic naturalism as uncompromising as that of the modern evolutionist, and a supernaturalism or acosmism which makes as little of the world as the *Maya* of the Buddhist — have all alike found a colourable sanction in Spinoza's teaching. A philosophy apparently as exact and logically coherent as the Geometry of Euclid or the Principia of Newton, has proved, in the hands of modern interpreters, as enigmatical as the utterances of the Jewish Kabbala or the mystical theosophy of the Neo-Platonists. To the vision of one observer, it is so pervaded and dominated by the idea of the Infinite, that he can describe its author only as "a God-intoxicated man." To the acute inspection of another, the theistic element in it is only the decorous guise of a scientific empiricism — a judicious but unmeaning concession to the theological prejudices of the author's time, or an incongruous dress of medieval scholasticism of which he had not been able wholly to divest himself.

Whilst some at least of those heterogeneous notions which have been fathered on Spinoza have no other origin than the mistakes of his modern critics, there are, it must be acknowledged, others which indicate real inconsistencies. It is true, indeed, that the controversies of subsequent times may easily read into the language of an early writer decisions on questions of which he knew nothing. "Philosophers of an earlier age," it has been said, " often contain, in a kind of implicit unity, different aspects or elements of truth, which in a subsequent time become distinguished from and opposed to each other." They make use, in a general and indeterminate way, of terms which later controversies have stamped with a special significance ; they may thus seem to answer questions which they never put to themselves, and may easily be got to pronounce seemingly inconsistent opinions on problems which they never thought of solving. The eager controversialist catches at his pet phrase or *mot d'ordre*, and hastily concludes that the old writer speaks in the distinctive tone of the modern polemic. But obviously the inconsistencies which thus arise are inconsistencies only to the ear. It may be possible to get Spinoza to side in appearance with the modern evolutionist or with the modern spiritualist, to make him an individualist after the fashion of Mill or Spencer, or a universalist who speaks by anticipation with the voice of Schelling. But if such attempts are made, they are mere philosophical anachronisms. The problems which they seem to solve are problems which, when the supposed solutions were given, could not even be propounded.

Yet it is impossible to ascribe the discordancy of Spinoza's modern interpreters only to the necessary ambiguity of their author's language. His philosophy is not a completely homogeneous product. It may rather be said to be the composite result of conflicting tendencies, neither of which is followed out to its utmost logical results. If we say in general terms that philosophy is the search for unity, the effort of thought to gain a point of view from which the contrast variously expressed by the terms the One and the Many, the Universal and the Individual, the Infinite and the Finite, God and the World, shall be reconciled and harmonised, then we shall look in vain, in the philosophy of Spinoza, for one consistent solution of the problem. No solution can be regarded as satisfactory which suppresses or fails to do justice to either of the extremes, or which, though giving alternate expression to both, leaves them still in merely external combination without being reconciled for thought. Yet, at most, the latter result is all that the philosophy of Spinoza can be said to achieve. There are parts of his system—such as the reduction of all finite individuals to modes or accidents of the absolute substance, and the assertion that all determination is negation—in which the idea of the infinite is so emphasised as to leave no place for the finite, or to reduce nature and man, all individual existences, to unreality and illusion. There are parts of his system, on the other hand—such as his assertion that the individual is the real, his ascription to each finite thing of a *conatus in suo esse perseverandi,* his rejection of general ideas as mere *entia rationis,* his polemic against teleology, his use of the term "Nature" as a synonym for "God"—which seem to give to the finite an independent reality that leaves no room for the infinite, or reduces it to an expression for the aggregate of finite things. Thus the system of Spinoza contains elements which resist any attempt to classify him either as a pantheist or an atheist, a naturalist or supernaturalist, a nominalist or a realist. As he approaches the problem with which he deals from different sides, the opposite tendencies by which his mind is governed seem to receive alternate expression ; but to the last they remain side by side, with no apparent consciousness of their disharmony, and with no attempt to mediate between them.

But though it may be conceded that the philosophy of Spinoza is not self-consistent, or contains elements which, if not irreconcilable, are unreconciled, it does not follow that the task of the expositor of Spinoza is limited to what is involved in this concession. Inconsistency may arise not so much from incompatible principles as from defective logic. Contradictory elements may have been admitted into a system, not because its author looked at things from different and irreconcilable standpoints, but because he failed to see all that his fundamental standpoint involved ; not because he started from different premisses, but because he did not carry out what was for him the only true premiss to its legitimate results. As moral defects assume an altogether different aspect according as they are regarded as the expression of a retrograding or of an advancing moral nature—as willing divergences or as involuntary shortcomings from its own ideal—so intellectual inconsistencies may mean more or less according to the attitude of the mind from which they proceed. It may be possible to discover, through all a man's thoughts, a dominant idea or general tendency, and to explain his inconsistencies as only unconscious aberrations from it. It may even be possible to discern, underneath apparent contradictions or abrupt transitions from one point of view to another, an implicit unity of aim—the guidance of thought by an unconscious logic towards a principle of reconciliation not yet fully grasped. And if any such dominant idea or implicit aim can be detected in a great writer, it cannot fail to throw light on the general character and bearing of his speculations, and it may enable us to pronounce whether and to what extent in his seeming inconsistencies he is only unfaithful to himself, or inadequately representing his own idea.

Now there are various conceivable indications by which we may be aided in detecting this undercurrent of tendency in the mind of a philosophical writer. We may be able, for instance, to learn something of the motive of his speculations—to discover in his previous spiritual history what it was that constituted for him, so to speak, the original impulse towards philosophy, and that secretly guided the process by which intellectual satisfaction has been sought. Or again, we may know something of the helps which have been afforded him in the search for truth, of the studies on which his opening intelligence has been fed, of the sources from which he has derived inspiration, of the books or authorities which consciously or unconsciously have moulded the substance or form of his thoughts. Or finally, we may have the means of viewing his system in the making, of watching the working of his mind and the development of his ideas from their earlier and cruder shape to the form which they have finally taken. We may be able thus to see which, if any, of the conflicting elements in his thought has gradually tended to prevail over the others, and to which of them therefore, though the victory to the last may be incomplete, the place of the ruling or characteristic principle must be ascribed. We may find it possible in this way to pronounce of the blots which disfigure his system in its final form, that they are not radical inconsistencies, but only irrelevances or excrescences foreign to its essential character.

Now we are not without such helps to the understanding of the Spinozistic philosophy. In the first place, we possess in the preface to the treatise 'Concerning the Improvement of the Understanding' an autobiographical fragment in which Spinoza narrates what may be termed the origin and development of his spiritual life, and from which we gain a clear insight into the motive and genesis of his philosophical system. In the second place, we have information, direct and indirect, as to Spinoza's early studies in philosophy. From his own testimony, from the internal evidence supplied by his writings, and from other sources, we know something as to the authors ho had read, the intellectual atmosphere in which he grew up, the authorities which may have influenced the formation of his opinions. Lastly, we have in Spinoza's earlier works the means of tracing the gradual development of those ideas which took their final systematised form in the 'Ethics.' Especially in the 'Treatise concerning God and Man,' which has been brought to light only in our own time, we possess what may be regarded as an early study for the 'Ethics,' embracing the same subjects and dealing with the same fundamental ideas, but presenting them in a cruder and less coherent form, and exhibiting the conflicting tendencies of the later work in harder and more unmodified opposition to each other. From these various sources some help may be derived towards the right apprehension of Spinoza's philosophy and the explanation of its apparent ambiguities and inconsistencies.

# CHAPTER I.

THE ETHICAL MOTIVE OF SPINOZA'S PHILOSOPHY — THE
TREATISE 'CONCERNING THE IMPROVEMENT OF THE
UNDERSTANDING.'

THE impulse towards philosophy was not in Spinoza's
mind a purely intellectual one. His philosophy is the
logical sequel to that of Descartes, but the Cartesian
philosophy only supplied or suggested a dialectic for convictions that were the independent growth of his own
moral and spiritual experience. He was prompted to
seek after a method of knowledge because primarily he
sought after spiritual rest. It was the consciousness
that the dissatisfaction and disquietude which the ordinary desires and passions engender had their ultimate
source in a false view of the world—in other words, that
the contemplation of the world from the point of view
of the senses and the imagination bred only perturbation
and unrest—which led him to ask himself whether that
point of view is not an illusory one, and whether it is
possible to penetrate beneath the shows of things to their
hidden essence. Nor is this account of the origin of
Spinoza's philosophy a mere conjecture. The introduction to the unfinished treatise above named is, as we

have said, a kind of spiritual autobiography, in which the author explains to us what were the moral difficulties and aspirations in which his speculative inquiries originated. He tells us what is the view of the true end and goal of human existence to which his own experience had led him, and he points out the means by which he conceived that that end could be attained. His philosophy took its rise, he tells us, not primarily in the search for intellectual satisfaction, but in the endeavour to discover some true and abiding object of love, something in finding which he would find a perfect and eternal joy—a joy which could not be found in the ordinary objects of human desire—in riches, honour, the pleasures of appetite and sense. All these objects experience proved to be deceptive and inconstant, difficult and uncertain of attainment, and when attained bringing only disappointment and disquietude.

"Our happiness," he says, "depends entirely on the quality of the objects to which we are attached by love. For, on account of that which is not loved, no strifes will ever arise, no sorrow if it perishes, no envy if others possess it, no fear, no hatred, no perturbation of mind—all of which come upon us in the love of things which are perishable, as are all those things of which we have spoken. But love to a thing which is eternal and infinite feeds the mind only with joy—a joy that is unmingled with any sorrow ; that therefore we should eagerly desire and with all our strength seek to obtain."[1]

The end of all human endeavour, therefore—that in which consists the perfection and blessedness of our nature—is union by love with an infinite and eternal

[1] De Int. Emend., i.

object. But love, according to Spinoza, rests on knowledge; or rather there is a point of view in which, for him, feeling and intelligence, knowing and being, are identified. The sure and only way to attain the end we seek is to know things as they really are, to disabuse our minds of error and illusion; and for this purpose what is chiefly needed is a discipline of the intelligence, " a method," as he expresses it, " of curing the understanding and of so purifying it that it may know things as well as possible and without error." But all knowledge, he repeats, has a value for him only as it is directed to one end and goal—viz., the attainment of that highest human perfection of which he had spoken—and everything in the sciences which does not bring us nearer to that end he will reject as useless. The task, therefore, which in this treatise he proposes to himself is the devising, not of a method of knowledge or organon of the sciences in general, but of a means of attaining that kind of knowledge, or of apprehending all things in that aspect of them, which will lead to the attainment of moral and spiritual perfection.

It is unnecessary, for our present purpose, to follow out in detail the successive steps by which Spinoza works out his conception of the true method of knowledge. The general drift of the treatise may be said to be this, —to set before us an ideal of true knowledge, and to point out the way in which that ideal is to be realised. In contrast with the kind of knowledge which constitutes the content of our ordinary unreflecting experience, that knowledge which can be said to be real and adequate must be intuitive or self-evidencing; it must apprehend its objects in their unity or their relation to each other as parts of one absolute whole; and it must see them in their right order, or in their relation to the first principle of knowledge, so that the order of our thoughts shall "correspond to the exemplar of nature," or represent the real order of things. The knowledge of the ordinary, unreflecting consciousness is, in the first place, merely second-hand and unintelligent, it is derived from hearsay, or from loose and unsifted experience. True knowledge, in contrast with this, must be that in which the mind is in immediate relation to its object, in which truth is seen in its own light, or, as Spinoza expresses it, "in which a thing is perceived solely from its own essence, or from the knowledge of its proximate cause." Ordinary knowledge, again, is disconnected and fragmentary, it looks at things apart from each other, or in the accidental order in which they are presented to the common observer of nature, or connected with each other only by arbitrary associations. In contrast with this, true knowledge is that which breaks down the false isolation and independence which popular imagination gives to individual objects; it regards the universe as a whole, in which no object exists for itself, or can be understood save in its relations to other objects and to the whole. It discerns, or seeks to discern, the real relations of things, or what is the same, the rational relations of the ideas of things; and therefore it is fatal to all such connections or combinations of ideas as rest on accident or arbitrary association. For the same reason, lastly, true knowledge is that which not only sees its objects as related to each other, but sees them in that definite relation of ordered sequence which is determined ultimately by the first principle out of which they spring. There are certain ideas on which other ideas rest. Spinoza rejects the "universals" of scholastic metaphysic as mere *entia rationis* or fictions of the imagination. Yet we are not left to the impossible task of attempting to collect or string together in thought the infinite multiplicity of finite and changeable things. There are certain ideas which come to us in the place of universals, and which gather up our knowledge into that unity which by means of the fictitious universals was sought after. "There are," he tells us in language the precise significance of which we cannot at present examine, certain "fixed and eternal things, which, though they are individual, yet on account of their omnipresence and all-comprehending power become to us as universals, or as genera in the definitions of individual changeable things, and as the proximate causes of all things."[1] Finally, there is one highest idea, that of "the most perfect Being," which is the source and explanation of all other ideas, as it represents the source and origin of all things. That knowledge therefore alone can be termed adequate which proceeds from and is moulded by this supreme or central idea. "That our mind," says he, "may thoroughly reflect the exemplar of nature, it must evolve all ideas from that which represents the origin and source of all nature, so that that idea may appear to be the source of all other ideas."[2]

Such, then, is Spinoza's theory of knowledge : how is it to be reduced to practice? What, in other words, is the true method of knowledge? What Spinoza says in answer to this question in the present treatise amounts to little more than this, that we should endeavour to

---

[1] De Int. Emend., xiv.  [2] Ibid., vii.

become possessed of what he calls "true ideas," and that
we should by means of the highest of all ideas seek to
reduce them to unity, or endeavour " so to order and
concatenate our ideas that our mind shall represent
objectively (*i.e.*, in thought) the formality (*i.e.*, objective reality) of nature, both as to the whole and as to its
parts." [1]

Spinoza does not atttempt here to investigate the relation of mind to nature, of thought to its object. He assumes that a true idea is something different from its
object, the idea of a circle from an actual circle, the idea
of the body from the body itself : but he takes for granted
that the former agrees with or adequately represents the
latter. To verify a true idea we need not go beyond itself.
" Certitude is nothing but the objective essence (the
idea) itself ; the way in which we perceive the formal
essence is itself certitude." [2] We may, indeed, have a
reflex knowledge of our ideas—make one idea the object
of a second idea, or, in modern phraseology, be not only
conscious but self-conscious. Yet, in order to the attainment of knowledge, it is no more necessary to know that
we know, than, in order to know the essence of a triangle,
it is necessary to know the essence of a circle. But
though it is possible to have true ideas without reflecting
on them, and even to reason correctly without a knowledge of logic or the principles of reasoning—ideas, both
in themselves and in their relations, being their own
evidence — yet this does not hinder that, for lack of
reflection and by reason of various prejudices, people
often mistake error for truth and go wrong in their
reasoning, so that " it seldom happens that in the inves-

[1] De Int. Emend., xii.          [2] Ibid., vi.

tigation of nature they proceed in proper order." Hence arises the need for method, "which is nothing but reflected knowledge or the idea of the idea." [1]

What this means is that we do not need to go outside of thought in search of a criterion of truth, inasmuch as this would virtually be the demand to excogitate a method of thought before we begin to think, to learn to swim before we go into the water. We cannot criticise the forms of thought without using them. Ideas must, so to speak, criticise themselves. In reflecting on them, making them objects of consciousness, they determine their own nature and limits, and so become capable of being used as the instruments of further knowledge.

"True ideas," Spinoza says, constitute themselves "the inborn instruments of knowledge" which the understanding makes for itself by its own native force. Having grasped a true idea, we have only to direct the mind's operations so as to make the given true idea "a norm according to which we shall understand all things." Method, in short, consists in bringing ideas to self-consciousness, and then in using them as the principles of investigation. Having a true idea—such as, *e.g.*, that of Causality—you become conscious of it, understand and define it ; and thenceforward it is no longer used at random, unintelligently, but becomes a principle of method or a guide in future inquiries. Knowledge thus acquired will possess, so far, the characteristics which have been laid down as constituting the ideal of knowledge ; it will rest on ideas or principles which are their own evidence, and it will, instead of a mere collection or combination of things

---

[1] De Int. Emend., vii.

arbitrarily associated, consist of parts related to each other by links of reason or necessary thought.

But there is a further and more important element which method must include ere it can be adequate to the whole field of knowledge. Knowledge must remain imperfect until we can contemplate all things from the point of view of their absolute unity. True ideas may serve as provisional instruments of thought; but their main use is that we may, like a workman who uses ruder implements to construct more perfect ones, fashion by means of them " other intellectual instruments, by which the mind acquires a farther power of investigation, and so proceeds till it gradually attains the summit of wisdom." [1] Each true idea, Spinoza seems to teach, furnishes us with a term of thought which serves so far to correct the false independence which imagination gives to individual objects; but that idea itself needs to have its individuality dissolved in a higher conception. As all things in nature " have commerce with each other, *i.e.*, are produced by and produce others "—are, in other words, reciprocally causes and effects—so each idea or term of thought is only a focus of relations, a transition point in a systematic whole; and ideas rise in importance according as they extend over a wider portion of the realm of knowledge. But if this be so, that knowledge must still be imperfect which stops short of the highest and most comprehensive idea in this intellectual hierarchy. Not only must individual objects yield up their false independence, but ideas themselves must surrender in succession their isolated authority, until we reach that which is " the

[1] De Int. Emend., vi.

fountain and source of all other ideas "—the idea, as Spinoza terms it, of "the most perfect Being."

"That method will be good which shows how the mind is to be directed according to the norm of a given true idea. Moreover, since the relation between two ideas is the same with the relation between the formal essences (objects) of these ideas, it follows that that reflective knowledge, which is that of the idea of the most perfect Being, will be more excellent than the reflective knowledge of other ideas ; that is, that method will be the most perfect which shows how the mind is to be directed according to the norm of the given idea of the most perfect Being." [1]

"If we proceed as little as possible abstractly, and begin as soon as possible with the first elements—*i.e.*, with the source and origin of nature—we need not fear deception. . . . No confusion is to be apprehended in regard to the idea of it (the origin of nature), if only we have the norm of truth, as already shown. For this is a Being single, infinite—*i.e.*, all being, and beyond which there is no being." [2]

"As regards order," again Spinoza writes, "and that we may arrange and unite all our perceptions, it is required that, as soon as it can be done and reason demands, we inquire whether there is any being, and, at the same time, of what sort, which is the cause of all things, as its objective essence is also the cause of all our ideas ; and then will our mind, as we have said, reproduce nature as completely as possible ; for it will contain objectively both its essence and its order and unity." [3]

What then, the question arises, are we to understand by this "most perfect Being," "Being, single, infinite, all-embracing," the idea of which constitutes, according to Spinoza, the first principle of knowledge ? Is it something above nature, outside of the cosmos of finite

---

[1] De Int. Emend., vii.  [2] Ibid., ix.  [3] Ibid., xiv.

things and relations, though itself the source or cause
of all things? Or is it, though the highest, only one of
the elements which constitute nature, the first principle
of the system of related phenomena, but itself essentially part of that system? Or again, is it only a synonym
for Nature, the totality of individual things and beings,
and is this identification of nature with " the most perfect Being " merely a concession to theological prejudices,
whilst really nothing more is meant than that the universe is to be conceived of as an ordered system of things?

According to one of the ablest of Spinoza's recent ex-
positors, " the idea of the most perfect Being includes,
if it is not equivalent to, the belief that the whole of
nature is one and uniform," which belief is " the very
first principle of science." " In knowing the 'most
perfect Being,' " he adds, " the mind also knows itself
as part of the universal order and at one with it, therein
finding, as we have to learn elsewhere, the secret of
man's happiness and freedom. What more Spinoza
may have meant is doubtful, that he meant this much
is certain." [1] Spinoza, he further explains, whilst " attached by an intellectual passion to the pursuit of exact
science," was also " attached by race and tradition to
the Hebrew sentiment of a one and only Supreme
Power ; " and in this he seems to find the explanation
of the fact that Spinoza clothed the purely scientific
idea of the unity and uniformity of nature in the theological guise of " the most perfect Being." Spinoza, he
tells us, " follows in form and even in language the
examples made familiar by theologians and philosophers under theological influence and pressure, who had

[1] Pollock's Spinoza, p. 136.

undertaken to prove the existence of a being apart from and above the universe. He does not simply break off from theological speculation, and seek to establish philosophy on an independent footing; he seems intent on showing that theological speculation itself, when reason is once allowed free play, must at last purge itself of all anthropomorphism and come round to the scientific view. Spinoza does not ignore theology, but provides an euthanasia for it." [1] Many of Spinoza's other modern interpreters have convinced themselves on various grounds that Spinoza's system is one of pure naturalism, that his highest principle does not go beyond the conception of an all-embracing, all-dominating, but unconscious nature-force, and that we should not misconstrue him if we substituted the word " Nature " for " God," wherever the latter occurs in his philosophy.

It cannot, we think, be questioned that the view taken by these writers is so far true that in Spinoza's system " theological speculation has," in Mr Pollock's graphic phrase, "purged itself of anthropomorphism." Spinoza's God is certainly not the supramundane potentate or "magnified man" of popular thought, or even the " all-wise Creator and Governor " of natural theology. Whatever else the idea of " the most perfect Being " means, it is an idea which is supposed to constitute a principle, and the highest principle, of knowledge —at once its own evidence and the evidence or explanation of the whole finite world. But an outside Creator or Contriver is a notion which explains nothing. Not only does it reduce the God who is placed outside the world to something finite, but it is essentially dualistic.

[1] Pollock's Spinoza, p. 166.

The link between God and the world, according to this notion, is a purely arbitrary one. To find in God the explanation of the world implies that the existence of the world and all that is in it is traceable to something in the nature of God, and not to His mere arbitrary will or power. A cause which thought can recognise as such is one which contains in it the reason and necessity of the effect, and which reveals itself in the effect. But a personified cause, which of its mere will produces an effect it might have refrained from producing, is an impossible conception. In such a conception cause and effect stand apart, and the gap is not filled up for thought by the interposition of an arbitrary, omnipotent will. To find in God the first principle of all being and of all knowledge implies a relation between the principle and that which flows from it—between God and the world—such that, in one point of view, God would not be God without it; and on the other hand, the world would not be what it is, would be reduced to unreality or nonentity, without God. Now this, as we have seen, is what Spinoza does, or attempts to do. The "most perfect Being," whatever else the phrase means, is a Being the idea of which is the first principle of knowledge, the key to the meaning of the whole system of being. Without this central principle, finite things and beings have no existence other than the illusory existence and individuality which imagination ascribes to them—are mere fictions and unrealities. And on the other hand, to anticipate Spinoza's favourite illustration, from this fundamental principle all things follow as necessarily as from the conception of a triangle follow the equality of its angles to two right angles, and all its other properties. If, therefore, Spinoza's system can only be redeemed from naturalism by the idea of an anthropomorphic God — the *deus ex machina* of popular theology—a pure naturalistic system it is.

The exclusion of the notion of an anthropomorphic God does not, however, of necessity reduce a system of philosophy to pure naturalism. A principle which explains nature is not therefore, to say the least, a part of nature. It is possible to derive from such a principle all that renders the facts of nature intelligible without regarding it as itself one of these facts. The definition of nature may indeed be so widened as to include in it the idea or principle which constitutes the world an ordered or rational system; but in another and truer sense that principle may, and properly must, be contemplated as something prior to and above nature. The treatise before us is, as above said, an unfinished work, and it does not contain except inferentially any explanation of what its author meant by the idea of the "most perfect Being." But if we take into view the general drift and intention of the work—if, in other words, we consider the motive from which it starts, and the general bearing of its theory of knowledge, we shall be led, I think, to see in Spinoza's "most perfect Being" something very different, at once from crude supernaturalism, and from the pure naturalism with which it has been sought to identify it.

1. The knowledge of the "most perfect Being" as the constitutive principle of the world is the formal expression of the result to which Spinoza was led by his search for that spiritual satisfaction and rest which he could not find in "the things that are changeable and

perishable." His examination of the principles of knowledge had given theoretical justification to his dissatisfaction with the ordinary objects of human desire, by
proving that these objects have no reality save the fictitious and illusory reality which imagination lends to
them. And the presumption with which he started,
and which indeed constituted the implicit ground of his
discontent with these objects — viz., that there must
exist "something eternal and infinite, love to which
would fill the mind with joy and with joy alone," now
finds verification in the rational idea of a "most perfect
Being," "a Being single, infinite, and beyond which
there is no being." Now, however intense may have
been Spinoza's "intellectual devotion to the pursuit of
exact science," the process just described is, we think,
one which that formula does not cover. If it did, then
the attitude of mind to which, under whatever modifications, the designation "religion" has been given, must
be something essentially indistinguishable from "the
passion for exact science." For, however foreign to
Spinoza's nature much that passes under the name of
religion must be pronounced to be, his account of the
mental experience that constituted the impulse to speculative inquiry is that of a process in which the very
essence of religion may be said to lie. If we pass beyond the "fetichism" of barbarous races, the mere in-
discriminating ascription of mysterious powers to material objects (which is as irrelevant to the religious
history of the world as the other phenomena of savage
life are to the history of morality and civilisation), the
religious life of man may be said to have its root in
what, for want of a better description, may be called

Pantheism. The dawn of religious feeling may be traced to the impression which experience forces upon us of the unsubstantial character of the world on which we look and of which we form a part. In different ways this sense of the illusoriness of the world may come to different men and different races, according to their less or greater depth of nature. The apparent shifting of the outward scene, the lapse of time, the impossibility of staying the passing moment to question what it means, the uncertainty of life and the insecurity of its possessions, may be to one what to another is its inner counterpart, the changing of our opinions, feelings, desires, which, even if the world remained steadfast, would perpetually make and unmake it for us. Or again, the sense of the illusoriness of life deepens into weariness and disgust or into a sense of shame and remorse, in the man who reflects on himself and feels himself the sport of it, who has detected the vanity of his desires and hopes, yet is powerless to emancipate himself from their dominion. Now it is this sense of the unreality of the world regarded from the point of view of ordinary experience which not merely gives rise to the longing for some fixed and permanent reality, "some Life continuous, Being unexposed to the blind walk of mortal accident," but is in itself, in a sense, already the implicit recognition of the existence of such a Being. Arguments from "design," which conclude from the existence of finite things to a God conceived of after the analogy of a maker of machines, are not a true expression of the natural history of religion. Such arguments are only the afterthought of an imperfect philosophy. It is not the reality, but the unreality, of

the finite world that gives rise to the consciousness of
God. It is not from the affirmation, but from the
negation, of the finite that the human spirit rises to the
conception of the infinite. And when we reflect on
what this process, this elevation of spirit means, we
discern that what is second in time is really, though
implicitly, first in thought. The very consciousness of
a limit is the proof that we are already beyond it. God
is not the conclusion of a syllogism from the finite
world, but the *prius* or presupposition which reveals its
presence in the very sense of our finitude and that of
the world to which we belong. The impression that
oomoo to us first in time is that the world is nothing;
but that impression would have no existence or meaning if the thought really though latently first were not
this—God is all. It is not, of course, meant that the
process we have described is one which all who experience it experience in the same manner. Like all nor-
mal elements of human experience it varies, as we have
said, with the varying character and the wider or narrower culture of individuals and races. In the deeper
and more reflective natures it manifests itself chiefly in
the consciousness of an inner life other and larger than
the life of sense, of a self that transcends the natural
desires. With widening experience of life this consciousness deepens, since wider experience only furnishes
new materials for the contrast between the multiplicity
of impressions and the self that is identified with none
of them. Advancing intellectual and moral culture
brings with it the profounder consciousness of an infinite possibility within us, of being greater than our
sensations and desires, of capacities to which the out-

ward life is not adequate. This consciousness, rightly interpreted, is a negative which involves a positive. It is the revelation in us of a something that is not of us, of a perfect, by comparison with which the imperfection of ourselves and the whole complex of finite existences is disclosed. Reflecting on the meaning of the discord between itself and its desires, the consciousness of a thirst that is unquenchable by the world becomes to such a nature the presumptive proof of " an infinite and eternal object, love to which would fill the mind with unmingled and abiding joy."

Now if there be any truth in the foregoing analysis of the movement of mind of which we speak, it is obviously one which cannot be identified with the processes of physical science, and the result of which could never be generated by empirical observation of the facts and phenomena of the world. It may be—if there be no other dialectic than the logic of the sciences, it undoubtedly is—a movement which reason does not justify, inasmuch as it puts more into the conclusion than is contained in the premisses, or rather, as we have seen, inasmuch as its conclusion is the negative of the premiss with which it seems to start. If it evaporates anything as " a dogmatic dream," it is not God but nature. The object to which it concludes is not one which is contained in, or can by any process of generalisation be extracted from the facts of nature, or identified with its " laws of coexistence and succession." If scientific experience be experience of change and laws of change, by no straining can this be identified with an experience which is that of an object beyond all change or possibility of change. At any rate, logical or illogical, scientific or

unscientific, the attitude of mind which Spinoza records
as that which constituted for him the impulse to speculative inquiry is identical, or in close analogy, with that
which in the history of mankind has been the origin and
secret nerve of what we mean by the word "religion."

2. But the negation of the finite is not the last step
in the process of which I have spoken. Neither religion,
nor philosophy which seeks to develop the logic of religion, can rest content with an idea of God from which
no explanation of the finite world can be derived. Even
if the independent existence of finite things be an illusion, the idea of God must contain in it a reason if only
for their illusory existence. The shadow, though it be
but a shadow, must have its reason in the substance it
reflects. To say that the infinite is the negation of the
finite, implies that there is in the infinite at least a
negative relation to the finite. But it implies something
more than this. The recognition of the inadequacy of
finite objects is not only the expression of the implicit
consciousness of an infinite object, but also of my relation
to that object. It is through something *in me* that I
am capable of pronouncing the verdict of reality and unreality. If therefore, on the one hand, I belong to the
finite world which, as an independent reality, is negated,
on the other hand, there is a side of my nature in which
I belong or am inwardly related to that infinite and
eternal reality which negates or annuls it. If I deny my
own reality as part of the finite world, I in one and the
same act reassert it as essentially related to God. It is
this which explains what may be termed the positive side
of that mental experience which formed the starting-
point of Spinoza's investigations. The inadequacy or

unreality of the finite was to him an implicit revelation, not only of an infinite and eternal object, but also of himself as in essential relation to it. And what he was thus implicitly conscious of he seeks to make explicit.

It is, we think, from this point of view that we must interpret Spinoza's attempt—partially fulfilled only in the fragmentary treatise before us, burdened with conflicting elements even in the later work in which it finds systematic embodiment—to reaffirm and explain the reality of the finite world in and through the idea of the infinite. But though in the present work the thought which forms the fundamental principle of his system is left undeveloped, it is possible, from the general drift and bearing of the treatise, to divine in some measure the meaning he attached to that principle, and the direction in which its development must lie. And, considered in this light, it is impossible, I venture to say, to find in Spinoza's philosophy only that pure naturalism with which it has been identified, or to regard the meaning of his "idea of the most perfect Being," as exhausted by any such formula as "the unity and uniformity of nature."

It is no doubt possible, as already said, so to define "Nature" as that it shall include both finite and infinite, the multiplicity of individual things, and the principle which gives them unity. If we mean by the universe all reality, then to say that there is nothing outside of it, that nature or the universe is all, is only an identical proposition.

Moreover, as we have seen, nothing can be more unquestionable than that Spinoza's God was no transcendent *deus ex machina*, existing apart from the world, or

connected with it only by the unintelligible bond of an
arbitrary creative act. Again, it may be conceded that
we do not as a matter of fact begin by forming a conception of God as the principle of all things, and then,
by a separate mental act or process of thought, bring this
conception to bear on the world of finite, individual
existences. Observation and experience are, it may be
granted, the only instruments of knowledge in this sense,
that the principle which gives unity to knowledge is
grasped, not apart from, but as inseparably implicated
with, the facts and phenomena observed or experienced.
But the real and only important question is, whether it
is Spinoza's doctrine that the individual, the things of outward observation, or the world as a collection or sum of
finite existences, are the sole constituents of knowledge
—whether there is not involved in real knowledge or
knowledge of realities, a principle of unity distinguishable from the manifold of phenomena, a universal distinguishable from the sum of particulars, an infinite and
eternal distinguishable from the finite and changeable,
not given by it, logically prior to it. If this question
be answered in the affirmative, it matters not whether
you give the name God or Nature to the universe ; in
neither case is Spinoza's system a pure naturalism.

Now it might seem, at first sight, to preclude any such
answer that, for Spinoza, individual things *are*, in one
sense, the only realities, and that he regards general
ideas or " universals " as one of the chief sources of error
and confusion.

" When anything," says he,[1] " is conceived abstractly, as

---

[1] De Int. Emend., ix.

are all universals, it is always apprehended in the understanding in a wider sense than its particulars can really exist in nature. Further, since in nature there are many things the difference of which is so slight as almost to escape the understanding, it may easily happen, if we think abstractly, that we should confuse them." And again : "We ought never, when we are inquiring into the nature of things, to draw any conclusions from abstract notions, and we should carefully guard against confounding things which are only in the understanding with those which actually exist."[1]

Whilst, however, here as elsewhere, Spinoza wages a constant polemic against the "universals" or abstract notions of scholastic metaphysic, and treats as nugatory any conclusions that rest on such premisses, this by no means implies that he excludes from knowledge every universal element—every element other than that which is generated by observation of particular facts. The very context from which the foregoing passages have been taken renders any such inference impossible. His denunciation of the abstractions of scholasticism is introduced expressly to contrast these false, with what he deemed true, universals. Deception arises, he tells us, in a passage already quoted, from conceiving things too abstractly.

"But," he adds, "such deception need never be dreaded by us if we proceed as little as possible abstractly, and begin as soon as possible with the first elements, that is, with the source and origin of nature. And as regards the knowledge of the origin of nature, we need have no fear of confounding it with abstractions. . . . For, since the origin of nature, as we shall see in the sequel, can neither be conceived abstractly,

---

[1] De Int. Emend., xii.

nor can be extended more widely in the understanding than it actually is, nor has any resemblance to things that are changeable, there is no need to fear any confusion in regard to the idea of it, if only we possess the norm of truth, and this is a being single, infinite, *i.e.*, it is all being and beyond which there is no being."[1] And again he says : " It is to be remarked that by the series of causes and of real entities, I do not understand the series of individual changeable things, but only the series of fixed and eternal things. For the series of individual changeable things it would be impossible for human weakness to attain to . . . because of the infinite circumstances in one and the same thing of which each may be the cause of the existence or non-existence of the thing ; since the existence of things has no connection with their essence, or, as I have just said, is not an eternal truth. It is, however, not at all necessary to know their series, since the essences of changeable individual things are not derivable from their series or order of existing, for this gives us nothing but external denominations, relations, or, at most, circumstances which are foreign to their inmost essence. The last is only to be sought from fixed and eternal things, and at the same time from the laws that are inscribed in these things as their true codes, according to which all individuals both take place and are ordered ; yea, these changeable things depend so intimately and essentially, so to speak, on those fixed things, that without them they can neither exist nor be conceived. Hence those fixed and eternal things, although they are individuals, yet on account of their omnipresence and all-comprehending power, are to us as universals or as genera of definitions of the individual changeable things, and as the proximate causes of all things."[2]

From these and other passages in the treatise it is impossible, we think, to avoid the conclusion that Spinoza's "nominalism" did not imply, *either* that indi-

[1] De Int. Emend., ix.      [2] Ibid., xiv.

viduals, finite objects, the facts and phenomena of
empirical observation, are the only realities, *or* that
there are not universals other than the abstract essences
of scholasticism which constitute a necessary element of
all true knowledge. In the first place, when we ask
what are the individuals of which it can be affirmed
that they constitute the only realities, it is to be considered that the individuality or independence which
ordinary observation ascribes to particular objects is no
real individuality. Ordinary observation contemplates
things under the external conditions of space and time,
and so it can begin and end anywhere. It conceives as
an independent reality whatever it can picture to itself
as such. Even scientific observation does not go beyond
the conception of the system of things as a multiplicity
of separate substances, each endowed with its own
qualities, and all acting and reacting on each other
according to invariable laws. But when we examine
more closely what this so-called individuality means,
we perceive that it is a mere fictitious isolation or independence, which it is the function of advancing knowledge to dissipate. Objects are not abstract things or
substances, each with a number of qualities attached to
it. The qualities by which we define the nature of a
thing are in reality nothing else than its relations to
other things. Take away all such relations, and the
thing itself ceases to have any existence for thought.
It is the qualities or relations which constitute its definite
existence : the substance in which they are supposed to
inhere, and which remains one and the same through all
the manifoldness of its properties, if detached from them
would have no meaning. At most, it would be but a

name for the bare abstraction of being or existence ; and
when we think away the predicates or properties, the
substance vanishes with them. But if the qualities by
which we determine any object are simply its relations
to other objects, then, inasmuch as each individual object
is directly or indirectly related to all other objects, completely to determine any individual, to see what it really
is, is to see it in its relation to all other objects. An
object cannot be perfectly individualised until it is perfectly universalised. In other words, knowledge of it
in its complete individuality would be knowledge of it
as determined by the whole universe of which it is a
part. True knowledge, therefore, does not begin with
individuals regarded as mere isolated singular things ;
nor is it the apprehension of the universe as a collection
of such individuals, nor any generalisation got from them
by a process of abstraction. In so far as it is knowledge
of the individual, it is of the individual which has become more and more specialised by each advancing step
in the progress of science, by every new and higher conception which exhibits it in new and hitherto unobserved
relations ; and the ideal of true knowledge cannot stop
short of the conception of each individual in its relation
to the highest universal, or seen in the light of the whole
system of being in its unity. It is this conception of
individuality to which Spinoza points when he speaks
of individuals as the only realities. For him the individuals of ordinary observation are as much unrealities,
figments of the imagination, as the abstract essences of
the schoolmen, they are "the individual, changeable
things the existence of which has no connection with
their essence," and the "accidental series" of which "it

is not at all necessary to know." The true " essences "
of individuals are to be discerned only in their relation
to what he calls " fixed and eternal things and their
laws, according to which all individuals exist and are
ordered," and " without which they can neither exist
nor be conceived," and, above all, in their relation to
that which is the " highest norm of truth, a being single,
infinite, and all - comprehending." So far, therefore,
from asserting that knowledge begins with individuals
regarded as the only realities, he tells us that " that
method of knowledge would be the most perfect in
which we should have an idea of the most perfect Being,
to the knowledge of which, therefore, it becomes us as
soon as possible to attain," and that our mind can only
reflect the exemplar of nature by deriving all its ideas
from that which reflects the source and fountain of
nature—*i.e.*, the " idea of the most perfect Being."

In the second place, it is implied in what has now
been said that Spinoza's " nominalism " does not involve
the denial of universals other than the abstractions of
scholasticism, as constituting a necessary principle or
factor of true knowledge. What are these universals,
and especially, what is that " idea of the most perfect
Being " which is the highest universal or first principle
of knowledge ? We have seen that a recent expositor
of Spinoza finds nothing more in it than the idea of
" the unity and uniformity of nature."

Even if we could suppose that by the " idea of the
most perfect Being " Spinoza meant nothing more than
the scientific conception of the unity and uniformity of
nature, the supposition would be fatal to the assertion
of his " thorough-going nominalism." Nominalism re-

gards individual substances as the only realities, and nature as, at most, a name for the collection or aggregate of such substances. But the unity and uniformity of nature is the first principle of all science. All scientific investigation proceeds on the tacit assumption that nature is not a chaos, but a system of invariable coexistences and successions constituting a self-consistent whole. "It is an assured fact that discoveries are not made without belief in the nature of things, by which I mean the sure trust that under all diversity of appearances there is a constant and sufficient order, that there is no maze without a clue. Belief in the nature of things is the mainspring of all science and the condition of all sound thinking."[1] But if this be so, it seems beyond question that a belief which is presupposed in all scientific observation and experience cannot itself be a product or part of that experience. It is from observation and experience that we learn what are the particular sequences of phenomena in nature, what are the particular causes or conditions of particular effects ; but the idea or principle of uniform sequence with which we start cannot itself be learnt from experience. To the unreflecting mind nature seems to reveal its own unity and uniformity. The objective world is a ready-made system, and the only function of intelligence is to observe and investigate what is already presented to it in its complete reality. Nature in its unity and uniformity is given to us, ready to be taken up into our experience ; the facts and phenomena and their unity and uniformity are things of the same order, and our knowledge of both comes from the same source. We

[1] Pollock's Spinoza, p. 142.

have before us a world organised into unity, and then our consciousness simply reproduces it. But a little reflection teaches us that this is not the true account of the process of knowledge. Our knowledge of nature as an ordered system implies a principle which is not natural, and which cannot be observed as we observe the facts of nature. Experience of difference implies already the presence of a principle of unity, experience of successions or changes the presence of a principle that is constant or self-identical. A process of change cannot be conceived to generate a consciousness of itself, still less to generate a consciousness of change according to a uniform method. In order to the minimum of scientific experience, the observation of a single sequence of related facts, there is presupposed in the observer the consciousness that the relation is an unalterable one, that the same conditions will and must ever give the same result; in other words, there is presupposed the idea of uniformity. But that which is the *prius* or pre-condition of all knowledge of the facts of nature cannot be itself one of those facts or the result of the observation of any number of such facts. The idea or principle, therefore, which is the necessary condition of all knowledge of nature, without which there could be for us no nature, and in the light of which all particular facts or objects are known—this, though it is not a universal, like the abstract essences of scholastic realism, may be said, in Spinoza's language, "on account of its omnipresence and all-comprehending power, to take the place of a universal, or a genus of definition of individual changeable things."

But by the idea of "the most perfect Being," can we

suppose that Spinoza meant no more than that of "the unity and uniformity of nature"? Or if he did mean something more, if the latter formula does not exhaust the meaning of the former or of the equivalent expression, "a Being single, infinite, and all-comprehending," can we form any conjecture as to what that something more is? The answer to this question would carry us beyond the contents of the work before us. This much at least we can gather from it, that Spinoza's speculative inquiries originated in his moral and spiritual aspirations, and that in both his endeavour was to rise above the illusoriness and unreality of the finite. The unrest inseparable from desires and passions that point only to finite and changeable things is itself implicitly the aspiration after an infinite and eternal object, in which the spirit can find perfect satisfaction and rest. And true knowledge, following in the steps of aspiration, discovers to us the unreality of the world as it appears to sense and imagination, and has for its aim to rise above the finite and to grasp that primary idea or first principle which is the source of all other ideas, in the light of which the fragmentary, contingent, confused aspect of things will vanish, and all things will be seen in their unity and reality as parts of one intelligible whole.

# CHAPTER II.

CONCEDING that the philosophy of Spinoza is not thoroughly self-consistent, we have said that it may be possible to discover what was the dominant idea or prevailing tendency in its author's mind, and to see in its inconsistencies, not so much the presence of irreconcilable principles, as an inadequate apprehension of the meaning and results of one leading principle. One help towards the right understanding of his system we have found in Spinoza's own account of the motive of his speculations, the impulse which originated and guided the process by which he endeavoured to attain intellectual satisfaction. Another help may be found in what we know of his early studies, and of the writers who may have moulded his mind or given a special direction to his thoughts.

Much ingenuity has been spent, perhaps we might say misspent, in tracing the supposed "sources" of Spinozism. Not only has it been regarded by many writers as the logical development of the Cartesian philosophy, but, in so far as it diverges from the latter, it has been represented as reflecting or reproducing the mystical theosophy of the Kabbala, or the ideas of Maimonides and other medieval Jewish philosophers, or the revived Platonism of Giordano Bruno and other writers of the fifteenth and sixteenth centuries.

But it is to be considered that the originality of a philosophical writer is not to be determined simply by the measure in which his ideas are traceable to earlier sources, or by the suggestions he has caught up from other minds. To lend real value to any contribution to philosophy it *must* reproduce the past, the sole question is whether the reproduction is a dead or living repro-duction, a *réchauffé* of old materials collected from various sources, or a revival of them, absorbed, trans-formed, renewed, by the quickening, transmuting power of speculative thought. On the other hand, no doubt, a great philosophical system must advance beyond the past; but the all-important test of the new element is, whether it is connected with the past as a mere arbitrary increment, or as the outcome of an organic development. The history of thought cannot, from its nature, be an arbitrary one. It is true that, as the formation of individual opinion may be deflected by a thousand acci-dents from the order of reason or rational progression, so the history of the thought of the world may be some-times the record of what is accidental and irrational—of errors, vagaries, reactions, incoherencies : but in both, in so far as there is real progress, it is a progress which must follow the order of reason—an advance by steps, each of which contains in it a reason for the next, each of which is at once the result and the explanation of that which preceded it. The merit, therefore, of any individual thinker, must be determined mainly by con-sidering whether he takes up and carries on the move-

ment of thought at the particular stage which it has
reached in his own day.   If his work have real or permanent value, it will be due, indeed, to his own productive activity, but to that as an activity which has
for its necessary presupposition the intellectual life of
the past, growing out of it and determined by it.   Consciously or unconsciously he must make that life his
own.   The originality of his work will consist, not in
his independence of the thought of the past, but in this,
that whatever ideas or suggestions he may have gathered
from various thinkers of various times, all his acquire-
ments have become fused in a mind that is, so to speak,
in sympathy with the dialectic movement of the spirit of
its time.   His greatness, if he be great, will be that of
one who has at once put and answered the questions
for the solution of which the age is pressing, given artic-
ulate expression to the problem of philosophy in the
form in which it is silently moving the thought of the
world, and either partially or completely furnished the
solution of it.

   That the merit of originality in the sense now indicated may be justly claimed for the philosophy of
Spinoza, we shall endeavour to show in the sequel.   But
though the solution of the problem of philosophy to
which he was led was logically involved in, and grew
out of the teaching of Descartes, it is not inconsistent
with this to say that it is one for which he was in some
measure prepared and predisposed by the intellectual
atmosphere of his early life, and by the literature and
traditions which created it.   In the ideas imbibed from
the speculative mysticism of the Kabbala, from the
teaching of medieval Jewish rationalists, and from the

Platonic or Neo-Platonic revival of times near his own, we may discern, though not the logical origin, at least the predisposing impulse towards the pantheistic side of Spinoza's philosophy.

## THE KABBALA.

No direct reference to the Kabbala is to be found in Spinoza's writings, with the exception of one sentence in the 'Tractatus Theologico-politicus,' the contemptuous tone of which has been supposed to settle the question of his indebtedness to Kabbalistic speculation. "I have read," says he, "and, moreover, been (personally) ac- quainted with certain Kabbalistic triflers, at whose folly I cannot sufficiently wonder." But this depreciatory judgment, it has been pointed out, has special reference to the arbitrary and grotesque method of interpretation by which Kabbalistic writers endeavoured to extract a hidden significance from the historical narratives and other parts of the Old Testament Scriptures ; and that his contempt for such vagaries does not extend to what may be termed the speculative element of the Kabbala seems to be placed beyond question by two passages in his writings in which Kabbalistic doctrines are referred to with at least a qualified respect. Replying to Olden- burg, who had urged that, in the work above named, Spinoza seemed to many to confound God and Nature, he says : "I hold that God is the immanent and not the transient cause of all things. That all things are in God and move in God I affirm with Paul, and perhaps also with all the ancient philosophers, and I might even venture to say with all the ancient Hebrews, in so far as may be conjectured from certain traditions, though these have been in many ways corrupted." [1]  The other passage is contained in the ' Ethics,' [2] where, with reference to his doctrine that " thinking substance and extended substance are one and the same substance, apprehended, now under this attribute, now under that," and that " a mode of extension and the idea of that mode are one and the same thing expressed in two different ways," he adds, " which truth certain of the Hebrews appear to have seen as if through a cloud when they affirm that God, the intellect of God, and the things which are the objects of that intellect, are one and the same thing."  To show that the reference here is to the Kabbala, the following passage has been adduced from a work entitled ' The Garden of Pomegranates,' an exposition of the Kabbalistic doctrine of "the Sephiroth" or Divine Emanations, by a celebrated Kabbalist of the sixteenth century, Moses Corduero.  " The knowledge of the Creator differs from that of the creature in this respect that, in the case of the latter, thought, the thinker, and the object thought of are different.  But the Creator is Himself knowledge, the knower, and the object known.  His knowledge does not arise from His directing His thoughts to things outside of Him, since in comprehending and knowing Himself, He comprehends and knows everything that exists. Nothing exists which is not one with Him and which He does not find in His own substance.  He is the archetype of all things that exist, and all things are in Him in their purest and most perfect form."  Notwithstanding the parallelism in this quotation, both in substance and expression, to the doctrine ascribed by Spinoza to " certain Hebrews," the reference is rendered somewhat

[1] Ep., 21.  [2] Eth., p. ii, Prop. vii. Schol.

doubtful by the fact that we have no evidence that Spinoza knew anything of the writer from whom it is taken, and also, that in the 'Guide to the Perplexed,' the well-known work of the Jewish philosopher Maimonides, from whom Spinoza elsewhere quotes, a passage occurs in which the same doctrine is maintained in almost the same terms.

It is not, however, in particular citations from the Kabbala that we find the most probable indications of the influence of its ideas on Spinoza's mind. Even the least incoherent of Kabbalistic works, the so-called 'Book Zohar,' can only be described as a strange conglomerate of philosophy and allegory, reason and rhapsody, of ideas from Plato and Aristotle and ideas from the Pentateuch, of Jewish traditions and oriental mysticism. But if we try to extricate from this curious composite the underlying speculative element, we find in it distinct traces of one particular phase or school of thought. Whatever the date or outward origin of the Kabbala, or its historic relation to Alexandrian metaphysic, the philosophy it teaches is simply Neo-Platonism in a fantastic guise. And through whatever channel they reached him, Spinoza's writings contain, we think, indications of a certain influence of Neo-Platonic ideas. It is necessary, therefore, to form some conception of the system of thought to which these ideas belong.

Neo-Platonism took its rise at a period when the old religions and philosophies of the world began to mingle, and (though the Greek element in it was the preponderating one) it attempted to produce a coherent system out of elements derived from Semitic theology, Asiatic mysticism, and the philosophies of Plato and Aristotle.

The main problem of Neo-Platonic speculation is that of the relation of the infinite and finite, of God and the world. Starting from a conception of the two extremes of this relation which made them absolutely irreconcilable, the whole system was the expression of one long effort to bridge over an impassable gulf—to deal with the idea of God conceived of as an absolute unity, beyond limitation or definition, so as, on the one hand, to make it possible for God to reveal Himself not merely in nature and man, but in an absolute formless matter; and on the other hand, for the human spirit to rise into communion with the divine. The solution of this absolute dualism which Neo-Platonism propounds may be represented by the two words *Emanation* and *Ecstasy.*

In the first place, the intense religious feeling which was the underlying motive of Neo-Platonic speculation, and the consequent endeavour to elevate the conception of God above all the limiting conditions of human existence, led to an idea of the First Principle of all things which is simply that of the absolutely indeterminate—that which can be thought of only as the negation of all that can be affirmed of the finite. God is the Absolute One, unity beyond all difference, to which no predicates can be attached, of which nothing can be affirmed or expressed. We may not think of Him as intelligent, for intelligence implies distinction between the knower and the object known. For a similar reason we may not ascribe to Him a will. "Strictly speaking, He is neither consciousness nor unconsciousness, neither freedom nor unfreedom, for all such opposites pertain to the realm of finite things. He gives life, yet Himself lives not, He is all and the negation of all." Even when we name Him

"the One," we must exclude any thought of numerical
unity, for that contains or implies the idea of multiplicity, and is meaningless when applied to that which is
above all distinction. "Only by negation can we define
Him. He is inexpressible, for all speech names some
definite thing; He is incomprehensible, for thought distinguishes between itself and its object; if we would
grasp Him, it is only by an act of intuition in which
the mind rises above thought and becomes one with
its object."

But when the idea of God has been thus rarefied to
an abstraction which is simply the negation of the finite,
every way back to the finite would seem to be cut off.
The Absolute One of Neo-Platonism, in which the explanation of all finite things is to be found, would seem
to be shut up in its own self-identity. In a unity so
conceived there is no reason why it should go beyond
itself to manifest or reveal itself in the manifoldness of
finite existence. The solution of the problem which
Neo-Platonism gives is contained, as we have said, in the
word "emanation." The self-involved imprisonment of
the Absolute which reason cannot break down, Plotinus
attempts to dissolve by the aid of imagination and pic-
torial analogy. "Everything," says he, "that is in any
degree perfect, and most of all, therefore, the absolutely
perfect, tends to overflow itself, to stream forth, and produce that which is other than itself yet an image of itself. Fire produces heat, snow cold, fragrant substances
odours, medicine healing. The most perfect cannot remain powerless, shut up in itself." Accordingly, that
Absolute which is above knowledge is conceived to
stream forth in a series of emanations, descending

through successive stages in which the irradiation becomes fainter and fainter, till it reaches the realm of
darkness, of that formless matter which is below knowledge. As Plato endeavoured to overcome the dualism
between the ideal and phenomenal world by the conception of a world-soul as a kind of mediator, so Plotinus
seeks to escape from a still more absolute dualism by expanding the Platonic conception into that of four descending stages of emanations, each of which successively
represents a lower degree of perfection. The first is the
ideal world or realm of ideas, in which the Absolute
One, the ineffable light which is indistinguishable from
darkness, becomes conscious of itself, or produces as the
image of itself mind or intelligence. This ideal world,
though in itself the archetype of all finite being, the
source of all the light and life of the phenomenal
world, is in itself incapable of any immediate relation
to it; and so, by the same emanational expedient, the
conception is formed of an intermediating principle, the
world-soul or realm of souls, related, on the one hand,
to the realm of ideas from which it emanates, and on
the other hand, to the realm of matter, by its impregna-
tion of which it produces the phenomenal world, and
time and space, which are the conditions of its being.
In this descending series we pass, circle beyond circle,
within the world of light and reality, till we reach its
utmost limit in the world of souls, beyond which lies
the sensible phenomenal world, which is produced by
the last circle of light casting forth its rays into the
darkness beneath. The phenomenal world is thus a
composite of light and darkness, being and non-being,
whose only reality is due to the radiance which pene-

trates it from the world above. Beneath it lies the
region of formless matter, which, as the opposite of the
First Principle, is designated Absolute Evil, in the sense
of pure negation or non-being. In the phenomenal
world it is redeemed from negation ; but that phenomenal
world is itself only a world of shadows, owing its reality
to the world-soul, as that in turn to the ideal world, and
both alike to the primordial unity, the only absolute, all-
comprehending reality. There, and there alone, all distinction, all mutation, cease ; the whole universe of
thought and being exists only as its transient image
or irradiation, and the reabsorption of that universe into
its primal source would be at once the vanishing away
of its finite existence and its return to the only absolute
reality.

In the second place, this last thought receives definite
expression in an ascending series of stages, in which aspiration, ending in ecstasy or ecstatic intuition, reverses
the process of the descending series of emanations. All
finite being strives after union with its origin. All individual existences in their separateness and transiency
are under an impulse which urges them backwards towards the centre from which they emanated. The individual soul, like the soul of the world, of which it is
a part, stands at the middle of this universe of emanations, and combines in itself elements at once of the
highest and of the lowest. As embodied it is a part of
nature and allied to the lower world of matter; as spiritual
it belongs to the ideal world and to the unity from which
it emanates, in estrangement from which it is in bondage
to a natural necessity separating it from its true home ;
and to that home, in obedience to its proper destiny, it

ever seeks to return. The steps by which this return is achieved repeat in reverse order those of descent. By knowledge or contemplative energy it emancipates itself from the bondage of sense, and remounts into the ideal world, the region where thought or intelligence finds nothing foreign to itself, but lives and moves in the pure atmosphere of eternal ideas. But even here intelligence has not reached its highest goal, the absolute unity to which it aspires. Even in the realm of ideas there is still division. The mind which contemplates objective truth, or which attains to knowledge by any dialectic process, is still not absolutely one with its object. There is a stage of spiritual exaltation higher than that of definite thought. There is a point where the last distinction, that of subject and object, vanishes, where thought dies away into feeling, intelligence loses itself in rapt identification with its object, and all sense of individuality is absorbed in that absolute transparent unity where no division is. This is the final goal of Neo-Platonic speculation, the " ecstasy " which can only be described as the extinction of thought from its own intensity, the striving of the finite spirit beyond itself till it is lost in God.

If we try to characterise this system generally, it may be described as a kind of poetical or imaginative pantheism. It does not succeed in overcoming the original dualism which is involved in the two extremes of an absolute, self-identical unity, and an absolute, formless matter. The former contains in it no reason for the existence of a world in which its latent riches shall be revealed, and the idea of emanation to which recourse is had is only the substitution of a metaphor for a rational principle. But in intention at least, it is purely pantheistic, or rather it belongs to that class of pantheistic systems to which the designation "acosmism" is more properly applied. The successive orders of emanations which constitute the world are only phantoms, unreal as the reflections in a mirror; its only reality is the absolute unity from which their phantasmal existence is projected, and *that*, as it was without diminution through their existence, remains without increase when they have vanished away.

If we endeavour to disengage from the arbitrary mythological and other ingredients of which the Kabbala is composed, the speculative element which gives it any value for thought, we shall find in it, as we have said, little else than a reproduction of Neo-Platonism. In the Book Zohar, the only part of the Kabbala which has any pretension to systematic connection, the fundamental idea is that of the "En Soph," or unlimited, with its ten "Sephiroth," or emanations. The former, the source from which all the life and light of the universe, all ideal and actual existence, flows, is described as "the unknown of the unknown," "the mystery of mysteries." "He cannot be comprehended by the intellect nor described in words, and as such he is in a certain sense non-existent, because, as far as our minds are concerned, that which is perfectly incomprehensible does not exist." [1] In other words, the Kabbalists, in their endeavour to exalt the conception of God above all anthropomorphic elements, refine it away till it becomes simply the abstract notion of being which is indistinguishable from non-being. This Absolute Being, unknowable

[1] Zohar, quoted by Ginsburg, *The Kabbala*, p. 6.

in Himself, can become known, even indirectly, only by becoming active or creative. But He cannot become immediate creator of a finite world : first, because to ascribe to Him intention and will would be to introduce finite determinations into His nature; and secondly, because an Infinite Being can produce only that which is infinite. Accordingly, in Neo-Platonic fashion, the Kabbala invents a mediating principle based on the figure of the radiation of light from an invisible centre. This principle, corresponding to the "ideal world" of Plotinus, is designated "the world of emanations," and is elaborated and arranged by the Kabbalists into successive trinities, each of which constitutes, on the one hand, one of the various aspects under which the "En Soph," or incomprehensible divine nature, is contemplated; on the other hand, the archetype of some one of the various orders of existence in the finite world. In their totality, gathered up into unity by the last emanation, which is the harmonising principle of the whole series, they are designated the 'Adam Kadmon,' the ideal or celestial man, inasmuch as, according to the Zohar, "the form of man contains all that is in heaven and earth, all beings superior and inferior, and therefore the ancient of ancients has chosen it for his own."[1] In order to constitute the mediating principle between God and the world, the Sephiroth are represented as partaking of the nature at once of the infinite and finite : as emanations from the infinite, they are themselves infinite; as distinguishable from the infinite, they are the first order of finite things. The finite world is not a creation out of nothing, but simply a further expansion or evolution of the Sephiroth. By a

[1] Zohar, quoted by Franck, *La Kabbale*, p. 179.

curious conceit the Kabbala supposes, prior to the existence of the present world, certain formless worlds,
abortive attempts at creation, so to speak, to have issued
from the ideal archetypal fountain of being and then
vanished away; and these it compares to sparks which
fly from a red-hot iron beaten by a hammer, and which
are extinguished as they separate themselves from the
burning mass.[1] On the other hand, in contrast with
these failures, the being of the actual world is due to
the continuous presence in it and in all it contains of a
measure, greater or less, of the luminous element from
which it springs. All finite existences are made in
descending series "after the pattern of things in the
heavens." "First comes the 'Briatic world,' which is
the abode of pure spirits; next, the 'Yetziratic world,'
or world of formation, which is the habitation of angels;
and lastly, the 'Assiatic world,' or world of action, which
contains the spheres and matter, and is the residence of
the prince of darkness and his legions."[2] Without following this theory of creation in the details of fantastic
imagery into which it is wrought out by the Kabbalists,
it may be observed in general that its characteristic principle, the emanational conception of the relation of the
world to God which is common to it with Neo-Platonism,
reappears in it in a form modified by Jewish mythological
traditions. The belief in angels and demons was deeply
rooted in the spirit of the Jewish people, and under its
influence the emanations of Neo-Platonism become personified into the angels of the Kabbala, and the world-
soul of the former becomes in the latter the Briatic
world, which is the habitation of pure spirits. In like

[1] Ginsburg, *l.c.*, p. 15.       [2] Ginsburg, p. 24.

     D

manner the phenomenal world of Neo-Platonism becomes
the Yetziratic world of the Kabbala ; and as the former
was constituted by the irradiation of light from above
into the darkness of matter, so in the cosmology of the
Kabbala the same result is brought about by the presence
of angelic beings pervading the whole realm of nature.
To every part and process of the material world—the
heavenly firmament, the orbs of light, the earth, the
element of fire, the revolution of the seasons, &c.—an
angelic ruler is assigned, and it is to the agency of the
angelic hosts that all the varied movements of nature
and their harmony and unity are to be ascribed.  Finally,
under the same personifying influence, the Neo-Platonic
realm of darkness, beneath the last circle of ideal life,
becomes, in the Kabbala, the Assiatic world, the habitation of evil spirits—a conception in which the demon-
ology of Jewish tradition and its wild imaginative
reveries come into strange conjunction with the results
of Greek speculative thought.

In the Kabbalistic theory of the nature and destiny
of man we find the same reproduction of Neo-Platonic
ideas under Jewish forms.  Man is the epitome of the
universe, the microcosm who combines in his nature all
the various elements which constitute the totality of being.
He is, says the Zohar,[1] " at once the sum and the highest
term of creation. . . . As soon as man appeared everything was complete, both the higher and lower worlds,
for everything is comprised in him ; he unites in himself all forms of being."  This is otherwise expressed by
saying that man is the earthly Adam, the image of the
heavenly Adam, the Adam Kadmon above described.

[1] Quoted, Franck, 229.

As the latter is simply an expression for the totality of Sephiroth, the eternal ideal archetypes of all that exists in the finite world, so, to say that man is the earthly image of the heavenly Adam is to say that all things in heaven and earth, from the highest to the lowest, are represented or expressed in the unity of his nature. He is at once spiritual and animal, divine and demoniacal— on the higher side of his being an emanation from the world of pure spirits, which is itself an emanation from the Infinite ; on the other hand, having relation through his fleshly nature to the material world and to that formless matter which is figured as the abode of the spirits of darkness. Finally, in its doctrine of the destiny of man and the world, the Kabbala reproduces, under a slightly modified form, the reascending stages of Neo-Platonism. As all individual souls, according to the Zohar, in their ideal essence, pre-existed in the world of emanations, so, having inhabited human bodies, and passed through the discipline of an earthly life (or through successive lives), they become emancipated from the blind power of nature which governs the animal life, and return to the source from which they emanated. In this reascending process two stages are distinguished, each marked by its own characteristics. From the servitude of the animal life the soul rises first into that real but still imperfect relation to the divine source of light in which knowledge is only reflective and obedience is more that of fear than of love. But there is, says the Zohar, a state of perfection in which the Eternal Light falls no longer indirectly and as through a veil on the spirit, but shines on it directly and full-orbed in immediate vision, and in which perfect love casts out fear. In this consummation of its being,

this state of intuitive vision and unmingled love, there is
no longer any division between the spirit and its object.
It has lost its individual character; all finite interests,
all activity, all return upon itself have vanished. Its
being becomes absolutely lost in the divine.[1] I have
said that the Neo-Platonic system leaves still in the
"formless matter" which lies beyond the last circle of
light an element of unsolved dualism, which its pantheistic principle of emanation has not overcome. But
the pantheism of the Kabbala is, in expression at least,
more uncompromising. In it the differentiation of the
primordial unity is succeeded by a more complete reintegration. Not even the lowest world of darkness, the
habitation of evil spirits, which is the analogue for the
"formless matter" of Neo-Platonism, is left in the final
crisis unreclaimed. The Kabbala knows no absolute
evil, no being doomed to everlasting separation from the
source of light. There will come a time when the world
of darkness will disappear, and even the archangel of
evil, "the venomous beast," will be restored to his
angelic name and nature, and when all orders of being
will have entered into the eternal rest, the endless
Sabbath of the universe.[2]

It is not, as we have said, in the theosophic mysticism
of the Kabbala, but in the dialectic movement of the
thought of his own time—a movement which found
independent expression where there could be no question
of Jewish influences, in the philosophy of Malebranche
and in the theology of the Reformers—that the true
genesis of Spinozism is to be discerned. But whilst
Descartes is the logical parent of Spinoza, there are

[1] Franck, p. 248.          [2] Ibid., p. 217; Ginsburg, p. 44.

traces in the 'Ethics,' and still more distinctly in the earlier treatise 'Concerning God and Man,' of his familiarity with Kabbalistic ideas, and these ideas may have constituted in a mind early imbued with them a predisposing tendency toward that view of the world and of its relation to God which lies at the basis of the Spinozistic philosophy. Whatever else Spinozism is, it is an attempt to find in the idea of God a principle from which the whole universe could be evolved by a necessity as strict as that by which, according to Spinoza's favourite illustration, the properties of a triangle follow from its definition. For the clear intelligence of Spinoza it was impossible to rest satisfied with a system in which metaphor plays the part of logical thought ; and accordingly, in his philosophy the emanation theory of the Kabbalists finds no place. Yet even in a system in which logical consecution is the supreme principle of method, there are traces of that attempt to effect by an arbitrary mediating principle what reason fails to accomplish, which is the main characteristic of Kabbalistic speculation. In one point of view the transition from the infinite to the finite is barred for Spinoza, as it was for the Kabbalists, by the idea of God with which he starts. If we interpret that idea by his own principle that "all determination is negation," what it means for him is the absolutely indeterminate, the bare affirmation of Being which is reached by abstracting from all determinations. It is true that he ascribes to God or absolute substance the two attributes of thought and extension, but these attributes are only distinctions relative to finite intelligence ; they do not pertain to the absolute essence of the divine nature, but are only ways in which the human understanding conceives of it. Beyond these attributes or determinations lies the indeterminate substance, of which nothing can be affirmed but that it is the self-identical unity into which no difference or distinction can enter. But in so defining the nature of God, Spinoza would seem to have rendered impossible all advance from this primary idea to anything further. In that of which nothing can be affirmed there can be no reason for the existence of anything else, and to find in it a reason for the existence of the finite world would be to find in it a reason for its own negation. To rehabilitate the finite world would be to reaffirm that by abstracting from which the idea of God has been attained; it would be to destroy God in order to derive the finite from Him.

Yet though in this point of view the fundamental principle of Spinozism would seem to preclude all further advance, it was, as above said, the intention of its author to find in that principle the explanation of all things. The whole finite world was to be so involved in the idea of God as to be deducible from it as certainly as the propositions of geometry from its definitions and axioms. To achieve this result it is obvious that either the fundamental principle as above defined must be modified, or some illogical expedient must be adopted to cure it of its barrenness. The latter alternative is that which Spinoza adopted. He attempted by means of a conception analogous to the world-soul of the Neo-Platonists, to mediate between the infinite and finite, and to gain for the latter a legitimate derivation from the former. Out of the rigid unity of absolute substance difference is to be educed; from an infinite which is in incommunicable isolation the finite world is to be derived. This problem Spinoza thinks to solve by conceiving of all individual finite existences as "modes"—*i.e.*, finite determinations of the infinite substance—and then escaping the contradiction implied in determinations of the indeterminate by means of the conception of what he terms "infinite modes." On the one hand we have the infinite, indeterminate substance—on the other, a world of finite modes or determinations; and in order to bridge the gulf between them we have a third something which, as its name implies, is so conceived as to be in affinity with both,—with the finite or modal world, as being itself a "modo"; with the infinite, as an "infinito" mode. In other words, Spinoza thinks it possible to conceive of modes which, though as such they belong to the finite, changeable world, are themselves infinite and unchangeable. The whole corporeal world may be represented as a single individual, a universal motion which, embracing all particular movements, remains itself eternally unmoved; and the whole spiritual world may be represented as a universal intelligence, which, embracing all finite ideas or intelligences, is itself unlimited or infinite. Thus these universal individuals having in them elements at once of infinitude and finitude, may constitute the transition from the one realm to the other. As infinite and eternal, they introduce no negation into the one absolute substance; as expressions for the totality of finite existences and of the whole series of phenomenal changes, they are in close relation to the finite world. It is not at present our business to criticise this notion; all we have to do is to point out that, whether suggested to his mind from his early studies in Jewish philosophy or not, there is at least a certain analogy between it and the Neo-Platonic conception, reproduced in the Kabbala, of an inter-mediating principle between the absolute unity and the world of finite existences, between the ideal world, in itself eternal and unchangeable, and the world of mutable things and beings.

Nor, on the other hand, is it impossible to discern in Spinozism a certain reflection of the reascending move-ment which forms the converse side of the Neo-Platonic system. As in the descending movement we have the stages of infinite attributes, modified by infinite modes, and these by an infinite number of finite modes, so in the return to God there is, so to speak, a retracing of the steps by which finite individualities have become differ-entiated from the unity of infinite substance in which all reality is comprehended. In the attitude of ordinary experience (*experientia vaga*) we contemplate the world as consisting of independent things and beings. But the independence we thus ascribe to them is illusory. As it is only by applying to space or extension, which is one and indivisible, the conceptions of number and measure, which are mere "aids of imagination," that we can think of it as made up of discrete parts, so it is only imagination which gives to ourselves and all other finite individuals a separate, independent existence. Not only does each finite mode exist only as determined by other finite modes in an infinite series, but by the very fact that it is a mode it has no claim to independence in regard to the infinite substance. The first step or stage of true knowledge, therefore, the commencement of our escape from the illusion of the finite, is that of our passing

from "vague experience" to "reason" or the rational
contemplation of the world. This kind of knowledge
Spinoza defines [1] as "that in which we contemplate things
not as accidental but as necessary;" and again,[2] as "that
in which we know things under a certain form of eternity." It is not the highest stage of knowledge, but it
is so far on the way to the highest that in it we are
rescued from the dominion of accidental associations;
we look at things no longer in the arbitrary relations of
time and place, but as linked together in necessary connection of cause and effect, so that all things are seen to
be what they are because they are parts of that series or
totality which, as above described, constitutes the "infinite modes" of the absolute substance. So regarded
they have in them, underneath all appearances of change,
an element of unchangeableness, of necessity, of eternity.
But beyond even this ideal aspect of things, there is a
higher attitude of mind which Spinoza designates *scientia
intuitiva*, in which we "proceed from an adequate idea
of a certain attribute of God to the adequate knowledge
of the nature of things." This stage of knowledge is
that in which we no longer reason about things, but
know them in their essence, no longer proceed inferentially, from premisses to conclusion, from causes to
effects, but as by immediate vision penetrate to the heart
and life, the inmost reality of the world. If there is
any element of mediation in this knowledge, it is only
in so far as it is that of an intelligence which sees all
things in God and in their relation to Him. At this
stage the finite mind has risen above itself and other
things as individuals, to contemplate them in their

[1] Eth. ii. 44.      [2] Ibid., cor. 2.

unity, as they are in God or as modifications of His attributes. Even its knowledge of God is no longer simply the knowledge which the finite has of the infinite, it is a part of the knowledge which God has of Himself. Moreover, it is to be noticed that, by his identification of will with intelligence, the reascending process is for Spinoza a moral as well as an intellectual one. The bondage of sense and the bondage of inadequate ideas is one and the same. To discern the illusory independence we ascribe to ourselves and to all finite things is to escape from it; to know the absolute law of necessity under which we lie is to become free; to know ourselves "under the form of eternity" is to rise above the sphere of time. It is the false reality which opinion and imagination ascribe to the finite that subjects us to the slavery of our desires and passions. Reason, in destroying their unreal basis, breaks the yoke. And when, finally, we have risen to that supreme attitude of mind in which we not merely reason from the idea of God as a first principle to the nature of things, but by the grasp of intuitive insight *see* ourselves and all things in the light of it, then with the very existence of our finite self the desires and passions that were implicated with it of necessity vanish. As we cease to know, so we cease to will or love, any object outside of God; and our love to God, like our knowledge of God, becomes one with that wherewith God regards Himself. Here as elsewhere in the philosophy of Spinoza there are elements which, as we shall see in the sequel, essentially distinguish him from the mystical Neo-Platonic theosophists; yet even in the foregoing sketch of the process by which he reaches that "intellectual love" which is for him the final goal of moral endeavour and aspiration, we may discern points of analogy to the Neo-Platonic "ecstasy" and to the Kabbalistic absorption in the " En Soph " which, in a mind steeped from early youth in Jewish literature and tradition, cannot have been altogether a matter of accident.

# CHAPTER III.

### THE MEDIEVAL JEWISH PHILOSOPHERS.

A VAST amount of learning and ingenuity has been expended on the question of Spinoza's supposed obligations to Maimonides, Chasdai Creskas, and other distinguished philosophic writers of his own race. Many parallelisms of thought and expression have been adduced by Dr Joël and others, and it has even been maintained that his debt to these writers seriously affects his title to originality as a philosopher. Such occasional coincidences, however, even if they had been more numerous and unambiguous than those on which this opinion rests, cannot without further consideration be accepted as proving the derivation of Spinozism from Jewish sources. Particular points of resemblance, as we have already said, mean more or less according to the general principles and point of view of the writers in whom they occur. The significance of an idea or form of expression can only be estimated in view of its organic relation to the whole of which it forms a part, and even exact verbal coincidences, so far from establishing the intellectual obligation of a later writer to earlier writers of a different school or standpoint, only go to prove, at most, that he was acquainted with their works. It is on this principle that we must judge of the alleged anticipations of Spinozism in the medieval Jewish philosophers. From one and all of these writers he differed, at least in this respect, that they served two masters, he only one. The conclusions they reached were the result of a compromise between reason and authority. Their aim in all they wrote was to reconcile philosophy with the teaching of Moses and the traditional dogmas of Judaism, and the result was even more unsatisfactory than in the parallel case of the scholastic philosophy. That result varied, indeed, in its character in different instances, according as the philosophic or the authoritative tendency predominated in the mind of the writer. In some cases Jewish dogma was manipulated by arbitrary interpretation into accordance with Greek philosophy, in others Aristotelian and Platonic terminology was crudely applied to the cosmogony of Moses and the theology of the synagogue. In all cases alike the issue of this forced alliance was a spurious one, which neither reason nor authority could claim as its own. Between such composite productions and a strictly reasoned system like Spinozism there can be no common measure.

A detailed examination of Spinoza's relations to the Jewish philosophers would carry us beyond the limits of this work. We must confine our remarks to that one of these writers to whom Spinoza has been said to owe the most, Moses Maimonides. The philosophical writings of Maimonides are characterised as a whole by the tendency above indicated, the endeavour to establish foregone conclusions. But perhaps the part of his philosophy in which this tendency shows itself least is that

which relates to the idea of God. In his treatment of
this subject the Jewish theologian is almost entirely subordinated to the follower of Plato and Aristotle. In
one passage of his most important work, the 'Moreh
Nebuchim,' or 'Guide to the Perplexed,' he adopts the
Aristotelian definition of God as νοησις νοησεως—*i.e.*,
thought which is its own object, pure, abstract self-
consciousness ; and in other passages in which he treats
of the divine attributes, the notion of abstract unity
involved in this definition is further rarefied into the
Neo-Platonic conception of absolute self-identity, a unity
which repels every element of difference. We have
already seen how, in the endeavour to clear the idea
of God from all anthropomorphic alloy, Neo-Platonism
endeavours to get beyond the stage at which there is a
distinction between thought and its object, and to rise
to a point of exaltation higher even than thought or intelligence, a unity in which this distinction vanishes.
Maimonides in different parts of his writings wavers
between these two conceptions. As Plotinus maintained
that the highest ideal of intelligence is that in which
the object of knowledge is no longer something external
to the knowing subject, but that pure self-contemplative
energy in which thought is the object of its own activity,
so Maimonides, still more closely following the Aristotelian dialectic, endeavours on the same principle to distinguish between divine and human intelligence. It is
of the very nature of thought or intelligence that it
grasps the " forms " or real essences of things ; and when
it does so, these forms are not something different from
itself, for it is only as active, as thinking these forms,
that it realises its own nature. Intelligence apprehend-

ing the forms of things, and the forms of things apprehended by intelligence, are only different expressions for one and the same thing, or the same thing regarded from different points of view. When, therefore, the human intelligence is in the state of actual thought, thought, the thinker, and the thing thought of, are wholly one. But man is not always in the state of actual thought. At first thought in him is only potential, a capacity of thinking which has not yet come into actuality; and even when intelligence in him has become developed, it is not always or continuously active. When the mind is at the potential stage of thought, or when the capacity of thinking is in abeyance, we can regard the power of apprehension and the object capable of being apprehended as two separate things; and further, inasmuch as a power can only be conceived of as residing in a being or nature which possesses it, to these two we have to add a third—viz., the mind in which the power of thought resides. But when we conceive of a universal and ever-active intelligence, an intelligence in which there is no unrealised capacity, no potentiality that is not actuality, and which does not apprehend at one time and cease to apprehend at another — when, in other words, we think of a mind to which no reality is foreign, in which the forms or essences of things are ever present, and which is eternal activity as well as potentiality,— then we have before us the conception of a being in which the threefold distinction vanishes. In a mind which ever thinks there is no separation of thinker and power of thought, nor of the power of thought from its own objects. In God, the absolute energy, the ever-active intelligence, thought, the thinker, and the object of thought, are one.

In the passage which I have here epitomised, the idea of God which Maimonides reaches is that which, if followed out and freed from the limitations which are connected with it in the Aristotelian philosophy, would lead to the modern conception of absolute, self-conscious, self-determining Spirit—of thought which at once reveals itself in the manifold differences of the finite world and from all these differences returns upon itself.

But in Maimonides not only does this idea remain undeveloped, but it is left in unreconciled contradiction with another conception of the divine nature on which he more frequently insists. In the false search for unity, or confounding that discreteness which destroys unity with that concrete fulness in which the highest unity consists, he sets himself to think of something higher even than intelligence, an absolute which is not the unity of subject and object, but the abstraction in which these distinctions are lost. An absolute unity is that from which every element of plurality or difference must be excluded. Our belief in the divine unity, therefore, implies that the essence of God is that to which no predicates or attributes can be attached. When we describe an object by attributes, these attributes must be conceived of either as constituting its essence, or as superadded to it. If the attributes of God are conceived of as constituting his essence, we fall into the absurdity of conceiving of a plurality of infinites, and further, of introducing into the nature of God that divisibility or compositeness which belongs only to corporeal things. If the attributes are thought of as superadded to the essence, then are they merely accidents and express nothing in the reality of the divine nature. By these and similar arguments, Maimonides convinced himself that such attributes as power, wisdom, goodness, cannot be understood as expressing any positive reality, and that even such predicates as existence, unity, &c., cannot, in the ordinary sense of the words, be applied to the divine essence. As applied to finite beings, existence is something separable from essence ; the idea of a house in the mind of the builder, for instance, being something different from the house as an actually existing thing : but in God existence and essence, idea and reality, are one and indivisible. When, again, we say of God that He is one, we must understand something different from the unity we predicate of finite things, for "unity and plurality are accidents belonging to the category of discrete quantity." When we pronounce a thing to be one, we add to its essence the accidents of its relations to other things ; but in God as an absolute or necessarily existing Being, unity and essence are one. The conclusion, therefore, to which Maimonides comes, is that the predicates by which we suppose ourselves to attain to a knowledge of God do not express any positive real ity in the divine nature, but can only be employed in a negative sense, to denote, not what God is, but what He is not; in other words, they are only expressions for our own ignorance. The essence of God is that pure absolute unity which lies beyond all plurality, and therefore beyond all predication, of which we can only say *that* it is, but not *what* or how it is.[1]

From the foregoing summary it is obvious that Maimonides does not advance beyond the Neo-Platonic conception of the nature of God. If any positive reference

[1] Moreh, i. 51-57

P.—XII.                                                    E

to him can be traced in Spinoza's writings, it is in the passage above quoted, in which he speaks in a somewhat slighting tone of some faint anticipation of his doctrine of the relation of the attributes of thought and extension to the divine substance as having dawned "as through a cloud" on the minds of "certain of the Hebrews." On the further question, whether on this point any indirect influence of the writers so designated can be traced in the philosophy of Spinoza, enough has already been said.

Whatever the relation of Spinoza's doctrine as to the nature of God to that of Maimonides, when we pass from this point to the teaching of the latter as to the relation of God to the world, the divergence between the two systems amounts to nothing less than radical inconsistency. Here it is no longer Aristotle but Moses who is the master of Maimonides. He is no longer an independent thinker, but a rabbi striving by special pleading to force philosophy into reconciliation with the creed of the synagogue. A philosophy which starts from the notion of a transcendent God, a self-identical unity excluding all distinctions, can find in itself no logical explanation of the existence of a finite world. The process from unity to difference becomes impossible when there is no element of difference *in* the unity. Even the Aristotelian conception of God as pure self-consciousness, pure Form without Matter, rendered it impossible to account for a world in which form was realised in matter. And the impossibility of the transition becomes still more obvious when the unity of self-consciousness is sublimated into the Neo-Platonic idea of a pure identity without difference. The only device by

which an apparent transition from the one to the many,
from God to the world, can, under such conditions, be
effected, is either to substitute metaphor for reason, as
we have seen attempted in Neo-Platonism, or, failing that
expedient, to take refuge in mystery and to account for
the world by a supernatural creative act. It is the
latter expedient which, under the constraint of the presupposed orthodox doctrine of a creation of the world
*ex nihilo*, Maimonides adopts. There is indeed one
remarkable passage in the 'Guide to the Perplexed' in
which the Neo-Platonic theory of emanation is distinctly
taught. How, he asks, can that which remains eternally
the same and unmoving be the cause of all motion and
becoming? And he answers by the following illustration : "Many a man possesses so much wealth that he
can not only bestow on others what they are in want of,
but can so enrich them that they in turn can enrich
others. In like manner there is poured forth from God
so much good that there emanates from Him, not only
spirit, but a sphere of spirits. This second spirit again
contains in it ever such a fulness that from it also
spirit and spheres of spirit are derived, and so forth
down to the last intelligence and the first matter from
which all the elements arose. This idea of God was
held by the prophets, and because this emanation of
God is limited neither by space nor time, they have
compared God to an eternal and inexhaustible fountain
pouring itself forth on all sides."[1] This passage, however, can only be understood as the passing lapse of an
unsystematic writer, adopting for the moment and for a
special purpose a theory inconsistent with his funda-

[1] Moreh, ii. 11, 12.

mental principles. It is scarcely necessary to show by formal quotations that the theory, if so it can be called, on which Maimonides rests as the only possible explanation of the existence of the finite world, is that which is expressed by the phrase, "creation out of nothing." In answer to the Aristotelian argument that creation in time would imply in God a potentiality which had not yet passed into actuality, Maimonides maintains that "the sole ground of creation is to be found in the will of God, and that it belongs to the nature of will that a thing takes place at one time and not at another."[1] "For all these phenomena of nature," he adds, "I see no law of necessity, but can only understand them when we say with the doctrine of Moses that all has arisen by the free will of the Creator."[2] "If I had any proofs for the doctrines of Plato," again he writes, "I would unconditionally accept them, and interpret allegorically the verses of Moses which speak of a creation out of nothing."[3] And then he proceeds elaborately to defend the Mosaic doctrine against the philosophic, which, in his opinion, would completely subvert religion, our belief in Scripture, and the hopes and fears which religion inculcates.

It need scarcely be said that we have here a doctrine which is irreconcilable, not only with the philosophy of Spinoza, but with any philosophy whatever. Whether Spinoza's doctrine of one substance, of which all finite things are only transitory modes, furnishes any adequate solution of the problem of the relation of the world to God, it is at least an attempt to find in the idea of God a first principle from which everything else follows by

[1] Moreh, ii. 18.    [2] Ibid., ii. 22.    [3] Ibid., ii. 25.

strict necessity. The finite world is for him that which " follows from the necessity of the divine nature—that is, all the modes of the divine attributes, in so far as they are considered as things which are in God, and cannot be conceived without God."[1] Even the theory of emanation is at least an attempt to solve the problem with which it deals. But the theory of creation out of nothing is simply the abandonment of the problem as insoluble ; and if it seem anything more, it is only because its real character is disguised by a meaningless phrase. The theory itself, as well as the world for which it would account, is created out of nothing.

It is unnecessary to follow the so-called philosophy of Maimonides into further details. Setting out from a point of divergence such as has just been indicated, it is obvious that in the subsequent course of their specula-tions Spinoza and Maimonides could never meet, and their occasional coincidences are such only to the ear. Maimonides, for example, like many thinkers of the same order, feels himself impelled to seek a basis for moral responsibility in a freedom of indifference or in-determinism, and from the difficulties involved in this conception he finds a ready escape in his theory of creation. He who begins by tracing all things to an arbitrary supernatural act can never be at a loss for a solution of particular speculative difficulties. "To man," says he,[2] "has been given complete freedom whether he will incline to the good or evil way. Here there is no law of causality as in outward nature, so that the will of man should be the effect of any cause, but man's own will is the first cause of all his actions." "But," he

[1] Eth. i. 29, schol.       [2] Yad-ha-chazakah, v. 4.

asks, "does not the assertion that the will is free stand in contradiction with the divine omnipotence? The answer is, Not so; for, as God has given to everything its own nature, so He has made it the nature of the human will that it should be free." In other words, the unconditioned freedom of the human will is not only not derived from but is in absolute contradiction with the nature of God, and must therefore be ascribed simply to His arbitrary will, and what is contradictory to God's nature ceases to be so when God Himself is the author of the contradiction. How far apart from Spinoza, both in matter and manner, lies this kind of reasoning, need not here be pointed out.

There is, however, one subject on which, viewed apart from the general principles of the two systems, their coincidence at first sight looks more than verbal—viz., the nature of physical and moral evil :—

"We must," says Maimonides,[1] "first of all consider whence evil comes, and what is the nature of good and evil. Only the good is something positive; evil, on the contrary, is only want of good, therefore a mere negation. Life, *e.g.*, is the combination of this form with this matter; the cessation of the combination or the division of the two is death. Health is harmony in human bodies, sickness arises so soon as the harmony is destroyed. God, therefore, can only be regarded as the author of evil in the world in so far as He permits change, and lets the world arise out of matter which is subject to change. But change is a thing that is necessary; that anything should begin to be implies the possibility of its passing away. And not only of natural evil but of moral evil must it be pronounced that it is a mere negation. It comes merely from a want of reason, and is nothing positive.

---

[1] Moreh, iii. 21.

Were men wholly rational there would be neither hatred, nor envy, nor error, which work destructively amongst men, just as blind men injure themselves and others through want of sight. Both kinds of evil are mere negations which God does not cause, but only permits. Both are consequences of matter from which the world and man have become, and yet from matter nothing better could arise."

Compare with this doctrine of evil the following passages from Spinoza :—

"With regard to good and evil, these indicate nothing positive in things considered in themselves, nor anything else than modes of thought or notions which we form from the comparison of one thing with another."[1]  "For my own part, I cannot admit that sin and evil have any positive existence. . . . We know that whatever is, when considered in itself without regard to anything else, possesses perfection, extending in each thing as far as the limits of that thing's essence. The design or determined will (in such an act as Adam's eating the forbidden fruit), considered in itself alone, includes perfection in so far as it expresses reality. Hence it may be inferred that we can only perceive imperfection in things when they are viewed in relation to other things possessing more reality. . . . Hence sin which indicates nothing save imperfection cannot consist in anything which expresses reality."[2]  "I maintain that God is absolutely and really (as *causa sui*) the cause of all things which have essence (*i.e.*, affirmative reality). . . . When you can prove to me that evil, error, crime, &c., are anything which expresses essence, then I will grant to you that God is the cause of evil. But I have sufficiently shown that that which constitutes the form of evil does not consist in anything which expresses essence, and therefore it cannot be said that God is the cause of it."[3]

To the cursory reader of these passages both writers

[1] Eth. iv. Pref.　　　[2] Ep. 32.　　　[3] Ep. 36.

seem to teach the same doctrine as to the nature of evil, and with a common object. To prove that God is not the author of evil, it seems to be the endeavour of both to show that no positive reality can be ascribed to it, and that physical and moral evil alike must be relegated to the category of negations or unrealities. But a little closer examination proves that a fundamental difference underlies this superficial similarity. The theory of Maimonides is essentially dualistic. To exonerate his supramundane Creator from the causation of evil, he adopts the Aristotelian distinction of form and matter, ascribing all that is positively good in the system of being to the former, and regarding evil as only the element of negation or limitation which necessarily clings to the latter. In so far as any finite being is redeemed from imperfection, the element of good that is in it is due to the divine causation; in so far as imperfection still adheres to it, it is to be ascribed, not to the positive agency of God, but, so to speak, to the intractableness of the materials with which He has had to deal. Matter is essentially mutable; pain, sickness, death are its inevitable conditions; only the life which arrests change and disintegration is due to God. Error and crime are not traceable to God, any more than the blunders and mistakes of the blind to the author of the organ of vision. If reason were perfect there would be neither error nor sin; and therefore the measure of knowledge and virtue which men possess is to be ascribed to the author of reason; that they have no more, and therefore yield to irrational passions, is simply another way of saying that they are finite. God wills the good element which reclaims finite beings from matter; the evil which shows that they are only partially reclaimed He can at most be said only to permit.

It is not our business to criticise this theory, further than to point out its essentially dualistic character, and therefore its discordance with every system which, like that of Spinoza, maintains the absolute unity of the universe. Not only does it start from the fundamental dualism of a supramundane Creator and a world lying outside of Him, but even in that world all does not spring from the will that creates it. God is not responsible for all that takes place in the world, simply because another principle, that of "matter," has there a *rôle* which is independent of Him, and over which He can achieve at best only a partial victory. Spinoza, on the other hand, knows nothing of such an external Creator, or of any element of matter which possesses substantiality and independence. For him there is but one infinite substance, outside of which nothing exists or can be conceived; and all finite beings, corporeal and spiritual, are only modes of that one substance. Interpreted in the light of this fundamental principle, Spinoza's language with respect to the non-positive nature of evil means something with which the doctrine of Maimonides has no relation. Finite things, as such, have neither in their existence nor their essence any substantial reality. Everything that has a real existence, everything in nature and man that can be said to have any positive reality, is a modification or expression of the divine nature, and everything else that seems to be is only unreality, nonentity. If, then, we ask how it comes that we regard anything as evil, or ascribe reality to things that are injurious or wicked, the answer is that

this arises from the false substantiation which imagination
or opinion gives to things finite. "Whatever we think
injurious and evil, and, moreover, whatever we think to
be impious, or unjust, or wicked, arises from this, that we
conceive things in a distorted and mutilated fashion." [1]
As by means of the conceptions of number and measure,
which are merely "aids of the imagination," we give a
false independence to discrete parts of space, which is
really one and continuous, so the negative element in
individual things and actions, which have no reality
apart from God, is only due to the false isolation or
limitation which the imagination or the abstracting understanding gives to them. Remove the fictitious limit
by which they are distinguished from God, and the
negation vanishes; the positive element, which alone
expresses their essence, is all that remains. Whether
this view of the nature of evil be tenable or not, it is
obviously one which has nothing in common with that
of Maimonides. For the latter, God is not the author
of evil, because the evil or negative element in things is
to be ascribed to another and independent source : for
Spinoza, God is not the cause of evil, because, from the
point of view of the whole, contemplating the system of
being in the only aspect in which it has any real or
affirmative existence, evil vanishes away into illusion
and nonentity.

[1] Eth. iv. 73, dem.

# CHAPTER IV.

### GIORDANO BRUNO.

ONE of the most remarkable writers of the transition period between medieval and modern philosophy is Giordano Bruno. His numerous works, poetical, scientific, philosophical, reflect the general characteristics of that period, modified in some respects by a strongly marked individuality. The revolt against authority, the almost exulting sense of intellectual freedom, the breaking down of the artificial division between things sacred and secular, human and divine, the revival of ancient philosophy, and resumption of its problems from a new and higher standpoint—these and other distinctive features of the spirit of the time, and along with these the intellectual unsettlement and unrest, the predilection for occult sciences and arts, the tendency to commingle the dreams and vagaries of imagination with the results of rational investigation which marked some of its nobler yet more undisciplined minds,—are vividly represented in Bruno's multifarious writings. In these it is vain to seek for systematic unity. They are the expression of a mind filled with intellectual enthusiasm, rich, versatile, original, yet undisciplined and erratic, feeling after truth, and making random guesses now in this direction, now in that, pouring forth with almost inexhaustible productiveness speculations, theories, conjectures, under the impulse of the moment or the varying influence of external circumstances and of the intellectual atmosphere in which he moved. Betwixt such a mind as this and the clear, patient, disciplined intelligence of Spinoza, it would seem impossible to find any point of contact, and in the absence of any direct evidence we might be disposed to regard Spinoza's alleged obligations to Bruno as nothing more than accidental coincidences. It is true, indeed, that the absence of any reference to Bruno in Spinoza's writings does not settle the question, inasmuch as Spinoza was undoubtedly conversant with, and derived important suggestions from, authors whom he does not quote. But without attaching any weight to Spinoza's silence, the positive proof of his obligations would seem, at first blush, to consist only of a few verbal coincidences scarcely avoidable in writers treating of the same subjects, and more than overborne by the lack of any real affinity of thought.

When, however, we examine more closely the general drift of Bruno's philosophical writings—the leading ideas which, though never developed into a coherent system, underlie his speculations concerning man and nature and God—we shall find in them not a little which may be regarded as a kind of anticipation of Spinozism. The idea which seems to have dominated the mind of Bruno, and which, by means partly of Aristotelian categories, partly of Neo-Platonic emanation theories, he seeks in his various writings to explain and defend, is that of the divinity of nature and man. He was in profound sympathy with the revolt against the medieval notion of a transcendent God, and a sphere of divine things absolutely separated from nature and the secular life of mankind. The course of religious thought during the scholastic period had tended more and more to obscure the Christian idea of the unity of the divine and human. The ecclesiastical conception of God had gradually become that, not of a Being who reveals Himself in and to the human spirit, but of a Being above the world, and to whom thought can be related only as the passive recipient of mysterious dogmas authoritatively revealed. The false exaltation thus given to the idea of God led by obvious sequence to the degradation of nature, and the individual and social life of man. The observation of nature lost all religious interest for minds in which the divine was identified with the supernatural, and which found the indications of a divine presence not in the course of nature, but in interferences with its laws. In like manner, and for the same reason, the specially religious life became one of abstraction from the world, and the secular life of man, its domestic, social, political relations, came to be regarded as outside of the sphere of spiritual things. It is easy to see how the reaction from this false separation of the natural and spiritual, the human and divine, should give rise, on the one hand, to the reawakened interest in nature which is indicated by the scientific revival of the sixteenth and seventeenth centuries, and on the other, to the pantheistic tendency in philosophy which gives their distinctive character to the speculative writings of Bruno. Both on the religious and the poetical side of his nature, Bruno recoiled from the conception of a supramundane God, and a world

in whose life and thought no divine element could be
discerned.   In the external world, in whose least
phenomena science had begun to perceive the hidden glory of intelligible order and law; in the inner
world of mind, to whose boundless wealth of thought
the consciousness of the time was becoming awakened,
Bruno seemed to himself intuitively to discern, not the
mere production of a distant omnipotence, but the immediate expression of a divine presence and life.   And
with the whole strength of his ardent nature he sought
to give philosophic form and verification to this intuitive
sense of a kingdom of heaven on earth.   But religious
and poetical feeling may instinctively grasp what reason
is inadequate to justify.   Bruno was a poet first and a
philosopher only in the second place.   And whatever indirect influence his writings may have had on a greater
mind, it needed a calmer intelligence and severer logic than
his own to overtake the task he set himself to accomplish.

   " The true philosopher," says Bruno, " differs from the
theologian in this, that the former seeks the infinite
Being, not outside the world, but within it.   We must
begin, in other words, by recognising the universal
agent in creation, before attempting to rise to that
elevated region in which theology finds the archetype of
created beings." [1]   Dismissing, then, the conception of
a supramundane God, it is Bruno's aim to show how
philosophy justifies the idea of an immanent relation of
God to the world.   When we examine his solution of
the problem, it is found to consist partly in a recurrence
to Neo-Platonic figures and analogies, partly in a manipu-

[1] De la causa, pincipio et uno—Wagner's edit., i. p. 175.   Cf.
Bartholmèss, J. Bruno, ii. p. 130,

lation of the Aristotelian categories of matter and form,
of potentiality and actuality.   To the former point of
view belongs his elaborate exposition of the notion of a
" soul of the world."   The universe is to be conceived
of as an infinite living organism, not created by any outward cause, but having the principle of all its existences
and activities within itself.   It is that beyond which
nothing exists, in which all things live, and move, and
have their being.   This inward, ever-active, creative
principle he compares to the principle of life in the root
or seed, " which sends forth from itself shoots, branches,
twigs, &c., which disposes and fashions the delicate
tissue of leaves, flowers, fruit, and again, by the same
interior energy, recalls the sap to the root."   It is in one
sense external, in another internal, to purely natural
things ; the former, because it cannot be regarded as
itself a part or element of the things it creates—the
latter, because it does not act on matter or outside of
matter, but wholly from within, in the very bosom and
heart of matter.   He represents this first principle again
as an " inner artist " of infinite productiveness and
plastic power ; but it differs from a human artist in two
respects : (1.) That the latter operates on matter which is
already alive or instinct with form, whereas in the case
of the former no such presupposition is involved.   He
argues, therefore, that though we may shrink from regarding the universe as a living being, yet we cannot
conceive any form which is not already, directly or indirectly, the expression of a soul, any more than we can
conceive a thing which has absolutely no form.   It
would be absurd, indeed, to regard as living forms the
productions of human art.   My table, as such, is not

animate; but inasmuch as its matter is taken from nature, it is composed of materials which are already living. There is nothing, be it ever so little or worthless, that does not contain in it life or soul.[1] The human artist, in other words, works from without to communicate his own thought to materials which are taken from nature, and which have already, as part of nature, a life and being of their own; but the divine or inner artist has no pre-existing materials on which to work. His art is creative, at once of the materials and of the infinitely diversified forms imposed on them. Creative and formative energy are in Him one and the same thing; and if He transmutes lower into higher forms of existence, the former are not taken from a sphere that is foreign or external to Him, but already instinct with His own life; and the latter are only the same life putting forth a new expression of its inexhaustible energy. (2.) It is only a slightly varied form of the same thought when Bruno tells us that in the divine or inner artist, in contrast with the human, the ideas of efficient and final cause are inseparable. In nature, he argues, the efficient cause cannot be separated from the final or ideal cause. Every reasonable act presupposes an end or design. That design is "nothing else than the form of the thing to be produced. From which it follows that an intelligence capable of producing all, and of raising them by a marvellous art from potentiality into actuality, should contain in itself the forms and essences of all things."[2] Since it is intelligence or the soul of the world which creates natural things, it is impossible that the formal

---

[1] De la causa, i. p. 241. Cf. Bartholmèss, ii. p. 135.
[2] De la causa, i. p. 237. Cf. Bartholmèss, ii. p. 134.

should be absolutely distinct from the efficient cause.
They must fall together in the inner principle of things.
Bruno expresses the same thing in another way when
he speaks of the universe as a living organism.    In
the work of a human artist the thought or conception
lies outside of the materials on which he works, and in
which it is by his plastic hand to be realised.    But the
thought or design which is at work in the creation of an
organised structure, is not a mere mechanical cunning
acting from without, shaping and adjusting matter according to an ingenious plan which is foreign to it.    Here,
on the contrary, the ideal principle or formative power
goes with the matter, and constitutes its essence.    Such
a principle is supposed to be present from the beginning,
inspiring the first minutest atom of the structure with
the power of the perfect whole that is to be.    The inner
principle, the life within, is both first cause and last ; it
makes the last first, and the first last.    When, therefore,
we apply this conception to the universe, what it brings
before us is, not an extramundane omnipotent agent,
creating and shaping things to accomplish an end outside both of himself and them—implying, therefore, something originally lacking both to himself and the matter
on which he operates—but a universe which contains in
itself the principle of its own being, a vast organism
in which the power of the whole is working from the
beginning, in which the least and most insignificant of
finite existences presupposes and manifests the end to be
realised, and in which the first principle is at once beginning and end of all.    Had Bruno realised all that is
contained in this conception, his philosophy might have
gone beyond that of Spinoza, and anticipated much

which it was left for later speculative thought to
develop.

But when we follow the course of his speculations, and
ask how from his fundamental thought he proceeds
to explain the nature of God, and His relation to the
world, we find that, under the limiting influence of
scholastic or Aristotelian categories, the inherent wealth
of his own idea escapes his grasp.　With him as with a
greater than he, the principle of abstract identity is in
fatal opposition to that of concrete unity, or if the latter
is faintly adumbrated in his conception of the soul of
the world as a self-differentiating, self-integrating unity,
the former speedily reasserts itself, so as to reduce the
idea of God to a meaningless and barren abstraction,
and the finite world to evanescence and unreality.

In order to determine the nature of the first principle
of all things, Bruno has recourse to the Aristotelian
distinction of "form" and "matter."

"Democritus and the Epicureans," says he, "hold that
there is no real existence which is not corporeal; they regard
matter as the sole substance of things, and assert that it is
itself the divine nature.　These, with the Stoics and others,
hold also that forms are simply the accidental dispositions of
matter. . . . A closer examination, however, forces us to recognise in nature two kinds of substances, form and matter.　If,
therefore, there is an active principle which is the constitutive
principle of all, there is also a subject or passive principle
corresponding to it, a something that is capable of being acted
on as well as a something that is capable of acting.　Human
art cannot operate except on the surface of things already
formed by nature; . . . but nature operates, so to speak, from
the centre of its subject-matter, which is altogether unformed.
Therefore the subject-matter of the arts is manifold, but the

subject-matter of nature is one, seeing that all diversity proceeds from form."[1]

In this passage and elsewhere, what Bruno seeks to prove is, that the conceptions of matter and form are correlative, that neither can be apprehended in abstraction from the other, and that the necessities of thought force us beyond them to another and higher conception, that of a primal substance which is neither matter alone nor form alone, but the unity of the two. We are led to the same result, he elsewhere shows, when we consider the supposed hard and fast distinction of substances corporeal and incorporeal. "It is necessary that of all things that subsist there should be one principle of subsistence. . . . But all distinguishable things presuppose something indistinguishable. That indistinguishable something is a common reason to which the difference and distinctive form are added." Just as sensible objects presuppose a sensible subject, intelligible objects an intelligible subject—

" So it is necessary that there be one thing which corresponds to the common reason of both subjects, . . . a first essence which contains in itself the principle of its being. If body, as is generally agreed, presupposes a matter which is not body, and which therefore naturally precedes that which we designate as properly corporeal, we cannot admit any absolute incompatibility between matter and the substances which we name immaterial. . . . If we discern something formal and divine in corporeal substances, on the same principle we must say that there is something material in divine substances. As Plotinus says, if the intelligible world contains an infinite variety of existences, there must be in them, along

---

[1] De la causa, p. 251.

with their characteristic differences, something which they all have in common, and that common element takes the place of matter as the distinctive element takes that of form. . . . This common basis of things material and immaterial, in so far as it includes a multiplicity of forms, is multiple and many-formed, but in itself it is absolutely simple and indivisible ; and because it is all, it cannot be itself any one particular being." [1]

Such considerations do not suggest the idea of a Supreme Being (an extramundane God), "but of the soul of the world as the actuality of all, the potentiality of all, and all in all. Whence, though there are innumerable individuals, yet everything is one." [2] "There is one form or soul, one matter or body, which is the fulfilment of all and the perfection of all, which cannot be limited or determined, and is therefore unchangeable." [3]

These quotations may suffice to show what is the general drift of Bruno's speculations. The result to which his reasoning leads is not that which he intended or supposed himself to have attained. His obvious aim was to attain to a first principle which should be the living source and explanation of all finite existences, material and spiritual. But owing to the false method by which he proceeds, what he does reach is, not a unity which comprehends, but a unity which excludes, all determinations—not a being which embraces in its concrete unity the whole inexhaustible wealth of the finite world, but an empty abstraction from which all content has been evaporated. Finding that the ideas of matter and form, and again of

---

[1] De la causa, Wagner, i. pp. 269, 270, 272.
[2] Ibid., p. 275.          [3] Ibid., p. 280.

corporeal and spiritual, cannot be held apart, but that
when we attempt to think it, each implies and falls over
into the other, he yet does not rise to a higher unity, a
unity which transcends, yet at the same time comprehends both.    Hence his only available resource is to find
his higher unity in that which matter and form, mind
and body, have in common when their differences are
eliminated.    But by thinking of that which mind has in
common with body, or form with matter, we do not reach
a unity which is higher and richer than both, any more
than we do so when we think of that which gold has in
common with silver or copper.    A generic unity, in
other words, is a mere logical abstraction which has
less content than the lowest individual it is supposed to
embrace.    In short, like many other thinkers before and
after him, Bruno conceived himself to be explaining the
differences and contrarieties of existence by the simple
process of eliminating or ignoring them.    And his first
or highest principle (which he identified with God), in
which he conceived himself to have reached the origin
and end of all things, was nothing more than the abstraction of " Being," which is logically higher, simply because
it is poorer in content, not merely than matter or mind,
but than the lowest of finite existences.

And if thus his idea of God or the infinite was depleted
of all content or reality, it fared no better, and for the
same reason, with his idea of the finite world.    What
he sought for was a first principle or " soul of the world,"
in which all finite existences should find their being and
reality.    The solution of this problem, therefore, implied
at once the nothingness of all finite being apart from
God, and their reality in God.    His fundamental notion

of an organic unity imposed on him the necessity of
explaining the universe as an organism in which the
members are nothing but dead, meaningless fragments in
separation from the life or vital principle of the whole ;
but also the necessity of showing that through their relation to that principle they cease to be such unreal
abstractions. His method certainly enabled him, as he
himself saw, to achieve the former of these results—
viz., that of reducing all finite existences, as such, to
evanescence and nothingness.

" In its externality," says he, " nature is nothing more than
a shadow, an empty image of the first principle in which
potentiality and actuality are one. . . . Thou art not nearer
to the infinite by being man rather than insect, by being star
rather than sun. And what I say of these I understand of
all things whose subsistence is particular. Now, if all these
particular things are not different in the infinite, they are
not really different. Therefore the universe is still one, and
immovable. It comprehends all and admits of no difference
of being, nor of any change with itself or in itself. It is all
that can be, and in it is no difference of potentiality and
actuality.[1] . . . Individuals which continually change do
not take a new existence, but only a new manner of being.
It is in this sense that Solomon has said, ' There is nothing
new under the sun, but that which is was before.' As all
things are in the universe and the universe is in all things,
as we are in it and it is in us, so all concur to one perfect
unity, which is sole, stable, and ever remaining. It is one
and eternal. Every form of existence, every other thing is
vanity, every thing outside of that one is nothing."[2]

But whilst Bruno thus proved the unreality of all
finite existences apart from the first principle, the soul

[1] De la causa, i. p. 281.          [2] Ibid., 283.

or substance of the world, what he failed to prove, and from the self-imposed conditions of his method could not prove, was that even in their relation to the first principle any reality was left to them. Regarded as that which is reached by abstraction from the limits of finite existences, the first principle does not explain, it simply annuls them. Their distinction from God is their finitude, and the withdrawal of their finitude, which makes them one with God, makes them lost in God. They are only figures carved out in the infinitude of space, and, like figures in space, they vanish when the defining lines are withdrawn.

Such then, in substance, is Bruno's contribution to that problem with which, directly or indirectly, all speculative thought attempts to deal. It would be to forestall the exposition of the Spinozistic system to attempt here, save in a very general way, to answer the question, What, if any, traces are to be found in it of the influence of this writer on the mind of its author? At first sight there would seem to be discordances as great between the leading ideas of Bruno and of Spinoza as between the glowing, imaginative, poetical manner and style of the former, stamped throughout with the personality of the writer, and the rigid mathematical mould, excluding every trace of personal feeling, in which the ideas of the latter are cast. What point of contact, for instance, can be discerned between Spinoza's view of the universe as a system in which all things follow from the idea of infinite substance by as strict logical deduction as the properties of a triangle from its definition, and Bruno's conception of an infinite organism in-

stinct with the freedom, the activity, the perpetual change
and variety of life, and in which the first principle is
for ever manifesting itself, with the spontaneity and inexhaustible productiveness of art, in the forms and
aspects of the world? Yet perhaps a closer examination
may lead to the conclusion that, with many apparent
and some real differences between the two systems, in
their essential principle and in the results to which it
leads, there is a real affinity between them. Both seek
to justify for thought that idea of the absolute unity of
all things which is the presupposition of all science and
of all philosophy. Both seek to explain the universe
from itself, to the exclusion of any external or arbitrary
cause, as implying a virtual abandonment of the problem
to be solved. In the idea of God both endeavour
to find, not an inexplicable supramundane Creator, but
the immanent cause or principle of the world. In both
there is a sense in which the words " God " and "Nature "
are interchangeable. In Bruno, the first principle is the
union of potentiality and actuality ; and whether you
consider it as a principle which realises itself in the
actual, and call it God, or as all actuality in relation to
its principle, and call it Nature, it is only one and the
same thing contemplated from different sides. In Spinoza,
Substance is that beyond which nothing exists or can be
conceived, and Nature—understood as the whole finite
world, including all possible modifications of an infinite
number of infinite attributes in their relation to Substance,
or in so far as they are expressions of it—is only another
name for the same universe regarded from a different
point of view. Finally, in both systems the logical re-

sult falls short of the aim and intention of the author, and the failure in both cases arises, to some extent at least, from the same cause—viz., the attempt to reach a concrete, by a method that can yield only an abstract, unity. We have seen how in Bruno the infinite living organism, which was his ideal of the universe, reduces itself to a God who is only a bare self-identical abstraction, in which the finite is lost or annulled. And in the sequel we shall find that Spinozism is, from òne point of view, the ambiguous result of two conflicting elements— a self-identical, undetermined substance which is all in one, and a world of finite individualities, each of which has a being and reality of its own. It is the obvious intention of the author to bring these two elements into the unity of a perfect system—to find in Substance the origin and explanation of finite existences, and also to bring back all the individualities of the finite world into unity in their relation to the one infinite substance. But the relation between the two elements is only asserted, never demonstrated. The absolutely undetermined is, by its very definition, precluded from going forth out of itself into a world of finite determinations ; and if we start from the latter, they can only be brought back to the former by the destruction of their finitude, and their absorption in the infinite all.

From these considerations it seems to follow that, whatever weight we attach to the external evidence of Spinoza's indebtedness to Bruno, in the movement of thought in both writers, in the principle from which they start, the end at which they aim, their partial success, and the reason of their failure, a close resemblance

may be traced. Whether, in point of fact, we can affili-
ate Spinoza's system to the speculations of his predeces-
sor is doubtful, but it must at least be conceded that
the philosophy of the former betrays tendencies which,
had he been acquainted with Bruno's writings, would
have led him to recognise in the latter a spirit akin to
his own.

# CHAPTER V.

### DESCARTES.

THE philosophy and the theology of modern times start from a common origin, and a certain analogy may be traced, at least in their earlier stages, in the course of development through which they passed. What first strikes us in studying that development is its apparent inconsistency with its origin. The principle of freedom is the common source of both, yet in both it speedily passes into a doctrine of absolutism which seems to be the complete negation of freedom. From a movement in which everything seems to be grounded on the individual consciousness, we are brought almost immediately to a theory of the universe in which God is so conceived of as to leave to the world and man no independence or reality. In religion, the assertion of the right of private judgment gives rise to a theology of absolute predestination and "irresistible grace." In philosophy the principle of self-consciousness, as the source of all knowledge and the criterion of certitude, develops into a system of uncompromising pantheism.

Yet a little reflection will show that the transition thus indicated involves no real inconsistency. The principle of the Protestant Reformation was, indeed, the assertion of spiritual freedom. It expressed the revolt of the reawakening religious consciousness against external mediation or authority in matters of faith. It is implied in the very idea of religion that the human spirit is essentially related to the divine, and that in seeking to realise that relation it is attaining to a deeper consciousness of itself. By whatever outward means the knowledge of God and of divine things may be conveyed to us, it is not religious knowledge until it has been grasped by the spiritual consciousness and has found its witness therein. The ultimate criterion of truth must lie not without, but within, the spirit. The voice of God must find its response in the heart and conscience of him to whom it speaks, and nothing can hold good for him as true or divine which has not received its authentication in the " assurance of faith." But whilst nothing, it would seem, can be more thoroughgoing than this assertion of spiritual freedom, it involves and directly leads to what might easily be regarded as the negation of such freedom. Religious knowledge is the revelation to man at once of freedom and of absolute dependence ; of freedom, because it is to consciousness that truth appeals, and by the activity of consciousness that truth is apprehended—of absolute dependence, because at the very first step of our entrance into the kingdom of truth, we find ourselves in a region where nothing can be made or unmade by us, in the presence of an authority which dominates our will and claims the complete submission of our thoughts. The very act of entering into it involves the renunciation of all individual opinions, inclinations, prejudices, of everything that pertains

to me merely as this individual self. It implies, moreover, the recognition by the individual self, not merely
of its finitude and dependence, but of its moral blindness
and weakness. Truth must find its witness in the consciousness; but the consciousness to which it appeals is
that not of the natural man, but of the spiritual. The
response which it awakens is that not of the individual
self, but of a higher or universal self, with which the
former is not in harmony. It is therefore the revelation
to me not merely of a universal reason to which the individual consciousness must subject itself, but of an
absolute moral authority, an infinite will at once in me
and above me, before which I am self-condemned and
helpless. Religion begins with the sense of moral guilt
and impotence; but the presupposition which this involves is that of an infinite will with which my finite
will is not in harmony, and to which it is only by the
absolute renunciation of any individual independence,
that I can ever be reconciled. It is from this point of
view that we can understand how, from the principle of
Protestantism, the early Reformers should be led to that
idea of God which constitutes the primary doctrine of
their theological system.

The principle which was at the root of the Protestant
Reformation found thus its first expression in the sphere
of religion, and it was here that the human spirit first
attained emancipation from that bondage to authority in
which it had been held. But the century of the Reformation is the beginning also of a new epoch in philosophy; and both in its origin and development, a close
analogy can be traced between the philosophical and the
religious movement. Speculative thought felt the same

impulse with religion to liberate itself from the presuppositions which had hitherto fettered it, and to assert its autonomy in its own sphere. And here, too, the individual consciousness seemed to employ its regained freedom only in subjecting itself to a new and more absolute limitation. In this point of view the philosophy of Descartes may be compared to the first assertion of religious liberty by the Reformers, and the philosophy of Spinoza springs from it by the same movement of thought which gave birth to the predestinarian theories of Luther and Calvin.

In general, the philosophy of Descartes expresses the effort of intelligence to bring all things within its own sphere, to find within thought the explanation of all the problems of thought. Formally stated, Descartes' search after an ultimate criterion of certitude was the endeavour to give to all that claims to be knowledge the form of self-consciousness. The process by which he represents himself as reaching this criterion is indeed, when closely examined, one which already virtually implies it. In the search for intellectual satisfaction he begins by resolving to reject everything which it is possible to doubt. When we examine the contents of ordinary knowledge, we find it to consist of a mass of unsifted and incongruous materials—of impressions, opinions, beliefs, which reason has never tested, and which have no other than an accidental connection with each other. They have been blindly accepted on authority or by tradition, they have fallen upon the mind in the form of instinctive impressions, they have been woven together by arbitrary associations. When reflection is awakened, there are none of them which it cannot doubt, and, at least provisionally, reject ;—not authoritative dogmas and beliefs, for these by their very definition have no inherent certainty ; not things we seem to perceive by the senses, for the senses often deceive us, and what once deceives may do so always ; not even mathematical propositions, for, as we are not the makers of our own minds, it is at least conceivable that they are the creation of some malicious or mocking spirit who has so constructed them as, even in their seemingly demonstrative certainties, to be mistaking error for truth. But when, by this process of elimination, I have got rid of or provisionally rejected one after another of the elements of that accidental conglomerate of beliefs which I have hitherto accepted, is there nothing that remains, no primeval rock of certitude, or fundamental basis of knowledge unassailable by doubt ? And the answer is, that when everything else has been doubted, there is one thing which lies beyond the reach of doubt, which in the very process of doubting I tacitly affirm. I cannot doubt the doubter. Doubt is thought, and in thinking I cannot but affirm the existence of the thinker. From everything else I can abstract, but I cannot abstract from myself who performs the process of abstraction. *Cogito, ergo sum.*

In this account which Descartes gives of the way in which he seemed to himself to have reached an ultimate principle of certitude, it is obvious that he tacitly presupposes from the outset the principle of which he is in quest. When he sets out by saying, " I will question everything which I can doubt," he virtually posits the " I " as the umpire by whose verdict everything is to be decided. In this, as in every other possible investigation which it can undertake, thought presupposes itself. In bringing anything to the bar of consciousness, consciousness presumes its own reality. Nay, we can go further, and say that in every act of intelligence, in the most rudimentary exercise of thought by which I bring any object before me, I presuppose myself as the thinking subject to which that object is referred. And this, further, enables us to see what is the real significance of Descartes' fundamental principle. As has been often pointed out, the proposition, " I think, therefore I am," is only in form syllogistic. As its author himself expressly says, it is not an argument based on the major premiss, " Whatever thinks exists," for the terms of that premiss would have no meaning save what is derived from the prior intuition of the unity of being and thought. *Cogito ergo sum* is, therefore, simply the expression of that unity as the ultimate datum of consciousness. In saying " I am conscious," the " I " and the consciousness predicated of it cannot be separated. In affirming the consciousness we affirm the I. Descartes' proposition, therefore, is the assertion of the indissoluble unity of thought and reality in self-consciousness as the fundamental principle on which all knowledge rests.

Descartes had now attained the principle of which he was in quest; but the inquiry would have been fruitless unless in that principle he had found not only that which is absolutely certain in itself, but that which is the source of all other certainties, the idea by means of which we can advance to rehabilitate the world which doubt has destroyed. If this principle is not to remain a mere barren abstraction, a form of knowledge without content, it must enable us to recover, as objects of rational and certain knowledge, what had been rejected as a congeries of unsifted beliefs. How, then, asks Descartes, shall we find in self-consciousness the key to all knowledge ? Now the failure or success of any attempt to answer this question must, it is easy to see, turn upon the sense in which the principle itself is understood. Whether the proposition, " I in thinking am," or more briefly, " I think," is to be fruitful or barren, depends on the part of it on which the emphasis is thrown. If the latter term be limited by the former, if, in other words, the thought or self-consciousness here affirmed be taken as merely subjective and individual, the proposition contains in it the beginning and end of all knowledge. In the empirical fact of his own self-consciousness there is nothing which enables the individual to transcend his own individuality. Thought that is purely mine can build for itself no bridge by which it can pass to a world that lies, by supposition, wholly beyond it. The future history of philosophy was to show, in the vain endeavours of the empirical psychologists, from Locke downwards, to solve this problem, that individualism imprisons the mind in its own isolated consciousness, and can never attain to the legitimate knowledge of the nature or even of the existence of any reality beyond it.

On the other hand, the principle of self-consciousness may be so construed as to become in itself the fruitful source of knowledge, and the test by which all knowledge can be evaluated. What it may be understood to mean is, that beyond all difference of thought and being, of thought and its object, there is a unity which alone makes this difference intelligible, a unity which is the first presupposition of all affirmation about the particular subject and the particular object. Or to state it differ-

ently, it may mean that whilst I can abstract from everything else, I cannot abstract from the being which is identical with thought. That being is not the being of my
particular self ; for that too, like every other particular
contingent existence, I can in one sense abstract from.
I can make it an object of observation, I can think of it,
and I can think it away, as that which was not and
might not be. But the self from which I cannot abstract, the self which is identical with thought, is that
for which not only I, this particular individual, am, but
for which and in which I and all things are. So far
from shutting me up in a mere subjective experience,
with a world of realities lying beyond and inaccessible,
self-consciousness, thus understood, is that which contains
in it the possibility of all knowledge. It is that which
is presupposed in all knowledge and to which all realities
are relative.

In which of these senses did Descartes understand his
own fundamental principle ? In his endeavour to re-
construct the world by means of it, did he employ it in
the sense in which it is altogether inadequate for the
task, or in the sense in which a system of knowledge
can legitimately be based on it ? The answer is, that
he did neither, but wavered between the two radically
inconsistent interpretations, and whilst his system contains much that implies or points towards the higher
view, he neither grasps it firmly nor carries it out to
its logical results. Yet even the arbitrary expedients
which he employs to extract more from his first principle than, in the narrower sense, it could yield, proves
that the wider construction of it was that towards
which he unconsciously tended, though it was left for

other and more consequent thinkers to discern its full
significance.

To say that self-consciousness is that to which all
things are relative, is to say that the world is an intelligible world, and that betwixt mind and matter,
thought and being, there is no essential division, and
no necessity, therefore, to go in search of some third
principle to mediate between them. Such a necessity,
however, Descartes creates for himself. The doubt or
provisional negation of external things by which the
affirmation of a conscious self had been reached, he
speedily hardens into an absolute negation. It is through
the opposition of a not-self that mind realises itself
How then can that conscious self which exists only as it
opposes itself to that which is not-self, which knows itself
only in abstracting from a world without, hold any intelligent converse therewith? In attempting to know
anything beyond itself, is not consciousness committing
a virtually suicidal act? This difficulty was rendered
more formidable for Descartes by the view he takes of
the essentially distinctive nature of mind and matter.
Mind and matter are independent substances, each having
its own determining or characteristic attribute. The
characteristic attribute of mind is thought or self-
consciousness, that of matter is extension, and these two
can only be understood in a sense which renders them
reciprocally contradictory. Thought or self-consciousness
is that which is absolutely self-included and indivisible.
We can ideally distinguish in it that which thinks and
that which is object of thought; but they do not lie outside of each other, they are indivisible elements in the
unity of self-consciousness. But if this *in*tensiveness is

the essence of mind, that of matter is the very opposite
or contradiction of this—*ex*tension, self-externality, existence which consists of parts outside of parts, without
any centre of unity.   Mind is self-consciousness ; matter, on the other hand, is absolute selflessness.   Now
then, between things which by their very definition are
reciprocally exclusive, can there be any communion ?
How can that whose very being is to be selfless become
related to that whose very being is to be a conscious
self ?   In passing into mind, matter must cease to be
matter ; in going forth to apprehend matter, mind must
cease to be mind.

The expedient by which ultimately Descartes endeavours to overcome this difficulty is, as we shall see,
that of arbitrarily depriving the two independent substances of their independence and reciprocal exclusiveness by reducing them to moments of a third and higher
substance.   Whilst the distinctive attribute which makes
each a substance with reference to the other remains,
their opposition is mediated by the absolute substance,
God, on whom the existence of both depends.    But this
attempt to overcome the dualism of mind and matter
presents itself first in a somewhat cruder and more
mechanical form.   Mind and matter are essentially opposed ; but God becomes the guarantee to mind of the
truthfulness of its ideas of matter.   Mind has no immediate certainty of the truth of these ideas ; it simply
finds them in itself.   They convey no assurance of any
objective reality corresponding to them.   It is conceivable, as was formerly supposed, that our notions of
material things, or even of the existence of an external
world, may be illusions.   But our idea of God is that

of an all-perfect Being, one of whose perfections is absolute veracity or truthfulness. If, therefore, in the mind which owes to Him its existence we find certain clear and distinct ideas of matter or of external realities, the veracity of God is the unquestionable security that these ideas are true. Ideas of things which we could not otherwise trust, we can trust as implanted in us by a God that cannot lie.

Arbitrary and forced as this method of solving the problem before him seems to be, what it really indicates is, that Descartes had discerned the inadequacy of a merely individualistic principle of knowledge, and had begun to see that the consciousness of the individual is implicated with a consciousness wider and more absolute than itself. And this becomes more obvious when we go on to consider how Descartes contrives, without any conscious departure from his fundamental principle, to extract from it the idea of God and the proof of His objective existence. In two ways consciousness seems to him to testify to something more absolute than itself. In the first place, he finds in it an idea which, from its very nature, cannot be traced to any finite source, and which therefore witnesses to an infinite Being as its cause or archetype. Whatever reality, he argues, any thing or idea contains, at least as much must be contained in its cause. If I find in myself an idea which contains more reality than is contained in my own nature or could be derived or collected from other finite natures, I may conclude that there is a being containing in himself an amount of reality transcending that of all finite existence. Such an idea is that of God, the infinite substance, and it could only have been implanted in me by an actually existing God.

To this argument it is easy to take exception, on the obvious ground that it presupposes the thing which it is intended to prove—that it seeks to deduce from consciousness, or one of the ideas of consciousness, a being who is to guarantee the veracity of consciousness ; and further, that it attempts to find *in* thought the proof of something outside of thought or unthinkable—in other words, to make thought transcend itself. Yet the flaw is only in the form, not in the real though implicit significance of the argument. The being who contains in himself all perfections is still a being thought of in a most definite way. Seeming to himself to have forced a path outward to a region beyond consciousness, Descartes is still within it ; and what he has really achieved is virtually to expand the sphere of self-consciousness till it embraces that which transcends all that is finite and individual. The secret nerve of the argument, and that which constituted its motive and significance, was, that there is an infinite element in thought, or that the consciousness of the individual, when closely examined, is seen to be implicated with or dominated by a universal consciousness, or a consciousness of the infinite.

The contrast between the apparent and the real significance of the argument becomes still more obvious in the second form in which Descartes presents it, and which is only a modification of the "ontological argument" of Anselm and Aquinas. The objective existence of God is involved in the very idea of God. Amongst the various ideas in our minds we find one, the highest of all—that of a Being supremely wise and powerful and

absolutely perfect; and we perceive that this idea, unlike
others, contains in it the characteristic, not of possible
or contingent, but of absolutely necessary existence. In
the same way, therefore, as from the fact that the idea
of a triangle necessarily involves that its angles should
be equal to two right angles, we conclude that every
triangle must have this property; so from the fact that
the idea of an absolutely perfect being includes in it
that of existence, we conclude that such a being must
necessarily exist. Here again the argument, though
faulty in the form in which Descartes presents it, is
valuable as indicating the untenableness of his original standpoint, and the inevitable tendency to read into
it a new and deeper meaning. If self-consciousness
is only individual, and we suppose a world of realities
lying outside of it, it is impossible to conclude from self-
existence or any other element of an idea in us that
there is any actual reality corresponding to it — any
more than, according to Kant's familiar illustration, I
can infer from the idea of a hundred dollars in my mind
that I have them in my purse. That equality of its
angles to two right angles is a necessary element of the
idea of a triangle, proves no more than that *if* any actual
triangle exists, it will possess this property; and that
necessary existence belongs to the idea of God, merely
proves that *if* there is a being corresponding to the idea,
he exists necessarily. By no straining, therefore, could
the principle of self-consciousness, if regarded as merely
individualistic, break down, in this case any more than
in any other, the barrier between the subjective self and
the world of realities opposed to it. But what Descartes
was really aiming at was a self-consciousness which is

not individual but universal, or the principle that the
real presupposition of knowledge is not the individual's
consciousness of himself as an individual, but the thought
or consciousness of a self which is beyond all individual
selves and their objects—that, viz., of universal or absolute intelligence.   Other existences may be contingent,
other things may or may not be; but behind all our
ideas there is one which, whether we are explicitly or
only implicitly conscious of it, so proves its reality from
thought, that thought becomes impossible without it.
Its absolute reality is so fundamental to thought, that to
doubt it is to doubt reason itself.   This was the goal to
which Descartes was tending.   Had he reached it, the
principle of individual freedom with which he started
would have converted itself into another form, which is
either the pantheistic suppression of freedom, or the re-
establishment of it on a deeper basis.   In his own hands,
however, it remained in the imperfect form in which it
served only to introduce into his system a new element
absolutely inconsistent with the principle from which he
started.

The foregoing view of the tendency and results of the
Cartesian philosophy will be borne out if we consider,
further, how near Descartes comes to the abandonment
in express terms of his original for a different standpoint; in other words, to the recognition of the truth
that it is not the consciousness of self but the consciousness of God which is the first principle of knowledge.   What he had represented to himself as the original certainty of self had been reached by doubting
everything else; but it was not the doubt that had
created the certitude, but the certitude that had cre-

ated the doubt. It was the implicit presence of a standard of reality that had led him to pronounce his first notions of things illusory and unreal. The idea that was the *prius* in the process of doubt was not that of the things doubted, but the idea or consciousness of self. In like manner when he comes to consider the relation of the idea of God to other ideas, or of the idea of the infinite to that of the finite, he expressly maintains that the idea of infinite and necessary being does not arise by abstraction or negation from that of finite, contingent being, but conversely, that it is the presence in the mind of the idea of infinite and necessary being that enables us to pronounce any other existences to be finite and contingent. " I ought not to think," says he, " that I perceive the infinite only by negation of the finite, as I perceive rest and darkness by negation of motion and light ; on the contrary, I clearly perceive that there is more of reality in infinite substance than in finite, and therefore that, in a certain sense, the idea of the infinite is prior in me to that of the finite." In other words, the idea of the infinite is presupposed in that of the finite ; the former is the positive idea, the latter produced merely by negation or limitation of it. It is really, though unconsciously, the idea of God from which we start, and from which our ideas of other existences as finite are derived. But if this be so, it is to be observed that we have here the complete subversion of Descartes' original principle of knowledge. For, in the first place, amongst the ideas of finite things to which that of the infinite is now pronounced the *prius*, must be included the idea of the finite individual self. And in the

second place, the *cogito ergo sum* was, as we can now
see, only his proof of God in another form.   In the
latter, he finds in his mind an idea which, in contrast
with all ideas of merely finite, contingent existences, is
that of infinite or necessary existence.   In the former
he found in his mind an idea which, in contrast with
all ideas he could doubt or deny, was absolutely certain.
The starting-point and the process are in both cases the
same.   What he denies or reduces to negativity and
contingency in contrast with the idea of God, is precisely the same with what he denied or reduced to
illusion and nullity in contrast with the idea of self.
The conclusion he reaches must be in both cases the
same.   And that the self of the one process is really
identical with the God of the other, is further obvious
from this, that doubt is possible, not through the certainty of self, but through the certainty of absolute
truth.   In doubting or denying anything, the tacit appeal
is not to a finite but to an infinite standard, not to the
idea of the subjective self, but to that of absolute objective reality.   The self of the *cogito ergo sum* was therefore not really the individual self, but that infinite which
he now pronounces to be the *prius* in thought of all
finite existences.

But though logically Descartes' own express admis-
sion implied the abandonment of his former for a new
principle of knowledge, he did not himself recognise or
admit the implication.   To save his own consistency he
has recourse to a distinction which is simply the acknowledgment of the unresolved dualism which characterises his system.   In order to retain the *cogito ergo sum*
as a first principle, whilst yet asserting that God or the

infinite is in thought the *prius* of the finite, he distinguishes between the principle of knowledge (*principium
cognoscendi*) and the principle of being (*principium
essendi*), assigning the former *rôle* to the Ego, the latter
to God. But a philosophical system fails by its own
showing, if it does not give to all with which it deals
the unity of *knowledge*. What, as a philosophy, it
undertakes to do, is to explain the world as an intelligible world—to trace rational relations between all
existences and orders of being, to make them members of one system by showing how all are expressions
of one principle to which all their differences can be
brought back. To make Being, therefore, something
apart from and irreducible to the principle of knowledge, is virtually to confess the inadequacy of the
system and of the principle on which it is based—to
save that principle by admitting that there is something
it cannot explain. For Descartes the true escape from
his dilemma would have been by admitting the conclusion to which his own hesitating language logically
pointed—that God or the infinite is first in knowledge
as well as first in being. To separate the existence of
God from the idea of God, and make the latter only the
proof of the former, was the impossible attempt to go
outside of knowledge for the explanation of knowledge ; and it was an attempt which his own account
of that idea rendered wholly arbitrary and self-contradictory. For what alone can be meant by an innate
or implanted idea of God is simply the indwelling or
activity of God in us. To infer the existence of God
from the idea of God, is to infer the existence of God
from the consciousness of it, or to infer the existence of

God from itself. There is no advance to something new in thinking of the existence of God, when in thought I have already His necessary existence. The idea is already the existence of God. " I think God, therefore God is," is no more a syllogism in which existence is inferred from thought than *cogito ergo sum* is such a syllogism. The existence and the thought are given in one act, inseparably united. It was because Descartes failed to perceive this that the unity to which his system tended was left still encumbered with a dualistic element.

Finally, it is to be remarked that the dualism which remains unresolved in Descartes' view of the relation of God and the world, continues of necessity unresolved in his conception of the relation of mind and matter, of soul and body. If the infinite be arbitrarily separated from the finite, the latter necessarily breaks into irreconcilable oppositions. Thought and being divided at the source cannot be united in the streams. Accordingly, mind and matter, the world within and the world without, remain, in Descartes' view, independent entities tied together only by an arbitrary bond. They are, as we have seen, so defined as to be each the absolute negation of the other. The two are conceived of only as substances reciprocally exclusive, and their very nature consists in *being* reciprocally exclusive. It would seem, therefore, impossible that two substances so defined should be united in one system or brought into any real relation to each other. To be so would imply that mind should cease to be mind, or matter matter—that mind should become extended, or matter think. All the devices, therefore, by which Descartes endeavours to include them in one system, are expedients to knit together what has been irreparably rent asunder. Mind has in it ideas of corporeal things; but these ideas have no real but only a representative relation to external objects, and they are not the mind's own, but due to an outside power who mechanically inserts or infuses them and vouches for their truth. Body and soul are not in themselves related to each other; they are not correlative factors of a whole which explains at once their difference and their unity, but independent substances brought and kept together by an external and unintelligible force. Thus matter and mind fall asunder, and that which is supposed to unite them does not unite them for thought. There being nothing in their own nature which unites them, an arbitrary act of power, even when it is designated omnipotent, explains nothing, but is merely another way of saying that somehow or another they are united.

There is indeed one form of explanation to which, with marks of hesitation, Descartes' language seems finally to point, and which, in so far as it is a conceivable explanation, indicates the ultimate goal to which his philosophy leads. The dualism which is only verbally solved by reference to an inexplicable act of power, finds at least a possible solution when the extended and thinking substances are subordinated to an absolute or infinite substance in which their differences are lost. But in order to this solution two things are necessary: in the first place, the subordinate substances must be deprived of their substantial character and reduced to attributes or accidents; and in the second place, the common substance in which they are united must be conceived of as something underlying yet different from both. And this, accordingly, is the process by which Descartes effected his final solution of the problem before him, the restoring to unity of his disintegrated universe. Substance, he tells us, is " that which so exists that it needs nothing else in order to its existence." But in this sense the notion cannot be applied to finite, created existences. Mind and matter retain, indeed, each its substantial character and distinguishing attribute with reference to the other ; but with reference to God they lose their independence and exclusiveness, and become, as absolutely dependent, moments or accidents of His being. Further, the supreme or absolute substance in which mind and matter find their reality must be something in which their distinctive characteristics no longer exist, a unity which is different from both. Though elsewhere, therefore, Descartes speaks of the nature of God as having a nearer affinity to mind than to matter, yet, contemplated as substance, he expressly declares that nothing can be predicated in the same sense of God and finite creatures. The qualities of matter He cannot have, for matter is divisible and imperfect ; and if thought can be ascribed to Him, it is in Him something essentially different from thought in man. God is therefore for us simply the unknown something which remains when we abstract from nature and man their distinctive attributes. He is neither matter nor thought, and if He can be conceived at all, it is only as the bare abstraction of Being which is common to both.

It is little wonder that Descartes' language should become hesitating and ambiguous when he seems to be led by his own logic to a conception which, instead of explaining the differences of the finite world, seems to suppress or annul them—which, having absorbed nature and man in God, reduces God Himself to a lifeless abstraction of which we can say nothing but that it *is*. But whilst Descartes, recoiling from the pantheistic abyss to the brink of which he had been led, refuses to commit himself in definite terms to this result, it was left for another and more resolute thinker to follow out his principles to their legitimate conclusion.

## NOTE.

The treatise ' De Deo et Homine,' which has been brought
to light in recent times, may be regarded as a kind of study
for Spinoza's greater and more systematic work, the ' Ethics.'
For the student of his philosophy its chief interest lies in
the fact that the ideas of the later work are here presented
to us in an inchoate and cruder form.　As the title indicates, the subject of the earlier work is the same as that of
the later; the succession of topics is the same in both,
and we find in them many coincidences both of thought
and expression.　But the earlier treatise is less coherent and
complete.　There is much in it—conceptions, definitions,
phrases, scholastic and theological formulæ—which are not
found in the ' Ethics,' and which can only be regarded as
survivals from a more immature stage of thought.　At the
outset Spinoza seems to be hesitating between different starting - points, and making trials of fundamental principles
which are essentially inconsistent.　There are many gaps in
the logical sequence of thought, dialogues are interposed
which interrupt the main argument, and an appendix is
added in which the doctrines of the work are re-discussed
from a different point of view.　But with all these differences the general character of the two works is the same.
They bear the stamp of the same mind, only of the same
mind at an earlier and a later stage of its philosophical development.　In the former we see the writer feeling his way
to ideas concerning God and man which reappear in the
latter, freed from irrelevances and inconsequences, as the
final result of his speculations.

It was my intention, as formerly indicated, to prepare for
the criticism and interpretation of the ' Ethics ' by a careful examination of the treatise ' De Deo et Homine.'　Such
an examination, however, would have extended this book
greatly beyond the limits assigned to it.　I have therefore been compelled to omit this part of my general plan.

# CHAPTER VI.

## THE ' ETHICS '—ITS METHOD.

THE point of view of a philosophical writer reflects itself,
not only in the substance of his teaching, but in the
form in which it is cast.   Clear speculative insight may
rise above the restraints of a false or defective method,
but cannot altogether withstand its influence.   Form
inevitably reacts on matter, method unconsciously modifies ideas or hinders their full expression and development.   From the form, therefore, of Spinoza's system
we may derive some help in the endeavour to apprehend
its general bearing and to discover the reasons both of
its success and of its failure, of what it does and of
what it leaves undone.

What Spinoza aimed at was a system of knowledge in
which everything should follow by strict necessity of
thought from the first principle with which it starts.
It is the function of reason to rise above the influence
of the senses, to strip away from the objects it contemplates the guise of contingency and independence with
which ordinary observation clothes them, and to see all
things related to each other under the form of absolute
necessity.   To this end it seeks to penetrate to the first

ground or presupposition of all thought and being, to grasp " that idea which represents the origin and sum of nature, and so to develop all our ideas from it that it shall appear as the source of all other ideas."

With such a conception of the nature of knowledge it is easy to see how Spinoza should regard the science of mathematics as affording the purest type of method, and should endeavour, as he has done, to cast his system in geometrical form. In geometry everything is based on the fundamental conception of space or quantity, and the whole content of the science seems to follow by rigid logical necessity from definitions and axioms relating to that conception. Might not the same exactitude, certainty, necessity of sequence be obtained for the truths of philosophy as for the truths of mathematics by following the same method ? It was probably some such anticipation that led Spinoza to give to his great work the form which is indicated by its title, ' Ethics demonstrated in Geometrical Order,' and to set forth his ideas, after the manner of Euclid, in a series of definitions, axioms, postulates, and of propositions and corollaries flowing from these by strict logical deduction.

To what extent the defects of Spinoza's system are to be traced to his method will perhaps appear in the sequel ; but it may be pointed out here that, from the very nature of the thing, a purely geometrical method is inadequate to the treatment of philosophical truth.

1. For one thing, philosophy must go further back than either mathematics or the sciences that treat of outward nature. These sciences may and do take much for granted ; philosophy admits of no unexamined presuppositions. The former not only deal with limited

departments of knowledge, and with things the existence
of which is regarded as already known, without asking
how they come to be known, but they employ categories
and forms of thought which they do not investigate, and
presuppositions which they do not pretend to do more
than verbally define. Even geometry may, in this point
of view, be called a hypothetical science. It presupposes
the objective existence of space, and employs, without
inquiry into its validity, the category of quantity. It
begins with certain definitions, *e.g.*, of a point, a line, a
surface, without examining into their origin or asking
whether they are mere arbitrary conceptions, or express
what is absolutely true and real. Philosophy cannot
content itself with such a method. It cannot follow
the example of mathematics and start with definitions and axioms, or employ in an uncritical way,
like the physical sciences, such categories as being,
substance, causality, &c. It must go back to the very
beginning, and, in a sense, create the matter with which
it deals. It must entitle itself to the use of its categories by tracing their origin and development, see them
coming to the birth in the pure medium of thought, and
evolving themselves in the necessary movement or process of reason. The special sciences may content themselves, each with its own provisional view of things, and
may relegate to philosophy the task of explaining and
verifying it. A philosophy which did so would need
another philosophy to examine and criticise it.

2. The geometrical method, when closely examined,
fails in that quality which constitutes, at first sight, its
peculiar attraction. It does not furnish to philosophy the
paradigm of a science in which everything follows by strict

necessity from its fundamental principle. In a philosophical system, according to Spinoza's favourite illustration, everything should follow from the primary idea by the same necessity with which the properties of a triangle flow from its definition. And it is true that, if we look only to the figures or ideal constructions represented in the diagrams of the mathematician, it is possible to draw out a series of propositions which follow by rigid deduction from the definitions of the figures. But if we test the value of geometrical science, not by what can be logically deduced from given premisses (and the illustration in question implies no more), but by what is involved in and can be deduced from its fundamental conception, then it fails to furnish what is implied in Spinoza's ideal of a philosophical system. For the idea of space does not evolve from itself a system of geometrical truth. There is no reason simply in the idea of space why triangles, circles, squares, &c., should arise in it. Such constructions are conditioned by and presuppose that idea, but are not produced by it. Space does not produce or evolve anything unless you, the geometrician, arbitrarily create or imagine in it lines, surfaces, solids, figured constructions of whatever kind. Being produced, they must relate themselves to each other according to the conditions which the conception of space involves ; and so you may rear upon these ideal constructions a vast system of geometrical truths of immense value in determining the relations of objects that admit of being regarded quantitatively. But neither these objects nor their relations, ideal or actual, are the necessary product of the fundamental conception. That conception has in it no principle of self-determination, and the determinations it gets are arbitrarily imposed on it from without. If, therefore, philosophical truth is to be, not a system in which by arbitrary synthesis you force its first principle to become fertile, but one in which that principle, by its own genetic power, necessarily determines or differentiates itself to all particular truths, then obviously it is a misconception to seek the type of such a system in the province of the mathematician.

3. The main objection to the employment in philosophy of the geometrical method is that the category on which it is based is inadequate to the treatment of spiritual things. Inevitable confusion and error arise from applying to one order of things conceptions or categories which are strictly applicable only to another and lower order of things, or in leaving out of account in the higher and more complex sphere all conditions and relations save those which pertain to the lower. Now the conceptions of space and quantity have their proper and exclusive application only to objects which can be conceived of as occupying extension or lying outside of each other ; whilst philosophy, in so far as it deals with things spiritual, has to do with a sphere where purely external or special relations vanish. In formal language, mathematical method is applicable only to the sphere of self-externality, but is incapable of dealing with thought or self-consciousness, which is the sphere of immanence or self-internality.

Mathematical science recommends itself by the clearness and simplicity of its conceptions and the demonstrative certainty of its results. But, however valuable within its own sphere, as compared with other sciences it may be said that its simplicity arises from its shallow-

ness or abstractness, and its certainty from its ignoring
of the very elements which, in the case of these sciences,
complicate the problems to be solved. Geometry, as we
have said, is based on the conception of space, and on
ideal constructions or figures in space. It abstracts from
all relations of actual objects, save those which arise
from their being extended—from all conditions save
that of not occupying the same parts of space with each
other. But this obviously is a way of looking at things
which is purely abstract; and conclusions reached with
reference to such abstractions do not apply, strictly speaking, to anything beyond the abstraction itself. Even
inorganic objects are incapable of being reasoned about
as if conclusions which are true of space and its parts
held good with respect to them. In the material world
there are indeed unities which are unities merely of aggregation—made up, that is, of parts which seem to be only
externally related to each other, and to be connected with
other unities only externally. But there are no material realities which are absolutely continuous or which
can be thought of as if their component parts were related to each other as the ideal parts of pure space, or
as if propositions with reference to lines, surfaces, solids
were unconditionally applicable to them. Nor, again,
are there any material realities which are not related to
each other in other ways than can be embraced under
the conception of spatial extension. Inorganic substances undergo chemical changes which do not admit of
being expressed simply in terms of quantity. Iron rusts,
but space does not, and the rusting is something more
than a change of spatial relations. Chemical changes,
in other words, involve other conditions than those of

space. In a chemical compound the unity is one
of which the elements have lost their independent
quantitative existence; their spatial individuality has
vanished in the neutral product. Still less do organic existences admit of being adequately dealt with
under the category of quantity. A living being is not
composed of parts which exist simply outside of each
other, and have only external or spatial relations to
each other. There is a sense in which in an organism
the whole is in every part, and the parts exist only in
the whole. In a mere material aggregate the whole is
simply the sum of the parts; but in a living unity, when
you have summed up all the parts, you have left out
something which escapes spatial measurement, and yet
which constitutes the very essence of the thing. It is
only when it ceases to be living that an organism de-
scends into the sphere to which quantitative measures
belong. And the reason is that its unity is not of parts
external to parts, but of parts which have their being in
and through each other—not a self-external but an immanent or self-internal unity. Least of all, when we
rise to the sphere of spiritual things,—when we propose
to consider the relations of God and man, to treat of
such things as intelligence, freedom, duty, immortality,—
can we adequately apprehend them by a method which
turns on quantitative relations. Organisms, whatever
else they are, are things which still occupy space, and
may therefore partially be apprehended by means of a
category which deals with objects externally related to
each other. But in the sphere of thought or self-consciousness we have absolutely transcended that of spatial
outwardness. The indivisible unity of self-consciousness

transcends all external difference. No thought or feeling is *beside* another. The self that thinks is not something outside of its thoughts. It is by a false abstraction that we talk of one faculty of consciousness as if it were a part or bit of mind separated by spatial division from other faculties. In every part of consciousness the whole is present. Nor, whatever we mean by speaking of one mind as greater than another, can we determine the greatness or littleness as quantitative magnitudes. We cannot conceive of Infinite Mind as something existing above or beyond finite minds; and if we say that Infinite Mind or Intelligence comprehends and transcends all finite minds, we cannot represent this relation as identical with that of a bigger circle or sphere to the smaller circle or sphere that is contained in it. We may speak in a figure of " larger, other minds than ours," but if the figure becomes more than a figure, if we let it govern or guide our ideas as to the nature of spiritual things, it will betray us into confusion and error.

Spinoza is often greater than his method. There are parts of his system which it is impossible to reconcile with the categories that in general seem to guide him. In the last Book of the 'Ethics,' especially, he seems to restore in a measure the very ideas, such as those of human freedom and individuality and of final causality, against which, in the earlier Books, he most strenuously contends. Perhaps the most valuable part of his philosophy is that in which his keen speculative insight rises above his self-imposed restraints. Yet, on the other hand, the method he adopts and the conception on which it is based furnish often the key to the meaning of his

ideas, and the explanation of the errors into which he is
betrayed ; and the general bearing of his system becomes
more intelligible when we consider it in the light of that
method, as a brief glance at some of its leading points
may suffice to show.

1. One of these points is his identification of the
infinite with the purely affirmative, of the finite or
determined with the negative. In one of his letters [1]
occurs the following passage : "As to the doctrine
that figure is negation and not anything positive,
it is plain that the whole of matter, considered indefinitely, can have no figure, and that figure can only
exist in finite and determinate bodies. He who says
that he perceives a figure, merely says that he has before
his mind a limited thing. But this limitation does not
pertain to the thing in respect of its being, but, on the
contrary, of its non-being. As, then, figure is nothing
but limitation, and limitation is negation, figure, as I
have said, can be nothing but negation." The same
principle is expressed in more general terms in another
letter,[2] where he writes : "It is a contradiction to conceive anything whose definition involves existence, or,
which is the same thing, affirms existence, under negation of existence. And since determination indicates
nothing positive, but only a privation of existence in the
nature conceived as determinate, it follows that that of
which the definition affirms existence cannot be conceived as determinate." Applying the principle here
enunciated, he in the same letter identifies the idea of
God, or of "a Being absolutely perfect," with that of
"a Being absolutely indeterminate," and argues that,

[1] Ep. 50.　　　　　　　[2] Ibid., 41.

" since the nature of God does not consist in a certain
kind of being, but in being which is absolutely indeterminate, His nature demands everything which perfectly
expresses being, otherwise it would be determinate and
defective." And the same doctrine, that " finite being is
negation, infinite being absolute affirmation," is laid down
in the ' Ethics.' [1]

In these passages the influence of what may be termed
a geometrical conception of the universe is obvious.
When we represent to ourselves the relation of infinite
and finite by that of space and its determinations, the
idea of the finite becomes that simply of privation or
negation. A figure in space has no individual reality ;
in so far as it has any positive reality, it is only the
reality that belongs to the part of infinite space which
its periphery cuts off ; and in so far as it can be said to
have any individual existence in distinction from infinite
space, that existence is not positive but negative, it is
created solely by cutting off or negating all of space that
is outside of it. Its very essence, therefore, is privation,
negation, want of being. Its sole being is non-being.
And this conception Spinoza applies to all finite or
particular existences. In so far as they have any reality,
it is not their own, but that which pertains to them as
parts of the being of the infinite ; and any apparent
individuality in them is not positive but negative—it expresses, not what they are, but what they are not. It is
true that we can pictorially represent to ourselves figured
portions of space ; but these constructions are purely
ideal, *entia rationis*, fictions of the mind. Space itself
has no parts ; it overflows, so to speak, these arbitrary

[1] Eth. i. 8, schol.

divisions and annuls them. And in like manner, it is possible for imagination to lend to particular finite beings, material or spiritual, an apparent independence or individuality. But this individuality is purely fictitious. It exists only for ordinary experience, which is under the control of appearances ; or for imagination, which regards as real anything that can be pictured. When thought penetrates to the reality of things, it discerns their individual independence to be an illusion ; it breaks down the false abstraction, and perceives the only reality to be that, not of the part but of the whole, not of the finite but of the infinite. It is obvious also what, from this point of view, is the only conception that can be formed of "a Being absolutely perfect." When we withdraw the arbitrary limits which distinguish the finite from the infinite, what we reach is simply that which is free from all limits or determinations, the absolutely indeterminate ; and as determinations are merely negations, the removal of all negations leaves us in the presence of non-negation, or of pure, absolute affirmation. As the very essence of the finite is *non esse*, privation or negation of being, so the essence of the infinite is simply pure Being, that which *is*, or that which cannot be conceived save as existing, seeing its very nature is one with existence.

We see, therefore, in so far as this part of his system is concerned, the narrowing influence of Spinoza's method. The conception of things on which that method is based excludes any other alternative than that of determination or indetermination. It excludes, in other words, another possible alternative—viz., that of self-determination, that is, of an affirmation which does not simply annul, but subsumes and includes negation.

Yet the way to this alternative lay open to Spinoza
when he had reached the last result which his method
could yield. For an affirmation which is reached by
negation, cannot ignore it. Apart from negation pure
affirmation has no meaning. A negative element enters
into its very essence. In itself, like the conception of
pure space on which it is based, it is a mere abstraction ;
it needs the negative or determinate as its correlate.
And when we have reached this point, we have got
beyond the contradictory elements of negation and affirmation to an idea which includes both. Thus the infinite, in the highest sense of the word, must be conceived not as the simple negation of the finite, but as
that which at once denies and affirms it. What this
view further implies—what is involved in the notion of
an infinite which does not annul, but realises itself in
and through the differences of the finite world—this is
not the place to show. Had Spinoza taken this further
step, it would have implied the reconstruction of his
whole system. As it is, the idea of a purely affirmative
infinite, or of a finite which is merely the illusory substantiation of imaginary distinctions in the infinite, had
it not been accompanied by other ideas, which, however illogically associated with it, modify or correct it,
would have left his system one of uncompromising
pantheism.

2. Connected with the foregoing, and in further
illustration of the relation of Spinoza's thought to his
method, we have to notice his denial of human freedom,
and his rejection of any other criterion of perfection
than that of amount or quantity of being.

In a system in which all things follow from the first

principle with the same necessity as the properties of a
geometrical figure from its definition, or a logical conclusion from its premises, individual freedom is, of
course, an impossible conception. The illusion of freedom, according to Spinoza, arises from the tendency
already noticed as belonging to ordinary thinking—the
tendency to see things abstractly or with the eyes of
imagination. The individual thinks himself free because
he is conscious of his desires and actions, but not of the
conditions that determine them. He can imagine himself to have acted otherwise than he has done, and can
ascribe to himself a capacity of so acting, for the same
reason that he can picture himself as an isolated and
independent being in the universe. But when he looks
at himself with the eye of reason rather than of imagination, he can no more think himself acting otherwise than
he has acted, than a triangle, if it were conscious, could
think its angles equal to three or four right angles or any
other number of right angles than two. For the same
reason the terms good and evil, virtue and vice, perfection
and imperfection, have, from Spinoza's point of view,
either no meaning or a meaning different from that which
ordinary thought attaches to them. " Were men born
free," says he—" that is, were they led by reason alone,
or possessed of adequate ideas of things—they could form
no idea of good and evil." We may create for ourselves
by the abstracting power of imagination fictitious
standards of human perfection, and judge men according as they fulfil or fall short of them ; but this is
merely a human way of looking at things. To the
divine intelligence what we call good and evil, as implying individual independence and freedom in relation to

the infinite, have no existence.   We compare men with
each other in view of this arbitrary standard, and regard
one as more imperfect than another ; but what separates
man from God, the absolutely perfect Being, is simply
his finitude, and no one finite being can be nearer to the
infinite than another.

There is, indeed, another side of Spinoza's teaching,
according to which, as we shall see, a certain independence or self-assertion, a tendency to maintain itself or
persist in its own being, is ascribed to each individual
existence.   But even here we find that the *quasi* moral
distinctions which this principle introduces, do not turn
on any conception of a universal element in man's nature,
a self deeper. than the natural self, to which merely
quantitative measures will not apply.   On the contrary,
what this supposed tendency or impulse points to is
simply the maintaining and increasing by each individual
of the *amount* of its being.   "Perfection and reality,"
says he, "mean the same thing." [1]   It is the possession
of more or less of this "reality" that distinguishes one
individual from another.   The more reality, the more
power of thinking and acting an intelligent being
possesses, so much the more perfect or virtuous he is.
"When I say that an individual passes from a less to a
greater perfection and *vice versâ*, I understand by this,
that we conceive that his power of action, in so far
as it is understood from his own nature, is increased
or diminished." [2]   The great principle of all spiritual
activity is thus simply the working out and enlargement
of our own individual nature.   Even if apparently unselfish motives, such as sympathy with and participation

[1] Eth. ii., def. 6.                    [2] Ibid. iv., Pref.

in the good of others, are admitted as possible principles of action, the ground of this possibility is that the happiness of the object of such affections contributes to the increase or expansion of our own individual being.

3. The influence of Spinoza's method betrays itself again in his rejection of a teleological conception of the relation of God to the world.

A philosophy which regards all things as following by logical sequence from the first principle, obviously excludes any question of the end or final cause of things. Such a principle does not aim at its results, or employ means to reach them. These results simply *are*, and cannot be conceived to be other than they are ; they do not arise as matters of foreseen design, but are absolutely determined by the nature of the principle with which we start. We may not ask, with respect to finite things or beings, why or for what end they exist, any more than we ask for what end the properties of a triangle exist. Of these we can only say that they are, or that they are because they are given along with the definition of the thing itself. And in like manner, of all finite existences we can only say, not that they point to or are explained by any ulterior end, but that they are because God is, or because they are the necessary determinate expressions of His being.

Spinoza's condemnation of a teleological view of the world is directed mainly against that kind of teleology which constitutes the so-called " argument from design." To view the world teleologically would, he urges, imply imperfection in God by conceiving of Him as aiming at an end outside of Himself. It would be to think of Him after the analogy of finite beings, who seek to give shape to their unrealised conceptions, or are impelled by the consciousness of wants to aim at objects which will satisfy them. "If God," says he, "works for the sake of an end, He necessarily seeks something of which He stands in need. . . . Theologians maintain that God has done all things for His own sake, . . . and therefore they are necessarily compelled to admit that God stood in need of and desired those things for which He determined to prepare the means."[1] But though a teleological view of the world, rightly apprehended, does not thus separate the end from the beginning, and therefore may be freed from the objection that it implies original imperfection in the author of it, it is obvious that in no sense can such a view be expressed in terms of quantity, or under that category on which the geometrical method is based. The idea of Final Cause is that of a unity which realises itself in differences, which, by its own inner impulse, gives rise to differences, yet ever maintains itself in them, and through these differences returns upon itself. It implies an organic process, in which neither the unity is lost in the differences nor the differences in the unity, but in which, the further the differentiation is carried, so much the richer does the original unity become. But, as we have already seen, a geometrical method is incapable of expressing any such living, self-differentiating, self-integrating unity. Space does not determine itself to its own divisions, or give rise to the determinate objects conceived as existing in it. Nor does space retract these arbitrary differences any more than it produces them; and when *we* have withdrawn them and restored the original unity and

[1] Eth. i., Append.

continuity of space, it has not become any richer by the process. The unity prior to the finite was complete in itself, and the arbitrary differentiation and reintegration has not increased its wealth. The differences are not preserved but annulled in the final unity, and it is the same self-identical unity at the end as at the beginning.

# CHAPTER VII.

## SPINOZA'S STARTING-POINT—SUBSTANCE.

THE starting-point of Spinoza's system is the idea of
" Substance," which he defines as " that which is in
itself and is conceived through itself—*i.e.*, that, the conception of which does not need the conception of another
thing in order to its formation."[1] This substance he
characterises as infinite, indivisible, unique, free, eternal, as the cause of itself and of all things, and as consisting of an infinite number of infinite attributes, two
only of which, thought and extension, are cognisable
by human intelligence; and he expressly identifies this
substance with God, whom he defines as "a Being absolutely infinite—that is, substance consisting of infinite
attributes, of which each expresses an eternal and infinite
essence."[2]

In beginning with this idea Spinoza is attempting
to realise his own theory of knowledge—viz., that "in
order that our mind may correspond to the exemplar of
nature, it must develop all its ideas from the idea which
represents the origin and sum of nature, so that that
idea may appear as the source of all other ideas."[3]

[1] Eth. i., def. 3.　　　[2] Ibid., def. 6.　　　[3] De Emend., vii. 42.

Philosophy, according to this view, begins with the universal, not the particular; it does not proceed by induction or generalisation from the facts of observation and experience, but it seeks to grasp the ultimate unity, the highest principle of things, and to derive or develop from it all particular existences. Its method is, not to reach the universal from the particular, but to know the particular through the universal.

But in thus endeavouring to find a first principle from which all things are to be evolved, does not Spinoza lay himself open to the charge often brought against philosophy, of neglecting or anticipating experience, and attempting to explain the world by *a priori* notions? Is not his system a flagrant instance of the unscientific method of metaphysicians who interpret nature by subjective theories, instead of, by patient observation and generalisation of facts, letting nature be her own interpreter? Suppose we could ever apprehend the unity with which he starts, would it not be the end rather than the beginning of knowledge? Science is ever seeking to embrace lower in higher and more comprehensive generalisations, and the ultimate goal to which the scientific impulse points may be a law which would comprehend all laws, a final principle which would transcend the inadequate and partial explanations of the world which particular sciences give, and achieve for them what they, each in its own province, attempt to do for the special phenomena with which they deal. But even if such a goal were actually attainable, would it not be so only as the last result of the long labour of science; and must not the hasty attempt to snatch at this unity by a mere effort of abstract thought be regarded as vain and futile ?

The answer in the case of Spinoza, as in that of all kindred thinkers, is that philosophy does not neglect experience, but only seeks to examine and criticise the presuppositions involved in it, to trace back to their ultimate ground the principles on which, unconsciously, ordinary and scientific thought proceeds ; and then to reinterpret experience—or, in one sense, to re-create it— in the light of the results thus reached. This account of its work implies that philosophy must, in a sense, reverse the order of ordinary and even of scientific experience, and beginning with the highest universal which thought involves, show how from it all lower universalities take their rise, and how the whole world of finite particular existences is transformed for thought by becoming linked in bonds of rational necessity to the first principle of all things.

The progressive method of knowledge then is, in one sense, based on and presupposes the retrogressive. Metaphysic does not pretend to create the world out of its own categories, still less to supersede the special work of science. On the contrary, it is through the discovery of the partial and inadequate explanation of things which the categories of science furnish that it is led to seek after a deeper satisfaction for thought, an interpretation of the world by higher principles, till it attains that final interpretation which is given by a principle that rests on no higher, but is seen by its own light. Reversing the process, it then seeks to show how all the previous stages of knowledge, from the highest to the lowest, become transformed in the light of the first principle of knowledge, or how all things are seen in their reality only when regarded as its expressions or manifestations.

Spinoza's method, then, is not justly chargeable with reversing the true order of knowledge. If his philosophy be found defective, the defect will lie not in his beginning where he did, but in the nature of the idea with which he began ; not in his attempt to start with a first principle from which all things might be derived, but in the idea with which he started being incapable of fulfilling the function assigned to it, and in his attempting to explain all things from this principle simply by analytic deduction. If modern philosophy has had more success in dealing with the problem, perhaps the reason may, in some measure, be that science, by its marvellous progress, has worked into the hands of philosophy in our day as it did not and could not do in his. The inadequacy of Spinoza's first principle is, in part at least, traceable to the fact that he found it possible, so to speak, to reach the infinite by a short cut ; whilst modern thought, in some measure, owes the greater richness and fertility of the idea which constitutes *its* starting-point, to the fact that it has had to attain that idea by a slower and severer process. The problem for Spinoza, by his own showing, was to find a first principle which would explain the universe, after the analogy of mathematical science, according to the simplest of categories. The problem which modern philosophy has had to face is that of finding a final interpretation of nature which must presuppose the previous interpretations of it by the whole range of the physical and biological sciences, and which must supply a principle of criticism of the categories on which these sciences are based, and itself at once comprehend and transcend them.

Spinoza's starting-point, the idea which is to be "the source of all other ideas," that which explains all else but needs no other idea to explain it, is "Substance," which, as already said, he defines as "that which is in itself and is conceived through itself." When we ask what Spinoza means by substance, we seem precluded by the very terms of the definition from all ordinary methods of explanation. The question what it is, seems to be answered simply by the affirmation *that* it is ; the question how we are to conceive of it, by what other ideas we are to be enabled to apprehend its meaning, seems to be met by the affirmation that it is that which can be conceived only through itself: we may understand all other ideas by means of it, not it by means of them.

But whilst thus we seem debarred from any direct explanation of the nature of substance, we may come at the answer indirectly if we consider, in the light of Spinoza's theory of knowledge, what is the point of view which this term is intended to express. We can understand the world, or bring our thoughts "into correspondence with the exemplar of nature," he tells us, as we have seen, only by "developing all our ideas from the idea which represents the origin and source of nature ;" and the idea which constitutes the "origin of nature," he elsewhere defines as that of "a Being, single, infinite, which is the totality of being, and beyond which there is no being." [1] From this we gather that, according to Spinoza's conception of it, true or adequate knowledge is that which starts from *the idea of the whole*, and for which all other ideas have a meaning and reality only as they are determined by or seen in the light of the idea of the whole. Whatever else substance means, therefore, by this term we are to understand this much at least—that idea of the whole or totality of being, in the light of which only can all individual things and thoughts be understood. This may be further illustrated by considering the contrast which elsewhere Spinoza draws between that "vague experience" of which popular knowledge consists, and that *scientia intuitiva* which is the highest and only real kind of knowledge. The separate, independent existence which popular thought ascribes to individual things and beings is no real existence. No object in nature is a single isolated thing. Each object is what it is only in virtue of its relations to other objects, and ultimately to the whole system of being. Ordinary observation looks at things superficially, or as to the outward eye they seem to exist, each apart from or side by side with the rest. Judging merely by the senses, it confounds externality in space with independent existence, and leaving out of view all deeper relations, it represents to itself the spatial separation of stones, plants, animals, as equivalent to an isolated or absolute reality. But when we cease to look at things after the outward appearance, and penetrate to their real nature, their isolated substantiality vanishes; we perceive them to be linked to each other by the inner bond of causality. Each in-

[1] De Emend. ix.

dividual thing forms part of an infinite series of causes and effects; its place, form, functions, activities, are what they are, not through itself alone, but through its connection with other beings, and ultimately with the whole universe of being. Not an atom of matter could be other than it is without supposing the whole material world to be other than it is; and to understand a single material substance, we must take into account not merely its immediate environment, but the causes or conditions which have created that environment, and so on *ad infinitum.* And the same principle applies to intelligent or spiritual beings; they, too, are successive existences which have only a semblance of individuality. By a trick of the imagination, we look upon ourselves as independent, self-determined individuals; but our whole spiritual life is involved in our relations to other intelligences, as theirs again in that of those who surround or precede them. Rightly viewed, each so-called individual is only a transition-point in a movement of thought that stretches back through the interminable past and onwards through the interminable future. Thus the substantial reality of individual existences vanishes, and we can apply the designation " substance " only to the whole, the totality of being which includes and determines them. That whole is the only true individual, the only being which " is in itself and is conceived through itself."

" All bodies," writes Spinoza in one of his letters,[1] " are surrounded by other bodies, and reciprocally determine and are determined by them to exist and act in a fixed and defi-

---

[1] Ep. 15.

nite way. Hence it follows that every body, in so far as it exists under a certain definite modification, ought to be considered as merely a part of the whole universe, which agrees with its whole, and thereby is in intimate union with all the other parts ; and since the nature of the universe is not limited, but absolutely infinite, it is clear that by this nature, with its infinite powers, the parts are modified in an infinite number of ways, and compelled to pass through an infinity of variations. Moreover, when I *think of the universe as a substance,* I conceive of a yet closer union of each part with the whole ; for, as I have elsewhere shown, it is the nature of substance to be infinite, and therefore each single part belongs to the nature of corporeal substance, so that apart therefrom it can neither exist nor be conceived. And as to the human mind, I conceive of it also as a part of nature, as having in it an infinite power of thinking, which, as infinite, contains in it the idea of all nature, and whose thoughts run parallel with existence."

By "substance," therefore, we are to understand, in the first place, the idea of the totality of being or the universe as a whole. Further, this substance is by its nature "infinite." It would be self-contradictory to suppose that any finite thing could be determined merely by a series of finite causes. We may trace back step by step the regress of causes by which each particular existence, material or spiritual, is determined to be what it is. But, however far back we go, we are dealing still with the particular or finite, which needs as much to be determined as the initial member of the series. If it was only by an illusory abstraction that we conceived of the latter as an independent individual, it is only by a like abstraction that we conceive of any aggregate of such individuals as having any reality apart from the whole. We may resolve any

particular thing into a larger whole of which it forms a
part, but that larger whole is itself but a fragment—" an
individual of the second order, but still an individual."
And though we may proceed in the same way by a
process of successive inclusions, correcting the conception of each lower unity by a higher, we can never
by any such ascending movement reach that of which
we are in quest—the infinite whole, the absolute unity
by which all finite things are determined to be what
they are.

But if we cannot reach the infinite, the substance of
all things, by seeking it through a receding series of
finite causes and effects, are we to conclude that the
quest is vain, that the object of inquiry is a chimera;
or if not, how is it to be attained? The answer of
Spinoza virtually is, that we need not ascend to heaven
to bring it down from above, for it is already in our
hands and in our mouths. " Every idea of any body
or existing thing necessarily involves the eternal
and infinite essence." [1] Our ordinary consciousness is
indeed, as we have seen, in one point of view, arbitrary
and illusory; but we have only to examine what is its
real content and meaning to perceive that it involves
what is virtually the consciousness of the infinite. All
knowledge of what is limited rests on an implicit
reference to what is unlimited. Every conception of a
particular space or body presupposes the idea of infinite
space or extension. Every particular idea implies a
virtual reference to an infinite thought. And the distinction of mind and matter, of ideas and things, would
be itself impossible save by a tacit appeal to the idea of

[1] Eth. ii. 45.

an infinite unity which lies beyond their difference. All finite thought and being, therefore, rests on the idea of Infinite Substance. And of this ultimate idea, this *prius* of all thought and being, it must be affirmed that whilst other ideas rest on it, it rests itself on no other. It cannot be proved by anything outside of itself, for no thing or thought could be or be conceived save on the assumption of it. It is beyond demonstration and inaccessible to doubt, for demonstration and doubt alike depend on and indirectly affirm it. It can only be defined as "that which is in itself and is conceived through itself."

What is to be said in criticism of Spinoza's fundamental principle has been already anticipated. That the individual can only be understood in the light of the whole system of being to which he belongs, that all the differences of the finite world presuppose and rest on an ultimate unity which is itself beyond demonstration or doubt, are propositions the soundness of which cannot be questioned. The weakness of Spinoza's doctrine may be said to lie in this, that his substance or infinite unity on which all things rest is not organic but abstract. It may be true to say that substance is that which is in itself and conceived through itself, or, otherwise expressed, that the thought or idea of God proves His being. But the significance and force of the so-called "ontological argument" lies in this, that the unity of thought and being to which it concludes is not an abstract but a concrete unity. The distinction between them, as it is a distinction in thought and to thought, is one which thought can transcend—nay, one which, when we bring to clear consciousness what is implied in it, thought in thinking it has already transcended. But the unity thus reached is the unity *of* the related elements, not something which merely lies beyond them; it explains and reconciles but does not annul them. What it expresses is, that thought and being, though distinguishable, are correlated elements in that ultimate unity of self-consciousness which all knowledge presupposes as its beginning and seeks as its goal. The Spinozistic substance, on the other hand, is reached, as we have seen, not by the reconciliation of opposed but related elements in a higher unity, but simply by abstracting from the difference of these elements. It is not the reason of these differences but the unity that is got by obliterating them. And as all differences vanish in it, so no differences can proceed from or be predicated of it. It not only contains in it no principle of self-determination, but it is itself the negation of all determinations. How then can Spinoza find in his infinite substance the source and explanation of the variety and multiplicity of existence? The answer to this question is contained in his doctrine of "attributes" and "modes."

# CHAPTER VIII.

SUBSTANCE AND ATTRIBUTES.

RIGHTLY to fulfil the function assigned to it as the first principle of knowledge, Spinoza's "substance" must be so conceived as to be, not only the presupposition, but the productive source of all finite being. It must be the ideal origin and explanation of things as well as that which transcends them. We must not merely be forced back to it as the unity which is above all differences, but also find in it that from which all differences are evolved. The transition, in other words, to the finite world must lie in the very nature of substance.

Does Spinoza's substance answer to this conception? That he deemed it capable of doing so is obvious. Substance is not merely *causa sui*, but *causa omnium rerum*. It is a unity which differentiates itself, first into "infinite attributes," then into "infinite modes," and these last again are modified by an infinite number of "finite modes." The world which is meaningless apart from it, the individualities which are only shadows and unrealities looked at in themselves, are redeemed from non-entity by the intuitive grasp of an intelligence which sees them instinct with the presence and power of "substance." All things are unreal viewed as independent or distinct from God; all things become real in so far as we can discern in them the self-affirmation of the divine nature. All thinking things, all objects of all thought, as Spinoza regards them, throb with the vital pulse of the universal life. The dead world becomes alive in God.

But though there can be no doubt as to the part which Spinoza intended his first principle to play, the first step he takes raises the question whether it is inherently capable of the function assigned to it—whether substance, as he defines it, is not so conceived as to be incapable, without giving up its essential nature, of passing from its self-involved unity or identity into difference.

This first step is that which consists in the ascription of "infinite attributes" to the infinite substance. "Substance" or "God" "consists of infinite attributes of which each expresses the eternal and infinite essence." [1] But of these infinite attributes, whilst we know that their number is infinite, only two, "thought" and "extension," are cognisable by human intelligence. What, then, is the ground or reason of this differentiation of the absolute unity? How does Spinoza find the attributes in his substance? To this question the answer seems to be, that whilst (1) there is nothing in the nature of substance, as Spinoza conceives it, which can logically yield, but everything to preclude any such element of difference, (2) failing such logical ground, he simply asserts without proof the differentiation of substance into attributes which he has empirically reached. In other words, the attributes are not differences to

---

[1] Eth. i., def. 6.

which substance determines itself, but to which it is determined *by us.*

(1.) As we have already seen, Spinoza's process to the infinite, the regressive movement by which he reaches substance as the ultimate unity of knowing and being, is simply the removal of the limit by which finite things are supposed to be quantitatively distinguished from the infinite. Number and measure are nothing but fictitious instruments of the imagination by which we break up the indivisible into parts. Space in itself is one and continuous, not made up of discrete parts. You cannot take one portion of space and isolate it from the rest, or say that one portion is here and the next there. Part runs into part, and it is only by a false abstraction that you can view them as separate from each other. "Figure," therefore, is "nothing positive."[1] And the same principle applies to all finite existences. The positive existence we ascribe to them is, when closely viewed, only negation or non-existence. To get to real or affirmative being we must negate the negation, withdraw the fictitious limit, and what we get as the real is simply the absolutely indeterminate, the logical abstraction of Being. To predicate differences of this colourless entity would be to introduce into it non-entity. A determined absolute would be a partly non-existing absolute. From this point of view, therefore, it would seem that Spinoza is precluded from attaching any predicates or ascribing any attributes to his absolute substance. To do so would be, as he himself says,[2] "to conceive under the category of non-existence that whose definition affirms existence."

[1] Ep. 50.  [2] Ep. 51.

(2.) Yet whilst by the very idea of substance Spinoza would seem to be precluded from giving to it any determinations, we find him passing at once from the notion of substance as the negation, to that of substance as the affirmation, of all possible determinations. The colourless blank becomes at a stroke filled up with a rich and varied content. The unity which was reached by abstraction from differences seems to be identified with a unity which contains all differences. Thought seems to re-enact the part for which imagination was condemned—that of dividing the indivisible, of introducing number and measure' into the absolute. Substance which, logically, is the purely indeterminate, passes into substance which consists of infinite attributes infinitely modified.

It is easier to discern the motive than to understand the logic of this transformation. Had Spinoza not refused to be led by his own logic, his system would have ended where it began. Philosophy, along with other things, comes to an end, in a principle which reduces all thought and being to nothingness. Moreover, it is not difficult to understand how Spinoza should seem to see more in the idea of substance than it legitimately contained. While he ostensibly rejected all determinations from it, in his thought an element of determination tacitly clung to it. Thought often supplies the hidden corrective of the theories we form about it. It is possible to devise a theory which implies the separation of unity and difference, of the universal and the particular, of affirmation and negation. But the opposite elements are really correlatives, and the rejected or excluded element secretly clings to the thought that denies it. It is impossible really to think an affirmative which affirms nothing in particular, or which is pure, blank affirmation devoid of all negation. When the particular vanishes from thought, the universal vanishes with it. Unity which carries with it no implication of diversity, becomes as meaningless a conception as that of a whole without parts, or a cause without effect. When, therefore, Spinoza began by rightly denying, or pronouncing to be *non esse*, the particular existences of the finite world *apart from* their unity, that to which his thought pointed was the assertion, not of pure abstract unity, but of the reality of these particulars *in relation to their unity.* The converse of the nothingness of the particular independent of the universal was, not the reality of the abstract universal, but the reality of the particular *in* the universal. From the negation of accidents without substance what thought sought after was, not the assertion of substance without accidents, but the assertion of accidents transformed into the necessary moments or attributes of substance, of substance realising itself in and through accidents. Though, therefore, the former of these alternatives—pure, abstract, indeterminate substance—was the logical result of his method, the latter was the real result to which the hidden, unconscious logic of his thought pointed. It was natural for him, therefore, tacitly to substitute the latter for the former, and so to pass, apparently by a leap, from the notion of God or Substance as the negation, to that of God or Substance as the affirmation, of all possible determinations.

But though it is possible thus to trace the real movement of Spinoza's thought, that movement was not a conscious one, and it was not thus that he justified his own conclusion. What he seemed to himself to have reached as the presupposition of all things' was the purely indeterminate self-identical infinite ; and the problem immediately arose, how to conceive of this infinite unity as, without abandoning its essential nature, passing into difference,—how to find in this moveless Absolute the explanation of the diversity and change-fulness of the finite world. The device which Spinoza falls upon to reach the diversity without tampering with the unity, is to regard the former as differences, not in the substance itself, but in substance *in relation to the finite intelligence which contemplates it.* "By attribute," says he,[1] "I understand that which the intellect per-ceives of substance as constituting its essence." It is, in other words, not the essence itself of substance, but that essence relatively to our intelligence. In one of his letters,[2] after defining substance, he adds,—"By attribute I understand the same thing, only that it is called attribute with reference to the understanding *attributing* a certain nature to substance." The relative or subjective character of the element of difference ex-pressed by attributes is further explained by various illustrations. He compares substance, *e.g.*,[3] to a surface reflecting the rays of light, which, regarded objectively, is called "a plane," but with reference to the observer is described as "white." "By a plane," says he, "I mean a surface which reflects all rays of light without altering them ; by a *white* surface I mean the same, with this difference, that a surface is called white with reference to a man looking at it." The same distinction

---

[1] Eth. i., def. 4.  [2] Ep. 27.  [3] Ibid.

is illustrated by the different names of the third patriarch, who in his proper character called Israel, is in one special relation called Jacob. Finally, in the following and other passages of his writings Spinoza expressly teaches that the true or absolute nature of God is something that lies beyond all conceptions formed of Him by finite intelligence : " If the will be supposed infinite, it must be determined to exist and act by God, not in so far as He is absolutely infinite substance, but in so far as He has an attribute which expresses the infinite and eternal essence of thought." [1]  " Being as being, by itself alone, as substance, does not affect us, and therefore it is to be explained by some attribute, from which yet it is not distinguished save ideally." [2]  To the same effect, in the ' Theologico-political Treatise,' [3] speaking of the various titles of God in the Hebrew Scriptures, he says that the name " Jehovah " points to " the absolute essence of God without relation to created things ; " whilst on the other hand " El Saddai " and other names express " attributes of God, and pertain to Him in so far as He is considered with relation to created things or is manifested by them."

Thus the ascription of attributes to God does not imply any tampering with the absolutely indeterminate unity of the divine nature, inasmuch as they do not characterise that nature in itself, but only as reflected in the finite intelligence. Finite intelligence cannot rise above itself, or see things otherwise than under the conditions that arise from its own nature. As man is himself a being at once spiritual and corporeal—in Spinoza's language, a " mode " or modification of thought and

[1] Eth. i. 32.  [2] Cogitat. Metaph. i. 3.  [3] xiii. 11, 12.

extension—he can know God only under these two
aspects or attributes. But we cannot conceive of the
infinite nature as exhausted by our ways of apprehending it. " The more reality or being anything has, the
more attributes belong to it." [1] " A being absolutely
infinite, therefore, is necessarily defined as being which
consists of infinite attributes, each one of which expresses a certain essence eternal and infinite." Though,
therefore, to us God is expressed only under the two
attributes of " thought " and " extension," to minds
differently constituted from ours the divine nature would
reveal itself in different ways, and to an infinite number
of minds or to an infinite understanding in an infinite
number of ways or by an infinite diversity of attributes.
" The infinite ways whereby each particular thing is
expressed in the infinite understanding cannot constitute
one and the same mind of a singular thing, but infinite
minds, seeing that each of these infinite ideas has no
connection with the rest." [2]

By yet another expedient does Spinoza find it possible to ascribe attributes to the infinite substance without infringing its purely indeterminate nature—viz., by
means of the distinction between what is "absolutely
infinite" and what is only "infinite in its own kind "
(*in suo genere*). To avoid the implication that by attaching predicates to substance we necessarily introduce
an element of finiteness or negation into it, he tries to
conceive of predicates which express something not negative but positive, not finite but infinite, and which
therefore limit neither the infinite substance nor each
other. Such predicates are the infinite attributes of

[1] Eth. i. 9.                           [2] Ep. 68.

God. All finite distinctions disappear in the infinite ; but we can conceive of distinctions which are not finite, in this sense that no one of them is limited either by the rest or by anything within its own sphere. We call a thing finite when it is bounded by another thing of the same kind, as one piece of matter by another ; but things of different kinds do not limit each other. Mental things are not limited by material, nor *vice versâ.* Ideas do not occupy space. Bodies are neither inside nor out side of minds. If therefore we can think of the attri bute of extension as that which has no limit within its own sphere, its infinitude is not infringed by the exist ence of another attribute of a wholly different kind, such as thought. It is no limitation of infinite exten sion that it cannot think, nor of infinite thought that it is not extended. We may conceive an infinite number of such attributes, each infinite in its own kind, and yet their infinite diversity implying no reciprocal limi tation. It may be said that if we conceive of an infinite number of such attributes as together constituting the nature of a being, each of them can express only a part of that nature, and therefore each must be regarded as a limitation of its infinitude. But Spinoza's answer to this objection virtually is, that it would be a valid ob jection if we conceived of infinite substance as *made up* of thought, extension, and other attributes. When we think of a thing as an aggregate or combination of quali ties, each of them is less than the whole, and expresses a limitation of nature. But the absolutely infinite sub stance is *not* the sum or totality of its attributes. Ac cording to Spinoza's peculiar conception, each of the different attributes expresses the same infinite reality and the whole of that reality. The attributes are not complementary properties, the omission of any one of which leaves the whole imperfect, but each the same perfect whole contemplated in a different aspect. They are not correlative members of an organic unity which have no independent reality apart from each other, but parallel, independent, equivalent manifestations of the same infinite object. Thought does not contain more or less of God than extension, but the content of both and of an infinite number of other attributes is absolutely the same. "Each attribute," says he,[1] "of one substance must be conceived through itself." "It is obvious," he adds,[2] "that though two attributes are conceived as distinct—that is, the one without the aid of the other—yet we cannot therefore conclude that they constitute two different entities or substances. For it is of the nature of substance that each of its attributes is conceived through itself (since all the attributes which it has have existed simultaneously in it), nor could one be produced by another; but each expresses the reality or being of substance. It is therefore by no means absurd to ascribe a plurality of attributes to one substance." From this point of view, therefore, Spinoza is enabled to combine the notions of absolute indeterminate unity with endless difference, or to conceive of an infinite multiplicity of attributes without tampering with the unconditioned unity of substance. The two expedients, however, by which he accomplishes this result, virtually resolve themselves into one. The attributes, though said to be infinite each in its own kind, are not really different in kind from each other. The con-

---

[1] Eth. i. 10.　　　　[2] Ibid., schol.

tent of each is precisely the same as that of any other, and the difference is only a difference in *our* way of looking at it. The difference in kind is nothing more than a difference of aspect. Spinoza's reconciliation, therefore, of diversity of attributes with absolute self-identical unity of substance, is simply that the diversity is a purely subjective one.

1. One obvious criticism on Spinoza's doctrine of attributes is that it presupposes what it is intended to prove. The definition of attribute is "that which intelligence perceives in substance as constituting its essence." But finite intelligence is itself only a "mode" or modification of one of the attributes of substance. The attributes, therefore, exist only through that which is simply a modification of one of them. The thought or intelligence which is the product of an attribute, is surreptitiously introduced to create the attributes. Thought, indeed, thinks itself and everything else ; and if the intelligence which differentiates the infinite substance were its own, there would be no paralogism in supposing infinite intelligence or self-consciousness to be the source or origin of the finite intelligence which knows it. But in the case before us, the absolutely infinite substance, as we have seen, is expressly distinguished from, or logically prior to, the attributes—that of thought as well as every other. Thought is only one of the aspects into which the absolute unity is diffracted ·by finite intelligence. Finite intelligence, therefore, is supposed to create that by which it is itself created.

2. The attributes are not derived from, but brought from without to, substance. To render the system coherent, the existence and distinctive character of the

attributes should arise out of the essential nature of substance. In the very nature or idea of substance an element of self-differentiation must be shown to exist, and *that* an element which does not tamper with its unity. In other words, substance must be conceived as a unity which has in it an impulse to go forth out of itself, to realise itself in the infinite determinations expressed by the attributes and their modifications, and yet in so going forth as remaining in unbroken identity with itself. Spinoza's substance, however, as we have just seen, not only does not contain, but is exclusive of, any such element of self-determination, and the determination expressed by the attributes are ascribed to a purely empirical origin. "*We* feel and perceive," says he,[1] " no particular things save bodies and modes of thought," and therefore we conclude that thought and extension are attributes of God. We represent to ourselves God as a " thinking thing " or an " extended thing." It is *we* who ascribe or bring the attributes to the substance, and the *we* has not been accounted for.

3. The accidental character of the attributes is indicated, not only in the origin ascribed to them, but also in their number and relation to each other. If substance is to have the character of a principle from which everything in the system is to be logically deduced, it should contain in itself the reason why such and no other determinations belong to it ; it should determine the order of their sequence, and show how each involves or is involved in all the rest. To say simply that a number of attributes cohere in one substance, is not to explain or give any rational idea of their unity, but

[1] Eth. ii., ax. 5.

merely to affirm that they are united. In the Spinozistic system extension, thought, and the other attributes are not organically related to each other. Each is absolutely independent of the rest—forms, so to speak, a completed whole in itself, and is to be conceived in and through itself. One attribute can no more be related to another than an object seen through a glass of one colour can be related to the same object seen through a glass of a different colour, or than an idea expressed in one language can be related to precisely the same idea expressed in another language. As it is perfectly indifferent to the object itself through how many differently coloured glasses it is seen, so it is perfectly indifferent to the nature of substance by what or how many attributes it is manifested. If Spinoza speaks of the diversity of attributes as infinite, the infinitude is not that which arises out of the essence of substance, but is only a numerical infinitude—the false infinite of endlessness or indefiniteness. In predicating of substance an infinite number of attributes, Spinoza relapses into the ambiguity which he himself had censured in a remarkable letter already quoted—the ambiguity, viz., of the term "infinite" as denoting *either* that which by its very nature is incapable of limitation, *or* that which exceeds every assignable limit. The infinitude which he ascribes to substance is of the former kind, and there is no legitimate connection between such an infinitude and the merely quantitative infinitude of attributes, the number of which exceeds any given or conceivable number.

4. In the letters which passed between Spinoza and his acute correspondent Tschirnhausen, some further de-

fects and inconsistencies in his doctrine of the attributes are brought to light. Amongst other pertinent questions, Tschirnhausen asks these two : First, whether it can be proved "that we cannot know any attributes of God other than thought and extension;"[1] or, more fully expressed, "why my mind, which represents a certain modification (of absolute substance), a modification which is expressed not only by extension, but in an infinite variety of ways, perceives only that modification as expressed by extension, and not as expressed through the other attributes?"[2] Secondly, whether, though it is laid down that every attribute is of equal content and significance with every other, "the attribute of thought is not really (as Spinoza defines it) of wider extent than any of the other attributes"?[3]

To the former of these questions Spinoza answers that "the power of a thing is defined solely by its essence, and that the essence of the mind is the idea of the body, which idea does not involve or express any of God's attributes save extension and thought.[4] Of this answer it may be said that, though from Spinoza's point of view it is no doubt conclusive, yet it betrays in some measure the insufficiency and even inconsistency of the principles on which it is based. In a philosophy in which thought is related to extension, mind to matter, as the conscious subject to its own object, Tschirnhausen's objection would, in one point of view, be unanswerable. For in such a philosophy there is nothing which lies outside the realm of intelligence, nothing which is not either known or knowable. If thought can apprehend extension, there is nothing which it cannot apprehend. If

[1] Ep. 65.          [2] Ep. 67.          [3] Ep. 68.          [4] Ep. 66.

human intelligence can transcend the distinction between itself and one attribute or manifestation of God, it thereby proves its capacity to transcend the same distinction in the case of every other attribute. Mind cannot be capable of apprehending its object in one aspect or two aspects and not in every other aspect. But, on the other hand, in a philosophy in which thought and extension, though regarded as attributes of one substance, are still conceived of as wholly independent of each other—as simply two parallel but unconnected expressions, amongst many others, of the divine essence—there is no reason in the nature of thought why, knowing one such attribute or expression, it should also know any other. The relation of parallelism does not carry with it what is involved in the deeper relation of consciousness to its object. An arbitrary connection does not imply the universal results of a necessary relation. In fact, the difficulty here is, not why, knowing extension, thought should not know everything else, but why it should transcend the gulf between itself and what is outside of it at all. In Spinoza's philosophy, that thought should overleap this gulf even in the one case of extension is an inconsistency ; but it is one of those happy inconsistencies which render it so fruitful and suggestive. It must be added, however, that from another point of view a philosophy which is based on the principle of self-consciousness would, though on different grounds, accept Spinoza's limitation of knowledge to extension and thought. For to such a philosophy extension is not, as Spinoza conceives, simply one amongst a multiplicity of attributes which intelligence in man happens to know, but it is the essential correlative of thought. It is not one amongst many things which thought can apprehend, but it is the necessary form of the object in its opposition to the thought for which it is. Extension and thought, in other words, are not *a* duality of attributes, but *the* dualism which constitutes the very essence of mind. If we conceive of God as Infinite Mind or Spirit, extension, instead of being one amongst an infinite number of attributes, is simply the form of objectivity through which alone is self-consciousness possible.

As to the second question, which does not seem to have been answered by Spinoza, it may be remarked that whilst, according to Spinoza's doctrine, every attribute expresses the whole of substance, and is of precisely the same value with every other, yet, inasmuch as all the attributes alike are relative to thought, or are "what intelligence perceives of substance as constituting its essence," thought has obviously in his system a wider function than any of the other attributes. In the case of man it knows the two attributes of which his mind and body are modifications, but it also, in the case of all other possible intelligences, knows the other attributes of which *their* natures are the modifications. If we conceive the attributes as running in pairs, thought will always be one of them. Each finite nature will be a modification of thought and of some other attribute which plays a corresponding part to extension in the nature of man. Thought has therefore a purely exceptional place in the scheme ; it is the correlate of all the other attributes. It is not simply one of the two attributes which human intelligence knows, but it is a universal factor in that knowledge of God which is possible for all finite intelligences.

# CHAPTER IX.

THE next step in the process by which Spinoza attempted to find in substance the first principle of all things, is that which is expressed in his doctrine of "Modes." The attributes, even if legitimately deduced, leave us still in the region of the infinite, and furnish no transition to a finite world. Though thought and extension are only expressions of substance, each in a certain definite manner, they are still infinite. The characteristic of being conceived through itself (*per se concipi*) belongs to the idea of attribute as well as to that of substance; there is nothing in it which points to anything beyond itself; it contains no element of self-differentiation by which the process to the finite might be mediated. The attributes, like the substance, are pure self-identical unities, and if they presuppose finite intelligence as the medium through which the colourless unity of substance is refracted, they only tacitly presuppose but do not prove it.

It is in Spinoza's doctrine of "Modes," and of their relation to substance, that we must find, if anywhere, the explanation of the existence of the finite world, and

of its relation to the infinite.    " By mode," says he,[1] " I
understand affections of substance, or that which is in
another, through which also it is conceived."   " Modes
can neither exist nor be conceived without substance ;
therefore they can exist only in the divine nature, and
can be conceived only through it."[2]   " Besides substance
and modes nothing exists, and modes are nothing but
affections of the attributes of God."[3]   Finite modes are,
further, identified with individual things (*res particu-
lares*), and of these it is said [4] that " they are nothing but
affections of the attributes of God, or modes by which
the attributes of God are expressed in a certain definite
manner."

What we gather from these various forms of state-
ment is, that, in contrast with Substance or God, who
alone is self-existent, all finite things have only an existence that is dependent on or derived from Him,
Their being is a being which is not in themselves,
but " in another "—that is, " in God."   What is meant
by the phrase " in another," or " in God," the following
passages may help us to understand :—

" Whatever is, is in God, and without God nothing can be
or be conceived."[5]   " From the necessity of the divine nature
an infinite number of things follows in infinite ways, as will
be evident if we reflect that from the definition of a thing
the understanding infers many properties which necessarily
follow from it — that is, from the very essence of the thing
defined."[6]   " The modes of the divine nature follow therefrom necessarily and not contingently, and that, whether we

---

[1] Eth. i., def. 5.

[3] Eth. i. 28, dem.

[5] Eth. i. 15.

[2] Eth. i. 15, dem.

[4] Eth. i. 25, cor.

[6] Eth. i. 16, dem.

consider the divine nature absolutely, or as determined to act in a certain manner. Further, God is the cause of these modes not only in so far as they simply exist, but in so far as they are considered as determined to any action." [1]

In these passages the relation of modes or finite things to God is represented by the equivalent forms of expression "following from God" and "caused by God"; and it is to be observed that in the last-quoted passage the causality of God with regard to modes is spoken of as of a twofold character—viz., that of the divine nature "considered absolutely," and that of the divine nature "in so far as it is determined to act in a certain manner." This distinction, to which Spinoza frequently recurs, and on the tenableness of which the coherence of his system may be said to turn, is more fully expressed in the following passages :—

"That which is finite and has a determinate existence cannot be produced by the absolute nature of any attribute of God; for whatever follows from the absolute nature of any attribute of God is infinite and eternal. It must therefore follow from God or from some attribute of God, in so far as He is considered as affected by some mode, . . . (or) in so far as He is modified by a modification which is finite and has a determined existence. This mode again must in turn be determined by another which also is finite, and this last again by another, &c., *ad infinitum.*" [2] Yet "it cannot be said that God is only the remote and not the proximate cause of individual things, except to distinguish them from those . . . which follow from His absolute nature." [3]

Thus the causality of finite things, considered as modes of God, is not the nature of God viewed absolutely, but that nature as modified by, or expressed in, the endless

[1] Eth. i. 29, dem.  [2] Eth. i. 28, dem.  [3] Ibid., schol.

regress of finite causes, or what Spinoza elsewhere calls
" the common order of nature and constitution of things,"
or the "connection of causes."[1] This idea reappears
throughout the whole system as a solvent of the difficulties involved in the relation of the purely indeterminate God to a world of finite individualities in time
and space. "The idea of an individual thing actually
existing is an individual mode of thinking distinct from
other modes," and is caused by God "not in so far as
He is a thinking thing absolutely, but in so far as He is
considered as affected by another mode of thinking, of
which again He is the cause as affected by another, and
so on to infinity."[2] "The human mind is part of the
infinite intellect of God; and when we say that the
human mind perceives this or that, we affirm that God
has this or that idea, not in so far as He is infinite, but
in so far as He is expressed by the nature of the human
mind, or constitutes the essence of the human mind."[3]
On the other hand, though the causality of individual
things is thus ascribed to God not as He exists absolutely
or infinitely, we find from other passages that there is
a sense in which they can be referred to the absolute or
eternal nature of God as their cause—*e.g.*

"It is the nature of reason to regard things not as contingent but as necessary. But this necessity of things is the
very necessity of the eternal nature of God, and therefore it
is the nature of reason to regard things under this form of
eternity." "Every idea of every particular thing actually
existing necessarily involves the eternal and infinite essence
of God." "By existence (of individual things), I do not mean
existence in so far as it is conceived abstractly and as a certain

---

[1] Eth. ii. 30, dem.   [2] Eth. ii. 9, dem.   [3] Eth. ii. 11, cor.

form of quantity ; I speak of the very nature of existence which is ascribed to individual things, because an infinite number of things follows in infinite ways from the eternal necessity of God's nature—of the existence of individual things as they are in God. For, although each individual thing is determined by another individual thing to exist in a certain manner, yet the force whereby each individual thing perseveres in existing, follows from the eternal necessity of the nature of God." [1]

Further, the two kinds of existence of individual things —that in which they are viewed as a series of causes and effects in time and space, and that in which they are viewed "under the form of eternity"—are expressly contrasted as follows · "Things are conceived as actual in two ways—either in so far as they exist in relation to a certain time and place, or in so far as we conceive them as contained in God and following from the necessity of the divine nature. When in this second way we conceive things as true and real, we conceive them under the form of eternity, and the ideas of them involve the eternal and infinite essence of God." [2]

In the light of these and other passages to which we shall refer in the sequel, we are prepared to examine what is Spinoza's conception of the relation of infinite or absolute substance to its "modes." When we ask what in his system is the relation of the finite world and individual finite things to God, the question is not settled simply by referring to his doctrine that all things exist in God, and that modes or finite things have no existence or operation independently of the infinite substance.

[1] Eth. ii. 44, cor., ii. 45, and ibid., schol.
[2] Eth. v. 29, schol.

Spinozism is not at once proved to be pantheistic by such expressions as these. For every system that is not dualistic, and for which the terms infinite and finite have any meaning, is pantheistic to the extent of holding that the world has no absolute or independent existence, and that the ultimate explanation of all things is to be found in God. Before pronouncing Spinoza a pantheist, therefore, the point to be determined is not whether he ascribes independent reality to finite things, but whether he ascribes to them any reality at all— whether his modes have any existence distinguishable from that of substance, and such that we can speak of an actual relation between the two. If, on the one hand, it can be shown that the existence he ascribes to modes is only a fictitious or fugitive semblance of existence, if the distinction of modes from substance is a distinction which is created by the imagination and has no objective reality, and if the unity into which all individual things are resolved is one which does not maintain but suppresses or annuls that distinction, then indeed his philosophy may justly be characterised as pantheistic. But, on the other hand, since real distinctions do not exclude but imply a unity which transcends them, if Spinoza's substance is a principle which subordinates but does not suppress differences, if his modes are the expression for a finite world which does not vanish, but constitutes a necessary and permanent moment in the unity of the infinite, then it is no proof of Spinoza's pantheism that he affirms that "whatever is is in God," and that modes are things that "exist only in God, and only through God can be conceived." In the passages quoted above, when read in the light of his general principles, there

is much to favour the former of these two constructions of his system ; but in these, as elsewhere, there
are expressions which refuse to lend themselves to a
purely pantheistic view of the relation of God to the
world.

1. The considerations that favour the former or pantheistic interpretation have already been adduced, and
need not here be repeated. They amount to this, that
individual finite things have no real existence distinguishable from that of absolute substance, but are
merely creations of the abstracting imagination.

"It is mere folly or insanity," he writes,[1] " to suppose that
extended substance is made up of parts or bodies really distinct from each other. . . If you ask why we are by nature
so prone to attempt to divide extended substance, I answer
that quantity is conceived by us in two ways : viz., abstractly,
superficially, as we imagine it by aid of the senses ; or as
substance, which can only be done by the understanding.
So that if we attend to quantity, as it is in the imagination,
it will be found to be divisible, finite, made up of parts, and
manifold. Again, from the fact that we can limit duration
and quantity at our pleasure, when we conceive the latter in
abstraction from substance, and separate the former from the
way in which it flows from things eternal, there arise time
and measure—time for the purpose of limiting duration,
measure for the purpose of determining quantity—so that we
may, as far as possible, imagine them. Further, inasmuch
as we separate the modifications of substance from substance
itself, and reduce them to classes in order, as far as possible,
to imagine them, there arises number, whereby we limit
them. . . . Whence it is clear that measure, time, and number are nothing but modes of thinking, or rather of imagin-
ing. But," he adds, "there are many things which cannot

---

[1] Ep. 29.

be conceived by the imagination, but only by the understanding—*e.g.*, substance, eternity, and the like. Thus, if any one tries to explain these things by means of conceptions, which are mere aids to the imagination, he is simply trying to let his imagination run away with him."

The drift of these and other passages which might be quoted is, not simply that modes, or individual finite things, have no existence independent of substance, but that they have no existence at all, save for a faculty which mistakes abstractions for realities. It is possible for the unreflecting mind to suppose itself capable of thinking the separate halves or minuter isolated parts of a line, but intelligence corrects the illusion. A line, it discerns, could as easily be made up of points lying miles apart as of points contiguous yet really isolated. The point it perceives to be a mere fictitious abstraction, an unreality, a thing which has no existence apart from the line, and when we think the line the point ceases to have any existence at all. And the same is true of lines in relation to surfaces, of surfaces in relation to solids, and of all existences in space in relation to space itself, which is the one infinite, indivisible reality. In like manner, when we regard the modes in relation to the infinite substance, we see that they are mere creatures of the imagination ; when we contemplate individual things from the point of view of intelligence, or as they really are, their illusory individuality vanishes, and the only reality left, the only being in the universe, is God, or Infinite Substance. And indeed it is only, Spinoza expressly affirms, when we leave out of view the fictitious differences which modes introduce into substance that the latter can be truly contemplated. "Substance is considered in itself—that is, truly—when we *set aside all its modifications* " (*depositis affectionibus*).

It is true that whilst Spinoza not only concedes but expressly teaches that modes or individual finite things have no reality in relation to the absolute nature of God, he yet contrives to ascribe to them, in a certain indirect way, a divine origin. " That which is finite," says he, in a passage above quoted, " and has a determined existence, cannot be produced or follow from the absolute nature of any attribute of God," for " whatever does so follow is infinite and eternal." And " every individual thing, or everything which is finite and has a determined existence, can only exist or be determined to act by another thing which is also finite, and this again only by another which also is finite, and so on indefinitely." " Only the infinite can follow from the infinite, the finite can follow only from the finite." How, then, does Spinoza reconcile these propositions with the assertion that modes " are conceived through the divine nature, and follow necessarily from it " ? The answer is, that he simply begs the question. " That which is finite," he tells us, " cannot be produced by the absolute nature of God or of any of His attributes ; . . . it must therefore follow from God, or some attribute of God, in so far as (*quatenus*) He is modified by a modification which is finite and has a determined existence, and this mode or cause must in turn be modified by another, &c." The only construction of which this proposition, taken in connection with what precedes it, is capable, is that it simply assumes without proof what has been already denied— viz., that individual finite things can be derived from God. The nature of God is such that it does not admit of modification, but finite things follow from it in so far as it *is* modified. Or, otherwise expressed, Spinoza presupposes the existence of finite things in order to prove it, or virtually makes God finite in order to express Himself in the finite. Finite things follow from God in so far as He is (already) modified by finite things. Every reader of Spinoza knows what an important *rôle* is assigned to this *quatenus*, and how often, by means of what is nothing more than a tautological phrase, he contrives to escape from difficulties and inconsistencies otherwise insuperable.

It may be said that Spinoza's reasoning here is not the bare *petitio principii* involved in the assertion that finite things follow from God in so far as they already follow from Him ; but that what he affirms is that they follow, not from individual finite things, but from the interminable series or connection of finite things, which is not finite but relatively infinite. But to this the answer is what, as we have seen, Spinoza has himself taught us, that by the spurious infinite of mere endlessness we do not rise above the region of the finite. An infinite quantity is a contradiction in terms, a phrase in which the predicate denies the subject. By no indefinite addition or aggregation of finites can we reach the essentially or absolutely infinite—that infinite from which Spinoza asserts that the finite can *not* be derived.

In the foregoing view of Spinoza's doctrine as to the relation of God to the world, we have considered it simply as a relation of the absolutely indetermined infinite to determined or finite things. But in some of the above-quoted passages, and elsewhere, we find him expressing this relation in terms of another category—viz., that of *causality.* " God is the efficient cause of all things that can fall under an infinite intellect." [1]   " God is the efficient cause not only of the existence of things but also of their essence." [2]  " The modes of any given attribute have God for their cause, &c." [3]  " Of things as they are in themselves God is really the cause, &c." [4] Now, as the relation of cause and effect is one in which we ordinarily think of the effect as something which, though dependent on the cause, actually emerges out of it into an existence of its own, the application of this category to the relation of God and the world would seem to give to finite things a reality which is not illusory or imaginative, a being which is not absorbed in that of infinite substance.   But it is to be considered that, in its proper sense, causality is not a category which is applicable to the relation of the infinite to the finite ; and if we attempt so to apply it, what it expresses is not the reality of the finite, but either the limitation or the non-reality of the infinite.

Causality is a category only of the finite.   The relation of cause and effect is one which implies the succession or (though not with strict accuracy) the coexistence of its members.   In the latter case it presupposes the existence of things external to, and affecting and being affected by each other.   In the former, it is a relation in which the first member is conceived of as passing into the second ; the cause, or the sum of conditions which constitute it, loses its existence in the effect or in the sum of the new conditions to which it has given rise.   The cause, in other words, is only cause in and through the con-

---

[1] Eth. i. 16, cor.      [2] Eth. i. 25.
[3] Eth. ii. 6.      [4] Eth. ii. 7, schol.

summated result which we call effect, and the very reality or realisation of the former implies, in a sense, its own extinction. In the impact of two balls the motion of the first becomes the cause of the motion of the second only when it has ceased to exist in the former ; the force which has existed as heat becomes the cause of motion only when it has exhausted itself of its existence in the one form and become converted into the other. But, obviously, in neither of these senses can we embrace the relation of the infinite and the finite under the form of causality. The infinite cannot be conceived of as external to, and acting on, the finite, as one finite body is outside of, and acts on, another ; in such a relation it would cease to be infinite. "God," says Spinoza, "is *omne esse.*" Beyond substance there is nothing real. Substance and its affections constitute the totality of existence, and is absolutely infinite. But this it could not be if its affections, instead of existing only in it and being conceivable only through it, had an existence capable of being acted on by it. Nor, again, can you speak of the infinite as a cause which, in producing the finite, passes wholly into it and becomes lost in it ; for, in that case, the existence of the finite would be conditioned by the non-existence or extinction of the infinite.

The inapplicability of the category of causality to the relation of infinite and finite is thus so obvious that Spinoza can only give a colour of relevancy to it by qualifying the term "cause" when applied to God so as virtually to destroy its meaning. "God," he tells us,[1] "is not the transient but the immanent cause of the

---

[1] Eth. i. 18.

world." He can only be designated cause of all things
in the same sense in which He is cause of Himself
(*causa sui*).[1] In other words, to obviate the contradiction involved in the idea of an infinite which is external to the finite, he modifies the notion of cause so as to
conceive of it as existing, not outside of, but wholly
within, the things which are said to be its effects; and
to obviate the further difficulty which thus arises, of
conceiving an infinite which passes away into the finite,
he again modifies the notion of cause so as to conceive
of it as maintaining its own independent existence at
the same time that it loses itself in the effect. But
though in the conception of a *causa omnium rerum*
which is at the same time *causa sui*, what Spinoza is
aiming at is the idea of a Being which remains one
with itself in all its changes, or of a self-differentiating,
which is at the same time a self-integrating, infinite, this
idea is one which in vain attempts to express itself
under the category of causality. The attempt so to
express it may be regarded as one of those indications
in Spinoza of the consciousness of another than the
purely negative relation of the finite to the infinite
which his own inadequate logic forced him to maintain.

2. The foregoing considerations seem almost conclusively to favour that view of Spinoza's doctrine of modes
which denies to individual finite things any existence
that is not fictitious and illusory. His derivation of
modes from substance would seem to be nothing more
than a reversal of the process of abstraction by which
the idea of substance was reached. It is not substance
which determines itself to modes, but we who, with a

---

[1] Eth. i. 25, dem.

show of logic, reintroduce into it the fictitious distinctions which the same logic had abolished.

But this account of Spinoza's doctrine would be incomplete if we did not point out that, however inconsistently they enter into it, there are elements of his system which refuse to lend themselves to the notion of the unreality of the finite world. Modes are not invariably represented as merely transient creations of the abstracting imagination. They have in them a positive element which remains even when on the negative side they have been resolved into the unity of substance.

Besides the tacit implication of another doctrine in the idea of a *causa sui* which is at the same time *causa omnium rerum*, the following considerations seem to point in the same direction :—

(1.) Even if modes are only transient forms, there must be a reason in the nature of substance for their existence *as such*. Though everything else in the finite world is resolved into negation, the negation itself is not so resolved. Evanescence itself does not vanish. When you have reduced all finite things to phantoms, insubstantial as the things of a dream, the dream-world itself remains to be accounted for ; and more than that, obviously the mind which perceives and pronounces that it *is* a dream-world cannot belong to that world. In ascribing to intelligence the function of rising above and abolishing the distinction from substance of finite things, Spinoza virtually exempts intelligence itself from the process of abolition. The criterion of the illusory cannot be itself illusory. If therefore, as Spinoza asserts, "that which is finite and has a determinate

nature cannot follow from the absolute nature of God,
for whatever does so follow is infinite and eternal,"
what this involves as to that intelligence which discerns
the nothingness of finite things is, not that it does not
follow from the absolute nature of God, but that it has
in it, in its very discernment of its distinction from God,
an element of what is infinite and eternal.

(2.) That Spinoza himself, despite of his own principle that "all determination is negation," recognises in
modes something that is not mere negation, is indirectly
indicated by the qualified form in which in the 'Ethics'
that principle is stated. "The finite," says he,[1] "is *in
part* negation " (*ex parte negatio*). The negation implied
in finitude is not complete but partial. There is, in
other words, a positive element in finite things, which
is not annulled when the fictitious distinction from the
infinite is taken away. There is an individuality which
survives the extinction of the false or spurious individuality. Nor is this implied only in the phrase "partial
negation." Besides the idea of God as the negation of
all determinations there are traces of another and opposite idea—that of the affirmation of all determinations.
For the indivisible unity in which all differences vanish,
Spinoza seems often, without consciousness of inconsistency, to substitute the infinite unity which comprehends
in it all possible differences.

"From the necessity of the divine nature," says he,[2]
"must follow an infinite number of things in infinite ways."
"There is not wanting to God materials for the creation of
all things from the highest to the lowest degree of perfec-

---

[1] Eth. i. 8, schol.        [2] Eth. i. 16.

tion—for the producing of all things which can be conceived by an infinite intellect." [1]  "There are two ways," says he in a passage already quoted, "in which things are conceived by us as actual—viz., either as existing in relation to a certain time and place, *or* as contained in God and following from the necessity of the divine nature.  In the second way we conceive them as true and real, under the form of eternity, and the ideas of them involve the eternal and infinite essence of God." [2]

And when we have reached the latter point of view, what we have ceased to see in finite things is not their individuality, but their finitude.  Their true individuality is not lost, for " every idea of an individual thing actually existing necessarily involves the idea of the eternal and infinite essence of God; . . . for the force by which each individual thing perseveres in its own existence follows from the eternal necessity of the divine nature." [3]  " In God there is necessarily an idea which expresses the essence of this or that body under the form of eternity," [4] and this idea is a certain mode of thinking which is necessarily eternal.[5]  What *is* lost, what of our former unreal view of things disappears, is their contingency, their transient, fugitive being as things of time and sense, for " it is of the nature of reason to contemplate things as they are in themselves—*i.e.*, not as contingent but as necessary," [6] not " as determined each by another finite thing, but as following from the eternal necessity of the nature of God." [7]

That there is, in Spinoza's view, an affirmative ele-

---

[1] Eth. i., Append.                  [2] Eth. v. 29, schol.
[3] Eth. ii. 45, dem. and schol.      [4] Eth. v. 22.
[5] Eth. v  23, schol.                [6] Eth. ii. 44, cor. 2.
[7] Eth. ii. 45, schol.

ment which remains to finite things when the negative element which seemed to distinguish them from the infinite is obliterated, an individuality which, taken up into the infinite, still exists and can be known through the infinite, these passages seem clearly to teach. But if we ask further and more definitely what that element is, and how it "follows from the infinite nature of God," the answer is by no means satisfactory. As to the first question, that element in the finite which lifts it out of the sphere of time into "the form of eternity" is, Spinoza tells us, the inherent impulse or endeavour of each individual thing to maintain itself or persevere in its own being. "No individual thing has in it anything by which it can be destroyed or which can deprive it of its existence; but, on the contrary, it is opposed to all that could deprive it of its existence."[1] There is in each thing an "endeavour (*conatus*) by which it seeks to persevere in its own being," and this endeavour "is nothing but the actual essence of the thing itself,"[2] and it is therefore something not conditioned by time, "it involves no finite but an indefinite time." But is not this conception of the self-maintenance or persevering in existence of an individual thing a simple tautology? Does it mean any more than this, that when we think of it as an existing thing, we cannot think of it as a non-existing thing? Is not the inherent capacity to persevere in existing simply the incapacity of the mind to predicate of a thing at once existence and non-existence? When we say that a thing necessarily perseveres in existence, do we say any more than that, so long as we think of it, we think of it as existing, or that the conception of

[1] Eth. iii. 6, dem.  [2] Ibid., 7.

existence excludes or contradicts the conception of non-existence ? Moreover, is not this perseverance in existing which is supposed to pertain to a thing as seen " under the form of eternity," a conception which is still conditioned by time ? We do not escape from the quantitative idea of duration merely by making it indefinite. Indefinite or endless duration is a form of time and not of eternity. As to the second question—viz., as to the relation of this self-maintaining element in the finite to God—all that Spinoza says amounts simply to the affirmation that it has its origin in the absolute nature of God, and is a determinate expression of that nature. " Although each individual thing," says he,[1] " is determined to exist in a certain way by another individual thing, yet the force by which each thing perseveres in existing follows from the eternal necessity of the nature of God." " Individual things are modes by which the attributes of God are expressed in a certain definite manner, &c." [2] How finite things can have in them a power of self-maintenance, a capacity of continuous existence flowing from their own nature, and yet have nothing in them which does not follow from the nature of God, is the problem to be solved, and Spinoza's only solution is simply to affirm that both propositions are true.

As the result of our inquiry we seem to have found in Spinoza's account of the nature of modes statements which, if not irreconcilable, he has made no attempt to reconcile. In accordance with the principle which generally governs his reasoning, the very essence of finite things is identified with negation or non-being ;

[1] Eth. ii. 45, schol.      [2] Eth. iii. 6, dem.

they not merely have no real existence apart from God, but existence in God is for them equivalent to extinction of existence. Yet, on the other hand, as we have just seen, to these same finite things Spinoza ascribes a positive, self-affirmative nature, an individuality which is inherent and essential, and which is not extinguished when the limits that divide the finite from the infinite are removed. And if thus Spinoza's two representations of the nature of finite things seem to conflict, equally conflicting are the corresponding representations of the nature of God. To the former representation of the finite corresponds the notion of a purely indeterminate, to the latter that of a self determining Infinite. In the one case the world is nothing and God is all ; in the other, the world is the manifold expression of the nature of God, and God the Being whose nature unfolds without losing itself in the innumerable individualities of the finite world. If Spinozism contained no other conception of the relation of God to the world than the first, we should be compelled to pronounce it a purely pantheistic system. Perhaps the second conception may be regarded as the expression on Spinoza's part of an unconscious endeavour to correct the inadequacy of the first. But the correction, whilst it obviates the imputation of thorough-going pantheism, and elevates his system above all other pantheistic philosophies, is still imperfect in this respect, that it implies a principle of self-determination in God which is without any speculative ground in his idea of the divine nature. At best, it only creates the demand for a more complete and self-consistent philosophy, and indicates the direction in which it lies.

# CHAPTER X.

Spinoza's system, so far as we have traced its development in the foregoing pages, leaves us still without any principle of mediation between God and the world. If, as we have just seen, it sometimes represents finite things as possessing an element of individuality which, taken up into the infinite, still remains, and therefore seems to imply a principle of self-determination in the divine nature, so far as we have gone this principle is simply affirmed, not proved; the gap between the infinite and finite remains unbridged. But there are certain passages in the 'Ethics' in which we meet with a conception not yet referred to, that of "Infinite Modes,"— a conception which may be regarded as an attempt to fill up the gap. As the very phrase indicates, "infinite modes" point to something which constitutes a link between the two worlds. As "modes," they belong to the sphere of the finite; as "infinite" modes, to that of the infinite. Despite of Spinoza's own assertion, that the finite can only follow from the finite, we have here a conception in which the ideas of infinite and finite are combined. The following are the passages in which the doctrine of infinite modes is most fully expressed : " Whatever follows from any attribute of God, in so far as it is modified by a modification which exists necessarily and as infinite through the said attribute, must also exist necessarily and infinitely;"[1] and conversely, " Every mode which exists both necessarily and as infinite, must necessarily follow, *either* from the absolute nature of some attribute of God, *or* from an attribute modified by a modification which exists necessarily and as infinite."[2]  Spinoza here speaks of certain modes or modifications of divine attributes, differing therefore from the attributes in this respect, that the latter are conceived through themselves, the former only through the attributes.  Further, of these modes he specifies two classes or grades : first, those which follow immediately from attributes ; and secondly, those which follow from attributes already modified : but to both the predicate "infinite" is applied.  One of Spinoza's correspondents[3] asks for examples of these two classes of modes, and conjectures that thought and extension may belong to the first, "the intellect in thought" and "motion in extension" to the second.  Spinoza, without waiting to correct the obvious error of finding in thought and extension, which are themselves attributes, examples of modifications of attributes, answers thus :[4] " Examples which you ask are, of the first class, in thought, the absolutely infinite intellect (*intellectus absolute infinitus*), in extension, motion, and rest ; of the second class, the form of the whole universe (*facies totius universi*), which, although it varies in infinite ways, remains always the same."

[1] Eth. i. 22.   [2] Eth. i. 23.   [3] Ep. 65.   [4] Ep. 66.

M

At first sight, Spinoza seems to be here attempting to combine ideas which are reciprocally exclusive. Substance and modes, he himself affirms, include all being. But in infinite modes we have a third something which belongs to neither category—which is neither " in itself " nor " in another," neither infinite nor finite, but both at once. If the absolutely infinite is " that which contains in its essence whatever expresses reality and involves no negation," is not an infinite mode as self-contradictory as a round square or a rectangular circle ? " Intellect," he tells us,[1] " whether finite or *infinite* " (and the same is true of the other infinite modes), belongs to the sphere of *natura naturata*—that is, to the order of things which exist only for the imagination and its quantifying forms of time and measure; yet, at the same time, these infinite modes are things which " cannot have a limited duration," but " must exist always and infinitely," or to which pertains the timeless immanent unity of the nature of God.[2]   In this conception of infinite modes there seems thus to be involved the same apparent contradiction with which theological controversy has made us familiar in the doctrine of the " Logos " or " Son of God," in which we meet with the same seemingly irreconcilable elements of subordination and equality with God ; of that which is " begotten," and therefore finite, and that which is consubstantial with God, and therefore infinite ; of that which is described as " eternally begotten," and therefore as belonging at once to the sphere of the temporal and to that of the eternal.   And that this is not a merely fanciful analogy, but one which was present to Spinoza's own mind, we learn from his earlier

[1] Eth. i. 32, cor.                    [2] Eth. i. 21, and dem.

treatise ' Concerning God and Man,' in which, with express reference to the subject before us, we find him thus writing :—

" As to the modes or creatures which immediately depend on God, of these we know only two—viz., motion in matter, and intellect in thought—of which we affirm that they have been from all eternity, and will be unchangeably to all eternity. . . . As to motion, therefore, that it is that which is in its nature infinite, and that it can neither exist nor be conceived through itself, but only by means of extension, . . . of all this I will only say here that it is a son of God, or a work or effect immediately created by God.  As to intellect in thought, this also, like the former, is a son of God, . . . created from all eternity, and continuing unchangeable to all eternity.  Its sole function is that of clearly and distinctly understanding all things in all times." [1]

Can the conception of infinite modes be freed from the contradiction which it thus seems to involve ?  The answer is, that though on Spinoza's principles the contradiction is really insoluble, yet in this conception we have an elaborate attempt to solve it.  Infinitude and finite individuality express ideas which, as Spinoza defines them, are reciprocally exclusive ; but when we examine what is meant by the phrase " infinite modes," we find that it involves, in opposite directions, an endeavour so to modify these ideas as to bring them into coherence.  On the one hand it introduces, at a lower stage, into the idea of the infinite, that element of activity or self-determination which is lacking to the higher ideas of substance and attributes.  On the other hand, it attempts to raise the finite world to a *quasi*

[1] De Deo, i. cap. 9.

infinitude which is denied to the separate individualities
that compose it.   The barren infinitude is thus rendered
fertile, and then finite things are so ennobled as to make
it possible to claim for them an infinite origin.   The
former side of this modifying process is expressed by
that class or grade of infinite modes which are "immediate modifications" of the attributes of thought and
extension ; the latter, by those which are modifications
of the second degree, of which Spinoza adduces only one
example, the *facies totius universi.*

1. Of the infinite modes which are immediate modifications of attributes, two are specified—viz., "motion
and rest" as modifications of extension, and "the absolutely infinite intellect" as the modification of thought.
Now, if we examine the function assigned to these
"immediate modes," we shall find that they are simply
the attributes of extension and thought, *plus* that element
of activity or self-determination which these attributes
lack, and yet which is necessary to make them the productive sources of finite things.   The very designation
"infinite mode" shows that Spinoza is here unconsciously seeking to introduce into his system the element
of difference or finitude which is excluded from the
abstract unity of substance.   From such an abstract
infinite, the purity of which can be maintained only by
the elimination of all distinctions (*depositis affectionibus*),
it is impossible to find any way back to the finite.   Nor
could it legitimately be made the living source of finite
existences save by transforming it from the abstract
unity which extinguishes difference into the concrete
unity of a principle in which all differences are at once
embraced and subordinated.   But whilst Spinoza's logic

debarred him from any such introduction of a negative
or finite element into the purely affirmative unity of
substance, or even into the infinitude *in suo genere*
which is the conception of attribute, the need for such
an element, if he would not arrest the descending movement of thought, asserts itself at the stage we have now
reached, and finds its expression in the conception of
infinite modes, or of an infinite which contains in it the
element of negation or finitude. With such a conception
a new principle of self-development is introduced into
his system. The barren self-identical infinite becomes
now an infinite which has in it the impulse to realise
itself in all the manifold individualities of the finite
world. That it is this principle of activity or self-
development which Spinoza is aiming at in the conception of infinite modes, becomes clear from the
examples he gives of these modes, and from what he
says as to their nature and function. Of extension the
infinite modification is "motion and rest"; and of
what he conceived to be the relation in this case of the
mode to the attribute, we have a clear indication in his
answer to inquiries on this point from his acute correspondent Tschirnhausen.[1] "It is very difficult," writes
the latter, "to conceive how the existence of bodies which
have motion and figure can be demonstrated *a priori*,
since in extension, considered absolutely, nothing of the
kind occurs." To this Spinoza answers by distinguishing his own from the Cartesian notion of extension."
"From extension, as Cartesius conceives it—that is, as a
mere inert mass—it is not only difficult, as you say, but
altogether impossible, to demonstrate the existence of

[1] Epp. 69-72.

bodies. For inert matter, as it is in itself, will persevere in its rest, and will not be excited to motion save by a more powerful external cause. And on this account I have not hesitated formerly to affirm that the Cartesian principles of natural things are useless, not to say absurd." In a subsequent letter, in answer to further difficulties propounded by his correspondent, Spinoza points out that Descartes' notion of extension breaks down by his own showing, seeing that he can only deduce the variety of things from extension by supposing it to be set in motion by God. Matter, therefore, cannot be explained by extension as Descartes defines it, " but must necessarily be explained by an attribute which expresses eternal and infinite essence." The further elucidation of this answer which Spinoza promises is not given, but his meaning is obvious. An attribute of God which explains the manifoldness of things only by calling in the co-operation of an arbitrary external force, is not what it pretends to be—viz., "that which expresses an eternal and infinite essence." It must not be supplemented by an outside mover, but must contain in itself implicitly the element of motion or activity. And this idea Spinoza conceives himself to have attained for his own attribute of extension by the proposition that motion and rest constitute its immediate infinite mode. In other words, extension, or what is here the same thing, matter, is not a mere passive inert mass, but contains in it, as equally essential moments, both motion and rest. It is to be noticed that motion and rest are here represented by Spinoza, not as two different things, but as constituting one infinite mode, parallel to that of " infinite intellect " in thought. His

motion is a motion which is self-terminated, or which is
not moved by anything outside of itself ; his rest is the
rest of that which is in intense and unchangeable activity.
In other words, his first infinite mode is simply self-
determined extension, or extension with the element of
activity or self-determination in it.

From purely infinite or indeterminate thought it is
as impossible to derive the manifold world of finite intelligences as from extension, considered as a mere inert
mass, to demonstrate the existence of bodies. Blank
self-identical thought remains one with itself. It is the
form of all ideas without the possibility of the actual
existence of any. Implicitly the whole wealth of the
world of intelligence is contained in it ; but it can never
realise that wealth, or become conscious of its own content, because to do so would be to introduce distinction
into that the very nature of which is to transcend all
distinctions. But what Spinoza wants is an infinite
thought which, while it remains one with itself, is yet
the productive source of an actual world of ideas and
intelligences. The only legitimate way in which this
could be achieved would be by transforming the idea of
God as Substance, with thought for its attribute, into
that of self-conscious Spirit or Mind. From this, however, which would have implied the reconstruction of
his whole philosophy, Spinoza was precluded, and the
expedient to which he had recourse was to introduce the
element of self-determination into thought under the
guise of an "infinite mode." "Intellect," though "absolutely infinite," is not absolute thought (*cogitatio ab-
soluta*), but only a certain mode of thinking, and therefore . . . must be referred not to *natura naturans*, but

to *natura naturata.*" [1]    By this means, without introducing difference into that which is " absolutely perfect
—that is, absolutely indeterminate "—Spinoza can claim
for the whole finite realm of thought a necessary derivation from the divine nature.    " Infinite intellect " is not
simply infinite thought, but that which *knows* infinite
thought and all that is contained in it.    " From the
necessity of the divine nature must follow an infinitude
of things in infinite ways—that is, all things that can fall
under an infinite intellect." [2]    " Active intellect, finite
or infinite, must comprehend the attributes and affections
of God." [3]    " The ideas of (even) non-existent individual
things or modes must be comprehended in the infinite
idea of God." [4]    Thus to " intellect," as an immediate
mode of thought, though it is said to belong to the
sphere of the finite (*natura naturata*), the predicate
" absolutely infinite " may be applied, inasmuch as there
is nothing in the realm of thought which it does not
comprehend.    Though it contains an infinite number of
determinations, they are, from first to last, *self*-deter-
minations.    Though, as the productive source of all
ideas, it is intensely and unceasingly active, yet, like the
parallel mode of extension, its activity is a motion
which is never moved.    As motion, which is at the
same time rest, is infinite, because it is motion which is
terminated only by itself, so intellect is infinite, because
its activity knows no limit that does not fall within its
own domain.    What, in short, Spinoza is aiming at by
the conception of " intellect " as an " infinite mode " of
thought, is the virtual introduction into his system of

[1] Eth. i. 31, dem.                    [2] Eth. i. 16.
[3] Eth. i. 30.                         [4] Eth. ii. 8.

what he had actually excluded from his idea of God—viz., the principle of self-consciousness or of thought as an active, self-determining principle which, in all its determinations, remains one with itself.

2. I have said that the conception of infinite modes is an attempt to bring into union the irreconcilable ideas of infinitude and finite individuality, not only in the way we have just considered—viz., by introducing the element of self-determination into the idea of the infinite—but also, from an opposite direction, by elevating the finite world into a *quasi* infinitude. Spinoza had laid down the principle that nothing can follow from the infinite save that which is itself infinite and eternal, and conversely, that "that which is finite and has a determined existence cannot be produced by the absolute nature of God." The world of finite individualities, therefore, can never be connected by necessary derivation with the first principle of his system, the absolute nature of God or an attribute of God, unless he can contrive to lend to that world such a guise of infinitude as will make it homogeneous with its origin. This he attempts to do by the second order of infinite modes or modifications of divine attributes in the second degree, the nature of which he exemplifies in the phrase "form of the whole universe." And the way in which he finds it possible to connect this totality of things with the absolute nature of God, is by ascribing to it, as a whole, a kind of infinitude and unchangeableness which does not pertain to the parts of which it is composed, taken individually. For this "form of the whole universe," "though it varies in infinite ways," though its constituent finite parts are determined each only by other

finite parts, and may be conceived to be endlessly diversified in their particular movements, yet taken as a whole, or as one composite individual, remains ever the same.[1] The individual parts are finite or determined; but as constituting together the whole universe, outside of which there is nothing to determine them, they are infinite. Here, therefore, we have an aspect of the finite world in which, in a being derived from the absolute nature of God, it fulfils the condition that nothing can be so derived which is not infinite and eternal. Under whatever attribute we contemplate this totality of things—whether as the aggregate of all corporeal things, or as the sum of all ideas—nothing is presupposed to it save "the absolute nature of some attribute of God, or of such an attribute modified by a modification which is necessary and infinite." The sole presupposition of the totality of finite bodies is the attribute of extension, conceived as self-determining, or under the infinite mode of motion; the sole presupposition of the totality of ideas is the attribute of thought conceived of under the infinite mode of intellect. If the phrase "*facies totius universi*" be regarded as embracing both the world of thought and the world of things, then we have here a point of view from which we can contemplate it as an infinite and eternal expression of the absolute nature of God.

If we ask what is the value of this attempt to mediate between the infinite or absolute nature of God and the finite world by the conception of "infinite modes," the answer can only be that Spinoza himself has furnished the proof of its inconclusiveness. The sum or aggregate of modifications is not equivalent to the unmodified; by

[1] Ep. 66, and II. Lemma 7, schol.

endless additions of finites we do not reach the true infinite ; the totality of relative, changeable things is no nearer than any one of them to the unchangeable absolute. Spinoza's finite modes, even when, by a *petitio principii*, he speaks of each mode as determined by God in so far as He is expressed by another finite mode, and that by others in endless series, are only contiguous, not essentially related, to each other. The whole finite world, in so far as we can conceive it at all, is broken up into an endless multiplicity of isolated atoms, and the attempt to sum them gives us only the false infinite of indefinite number, which leaves us no nearer the true infinite at the end than at the beginning.

It may be possible, indeed, in another way to discern a real infinitude in the multiplicity of finite things. As a living organism is a unity which is not the sum of its parts, but prior to yet expressing itself in each and all of them, so it may be possible to conceive of the *facies totius universi* as an infinite organic whole, every infinitesimal portion of which is instinct with the universal life, every part of which lives in and through the rest, and all together constitute, not an aggregate outwardly related to, but a corporate unity which is the living expression of its infinite author. But though Spinoza undoubtedly aimed at a view of the universe in which all finite things should be seen to follow from, and constitute a necessary expression of, the absolute nature of God, we seek in vain in his dialectic for any such principle of organic coherence between the individualities of the finite world and the infinite substance. By his own acknowledgment his " infinite modes " belong still to the sphere of *natura naturata*, and the gulf between them and his *natura naturans* remains unbridged.

# CHAPTER XI.

## THE NATURE AND ORIGIN OF THE MIND.

THE Second Book of the ' Ethics,' to which the above
title is prefixed, opens with the following words : " I
will now explain the results which must necessarily follow from the nature of God, or of the Being eternal and
infinite ; not, indeed, all these results, . . . but only those
which can lead us to the knowledge of the human mind
and of its highest blessedness." In these words we have
the key to the subsequent course of Spinoza's speculations
with respect both to the intellectual and the moral
nature of man. Here, as in his former work on ' The
Improvement of the Human Understanding,' his aim is
not a theoretical but a practical ·one—not primarily the
search for intellectual satisfaction, but the discovery of
the way to spiritual perfection and blessedness. But as,
in his view, all moral advancement rests on and is in
one sense identical with intelligence, the true way to
perfection is to disabuse our minds of error and illusion,
and to gain a point of view from which we shall see
things as they really are. His inquiry into the nature
of the human mind, therefore, resolves itself into the
question whether, from its very nature, human intelli-

gence is capable of adequate, or only of inadequate or imperfect knowledge. Spinoza's doctrine of "finite modes" contains two different and apparently irreconcilable views of the nature of individual finite things—that in which the finite is represented as destitute of any positive reality, and that, on the other hand, in which the negation involved in the notion of the finite is only a *partial* negation, leaving to it still a positive element, "a force by which each individual thing perseveres in existence, and which follows from the eternal necessity of the divine nature." And what is true of finite things is equally true of our knowledge of them. The finite mind, like all other finite things, has, on the one hand, an existence that is merely negative and illusory; the idea of the finite is itself finite, limited and determined by other finites, and incapable of rising above itself. On the other hand, it has in it an element which is not mere negation, which transcends the limits of the finite and relates it to the absolute nature of God. In the former aspect, in its actual, empirical reality, it contemplates all things only under the form of time; it looks on the world from the point of view of sense and imagination, broken up into fictitious individualities, or into things which have only accidental relations to each other in time and space. In the latter aspect, it sees all things from the point of view of reason or intelligence, as having in them a nature that is not unreal and relations that are not accidental, but which "involve the eternal and infinite necessity of the nature of God;" it sees them "under the form of eternity."

Now whether this twofold existence and activity

which Spinoza ascribes to the human mind is not, when closely examined, an impossible and self-contradictory notion, need not here be considered; what we are at present concerned to notice is, that it is obviously Spinoza's aim, both here and in the more strictly ethical part of his system, to represent the lower or finite aspect of human nature as an imperfect stage of man's being, and the higher or infinite aspect as the goal of perfection to which, by its very essence, it is capable of attaining.

The human mind, as we first contemplate it, is imprisoned in the finite. It is an individual amongst other individuals, a link in the endless series of existences, to parts of which only it stands in immediate relation. Its knowledge is only of the particular; it is a finite mode which has for its object only another finite mode; and it has no knowledge of other things save in their accidental relation to its own particular being—no knowledge, therefore, which is not at once fragmentary and confused. The mind is thus in its origin simply " the idea of an individual thing actually existing, or an individual mode of thinking; " and its whole conception of things is determined by this individual reference.

But though it would seem to be impossible, on Spinoza's principles, that the individual finite mind should, without ceasing to be finite or losing its individuality, attain to any higher knowledge, it is implied in his whole treatment of the subject, that the mind is capable of emancipating itself from the particular, and of attaining to a knowledge of things from a universal point of view. There is a stage of human intelligence in which it has become liberated from accidental associations and can contemplate things not as they are merely in relation to our own individuality, but as they are in their own nature and in their necessary relations to each other. At this stage of knowledge the mind has ceased to be dominated by the senses and the imagination; its objects are not mere transient phenomena, but permanent laws. But beyond this there is a yet higher stage. Even the second stage of knowledge, in which we connect things under necessary principles and laws, rests on and involves the highest principle of all, "the very necessity of the nature of God." But there is a form of knowledge of which this principle is not merely the implied basis but the very essence—that which Spinoza designates "intuitive knowledge," "which proceeds from an adequate idea of the absolute essence of certain attributes of God to the adequate knowledge of the essence of things." When it has reached this highest stage of intelligence, the mind, starting with the unity which is present in all knowledge, sees all things in the light of it; it discerns the immanence of the infinite in the finite, and regards the finite as real only in so far as it has the infinite in it. Thus Spinoza's inquiry into the nature of the human mind begins with the definition of the mind as "the knowledge of the body," and ends virtually with defining it as the knowledge of God and of all things in God. Its first consciousness of things is from a purely individual, but it is capable of rising to a universal standpoint. Lost at first in the confused and inadequate ideas of sense and imagination, human intelligence has in it the capacity of rising above itself.

of seeing things no longer in *ordine ad individuum,* but
in their objective reality and necessary relations ; and
finally, it is capable of reaching a point from which
by the intuitive grasp of reason it can discern all
individual things, and all relations of things in their
absolute unity, as expressions of "the eternal necessity
of the divine nature."

I. If now we examine a little more closely the course
of thought of which the foregoing is an outline, the first
important proposition in Spinoza's account of the nature
of the mind is that the human mind is "the idea of the
body." "The first," says he, "which constitutes the
actual being of the human mind is nothing else than
the idea of an actually existing individual thing," and
"the object of the idea which constitutes the human
mind is the body—that is, a definite actually existing
mode of extension and nothing else." [1]

The proof that the mind is the idea of the body is
simply an application to the nature of man of Spinoza's general doctrine of the attributes of thought and
extension, and of the modes as parallel expressions of
these attributes. Substance is both a "thinking thing"
and an "extended thing"; but thought and extension,
and their respective modes, are not essentially different,
but only different expressions of one and the same
thing. To every mode of thought a mode of extension
corresponds, the order or series of thoughts is the same
as the order or series of things, and every actually
existing thing may be regarded as a modification both
of thought and extension. We say of man that he is
composed of body and mind,[2] but the body and the

---

[1] Eth. ii. 11 and 13.					[2] ii. 13, cor.

idea of the body are one and the same thing, contemplated, now under one attribute, now under another. The two worlds of mind and matter, thoughts and things, are thus absolutely separated from each other. Though completely correspondent, they are absolutely independent, and idealistic explanations of physical, and materialistic explanations of mental phenomena, are equally precluded. In Spinoza's theory there is as little room for the *deus ex machina* of Descartes as for the "occasional causes" of Geulinx or the "pre-established harmony" of Leibnitz, to explain the relation of body and mind and the correspondence of bodily and mental acts ; for relation implies difference, and in this case there is no difference, but only one and the same thing contemplated in different aspects. We may, indeed, refer both mental and material phenomena to God as their cause, but we can refer the former only to God or Substance as thinking thing, the latter to God or Substance as extended thing. To trace the existence of any material object to the "will of God" would be to explain by the attribute of thought what can only be explained by the attribute of extension. A circle and the idea of a circle are one and the same thing, conceived now under the attribute of extension, now under the attribute of thought ; but we cannot explain the ideal circle by the actual or by any mode of extension, but only by thought and modes of thought, and *vice versâ*. Body and mind, in like manner, are to be conceived each as a mode of its own attribute ; and the only union of the two of which we can speak, is involved in the proposition that for everything that exists "formally " —*i.e.*, as a modification of extension—there exists something exactly parallel "objectively"—*i.e.*, as a modification of thought.

What, then, from this view of the nature of things, are we to understand by Spinoza's definition of mind as "the idea of the body"? In the first place, it might seem that there is much in man's spiritual nature which this definition does not embrace. By defining it as an "idea" or mode of thought, does not Spinoza leave out of sight such essential elements of that nature as feeling, desire, will, &c., and reduce it to something purely intellectual? The answer is, that, in Spinoza's view, knowledge, the objective knowledge of the human body, precedes all other forms of consciousness and constitutes the fundamental essence of man's mental nature. No emotional or volitional element can exist without presupposing thought, and the latter can exist without the former. Thought is not one among many co-ordinate faculties, each having its own peculiar function, its own time and mode of action; it is the principle which underlies all the many-sided aspects of our spiritual life, and of which these are but various specifications. "Modes of thinking, such as love, desire, or affections of the mind, by whatever name they are designated, do not exist unless there exists in the same individual an *idea* of the thing loved, desired, &c. But the idea may exist without any other mode of thinking."[1]  "The essence of man is constituted by modes of thinking, to all of which the idea is by nature prior, and it is only when that exists that the other modes can exist in the same individual. Therefore the idea is the first thing constituting the being of the human mind."[2]

[1] Eth. ii., ax. 3.            [2] Eth. ii. 11, dem.

But, secondly, even if we accept the doctrine that the ideal element is that to which all other elements of man's spiritual nature may be reduced, this doctrine, it may be said, does not to the modern ear seem to be expressed by the proposition, "the mind is the idea of the body." Modern thought conceives of mind as the conscious, thinking self to which ideas are referred, the rational nature, which is not one idea but the source or subject, at lowest, "the permanent possibility," of all ideas. But the explanation of Spinoza's phraseology lies in this, that mind, as anything more than the idea of the body (or of "affections" of the body), is for him a mere abstraction. It is only by a fictitious, imaginative generalisation that we conceive of any abstract faculty of thinking, feeling, willing, apart from particular thoughts, feelings, volitions ; so it is only by carrying the same fictitious generalisation still further that we conceive of an abstract entity called "mind," which is no particular mental activity, but a capacity of all activities. Such a conception belongs to the same fictitious region with the conception of "lapidity" in relation to stones, or "aquosity" to streams. "There is," says he,[1] "in the mind no absolute faculty of understanding, desiring, loving, &c. These and similar faculties are either entirely fictitious or merely metaphysical entities or universals, such as we are accustomed to create from particular things. Thus the intellect and the will stand in the same relation to this or that idea or this or that volition, as lapidity to this or that stone, or man to Peter and Paul." "The mind is a fixed and definite mode of thought, and not the free cause of its actions."[2] Mind

---

[1] Eth. ii. 48, schol.          [2] Ibid., dem.

is for Spinoza, not a general capacity of knowledge
without definite content, but a definite knowledge of
definite things, an individual mode of thought which
has for its object an individual mode of extension, the
idea of the body or of the 'affections' of the body."
Are we, then, to understand that for Spinoza there is no
such conception as a conscious self, a permanent ego or
subject, to which all mental experiences are referred?
Is the human consciousness nothing but a succession of
isolated thoughts, feelings, &c., bound together by no
principle of unity? To this question the answer can
only be that, though Spinoza's philosophy contains
elements which, as we have often seen, are inconsistent
with his fundamental principles, there is for him, according to these principles, no unity or unifying principle of ideas that stops short of that ultimate unity of
all things which lies in God. We may group a number
of the simplest bodies (*corpora simplissima*) by aggregation, or by the constant relation of their motions to each
other, into a combined or corporate individual, and these
again, by a similar process, into larger individuals; in
like manner we may combine the simplest ideas, or ideas
of the simplest bodies, into the more complex idea of an
individual body, which is the aggregate of many such
simpler elements, and from that again we may rise to
the idea of a larger and more comprehensive individual.
But all such unities, the most comprehensive alike with
the smallest, are artificial creations of the imagination,
which can ascribe to the part an independent unity that
exists only in the whole. The unity of all modes of
thought, of all modes of extension, lies solely in the
attribute which each mode expresses in a certain definite

manner ; and the attributes themselves are only different
expressions of the one ultimate and only absolute unity,
that of Substance or God.   As a mode of a divine attribute, therefore, the human mind has no independent
individuality or self-consciousness.   " It is," says Spinoza,
"part of the infinite intellect of God ; and when we
say that it perceives this or that, what we affirm is that
God has this or that idea, not in so far as He is infinite,
but in so far as He is manifested through the nature of
the human mind, or constitutes the essence of the human
mind." [1]

By the phrase " idea of the body," we are thus to
understand that particular mode of thought called the
human mind which corresponds to that particular mode
of extension which we term the human body.   Mind,
in other words, is the correlate in thought of body in
extension.   It has been alleged that here, as elsewhere,
Spinoza wavers between two entirely different senses of
the word " idea "—that, viz., in which it means, as just
explained, the mental correlate of a certain modification
of matter, and that in which it means the *conception of*
that modification.   It is one thing to say that there
exists in thought an idea which is parallel to the thing
we call body, and another thing to say that the body is
the object of that idea.   The relation expressed in the
former phrase is something quite different from the relation of the knower to the known, which is the relation
expressed in the latter.   A constant relation of the mind
to the body does not imply that we are always thinking
of the body, nor a relation of the mind as a whole to the
body as a whole that there is a complete knowledge of

[1] Eth. ii. 11, cor.

the body in every man's mind, or that every human being is " an accomplished physiologist." Yet a confusion of these two uses of the term " idea " is to be traced, it is averred, in much of Spinoza's speculations, and to this cause are to be ascribed some of his gravest errors.[1]

If, however, we look to the whole drift of Spinoza's doctrine, it must, I think, be acquitted of this alleged ambiguity. Though, unquestionably, the idea of the body is, according to Spinoza, an idea which has the body for its object, yet neither directly nor by implication does Spinoza confound the idea of the body with the physiologist's knowledge of it. The human mind is a mode of thought, but relation to an object is of the very essence of thought. Spinoza, we have just seen, rejects any such notion as that of an empty, abstract mind or subject, a capacity of thinking apart from the actual thought of a particular object. There is no thought or idea which is not the thought or idea *of* something. What, then, can be the special object of the idea which is a particular mode of thought if not the particular mode of extension which corresponds to it? For man the whole universe of being consists of thought and extension, and their modifications. Outside of itself, therefore, there is nothing for the individual mind to think, nothing that for it immediately exists, save the individual mode of extension which is the obverse, so to speak, of itself. In being the mental correlate of the body the mind *thinks* the body. There is no confusion, therefore, of correlation and relation in saying that the idea that is correlated to the body is the

[1] Pollock's Spinoza, p. 132.

idea which has the body for its object, or, in brief, that
the mind is the idea of the body.

But though the mind is, primarily, the idea of the
body, Spinoza in so defining it neither identifies, nor is
logically bound to identify, this idea of the body with
the scientific knowledge of it, or to maintain anything
so absurd as that "every human being must be an
accomplished physiologist." As a matter of fact, he
expressly teaches that the knowledge of the body which
is the content of this "idea" is very imperfect and
inaccurate knowledge. "The human mind," says he,
"does not involve an adequate knowledge of the parts
composing the human body." "The idea," again he
writes, "of each affection of the human body does not
involve an adequate knowledge of the human body
itself;" and again, "The idea of the affections of the
human body, in so far as they are related only to the
human mind, are not clear and distinct, but confused." [1]
Nor does his theory force him to hold any more than
this. The idea of the body and the body correspond to
each other; but the correspondence is between the idea
as this finite mode of thought, dwelling in the region of
imagination or sensuous perception, and the body as this
finite mode of extension apart from its relations to the
whole system of the physical universe. In this point of
view "the body" no more includes its whole organic
structure and functions as they are contemplated by the
anatomist or the physiologist, than "the idea of the
body" or the mind includes its whole constitution and
relations as they are contemplated by the psychologist
or the metaphysician. Between the *adequate* idea of

[1] Eth. ii. 24, 27, 28.

the body, indeed, and the body as it really is, there would be a perfect correlation, and the relation in this case would be that of scientific knowledge ; but the correlation implied in Spinoza's definition of the mind, is not between the body as it really is and the scientific mind, still less between the former and the unscientific mind, but between body as a finite mode of matter, and mind in that attitude which is for the ordinary consciousness its first crude conception of things. If it be said that, after all, the body is as it is to the perfect physiologist, the answer is that the perfect physiologist is God, who is also the body as it is in reality—*i.e.*, as determined in relation to the whole of extension, and therefore in all its physical relations. Mind is the idea of the body, and only so as it is the idea of itself ; but the consciousness is as imperfect in the one case as in the other. Idea and object, therefore, are here exactly correspondent. Relation includes no more than correlation, and there is no confusion between two different things—between the body as the condition of thought, and the body as the object of thought. What makes our knowledge at this stage superficial and confused, we shall see more fully in the sequel.

II. The first important point in Spinoza's inquiry into the nature of the human mind is the definition of the mind as the "idea of the body." The second is the further characterisation of the mind as the idea of itself, the doctrine of *idea mentis* or *idea ideæ*. This further step may be expressed by saying that the first determination is that of mind as consciousness of an object, the second that of mind as self-consciousness. As "the mind is united to the body because the body is the object of the mind, so . . . the idea of the mind is united to its object, the mind, in the same way as the mind is united to the body ; " the only difference being that " mind and body are one and the same individual regarded, now under the attribute of thought, now under that of extension," whereas " the idea of the mind and the mind are one and the same thing regarded under one and the same attribute, that of thought." [1]

The proof of the doctrine of *idea mentis* is twofold, (1) from the nature of God, (2) from the nature of mind itself as " the idea of the body." (1.) The human mind, as we have seen above, is, according to Spinoza, " part of the infinite intellect of God." To say that the mind perceives anything is to say " that God has this or that idea, not in so far as He is infinite, but in so far as He constitutes the essence of the human mind." But it is involved in the divine attribute of thought that " there must necessarily exist in God an idea both of Himself and of all His affections, and therefore an idea of the human mind." [2] " The idea of the mind and the mind itself exist in God by the same necessity and the same power of thinking." [3] The human mind, therefore (or God as constituting its essence), has an idea of itself.

(2.) The same thing is proved from the nature of mind itself, regarded as " the idea of the body." " The idea of the mind, or the idea of the idea, is simply the form of the idea considered as a mode of thought without reference to its object. For one who knows anything, in the very act of doing so knows that he knows

---

[1] Eth. ii. 21, dem. and schol.
[2] Eth. ii. 20, dem.       [3] Eth. ii. 21, schol.

it, and knows that he knows that he knows it, and so on *ad infinitum.*" [1]

What it is of most importance to remark as to this doctrine of *idea mentis* is that, notwithstanding Spinoza's assertion of the absolute independence and equality of the two parallel series of modes, a richer content is here ascribed to the mental than to the corporeal side. The idea of the body corresponds to the body, but there is nothing in the latter which corresponds to the idea's consciousness of itself. The body, as a mode of extension, has relations to other modes of extension, and the idea which constitutes the mind has relations to other modes of thought; but in the series of ideas there is interposed a relation which has nothing parallel to it in the series of material modes—viz., the relation of each idea to itself. In returning upon itself, mind is not the correlate in thought of anything that takes place in extension. It possesses a self-activity, a power of self-reflection, which has no existence in matter. In his whole doctrine, indeed, as to the relation of the ideal and the material, we find an unconscious preponderance ascribed to the ideal side. In the very definition of mind as the idea of the body, there seems to be attributed to it a power to transcend the gulf between thought and things, which is not ascribed to the latter. Matter, so to speak, becomes idealised, but mind does not become materialised. It is not by any influence or impression of the body on the mind, but by the mind's own inherent activity, that it knows the body, or has the body for its object. "It would be absurd," says Spinoza, "to think of the idea as something dumb, like a picture in-

[1] Eth. ii. 21, schol.

scribed on a tablet, and not as a mode of thinking, as intelligence itself." [1]  "By idea," says he elsewhere,[2] " I
understand a conception of the mind which it forms because it is a thinking thing.  I say conception rather
than perception, because the word 'perception' seems
to indicate that the mind is passive to the object, but
'conception' seems to express the activity of the mind."
In being the idea of the body, mind is not passive but
active, and its activity is the purely internal, self-originated activity of thought.  Moreover, as we have just
seen, its inherent activity manifests itself in a wholly
original manner, to which there is nothing corresponding
in the body—viz., as reflection on itself.  It is not
merely the idea of the body, but it makes that idea its
own object; and in so doing, as Spinoza teaches, it is
its own criterion of certitude.  In knowing, it knows
that it knows.  The truth of its knowledge is self-cer-
tified.  The content of every true idea carries subjective
certainty with it, and the " form " or characteristic property of the idea is something that pertains to it, "in
so far as it is considered as a mode of thought, *without
reference to the object.*" [3]  Finally, we shall afterwards
see that Spinoza ascribes to mind not merely an activity
independent of the body, but a power to control and
modify the body and its affections.  The mind masters
the passions by the very act of thinking them, or "by
forming clear and distinct ideas of them ; " [4] and when
it is thus liberated from passion, it can order and concatenate its ideas according to the order of reason.  But,
as ideas are ordered and connected in the mind, so are

---

[1] Eth. ii. 43, schol.            [2] Eth. ii., def. 3.
[3] Eth. ii. 21, schol.            [4] Eth. v. 3.

the affections of the body or the images of things in
the body. "So long," he therefore concludes, "as we
are not assailed by passions which are contrary to our
nature, we possess the power of ordering and connecting
the affections of the body according to the order of
reason." [1]  Notwithstanding, therefore, his denial of any
causal nexus between mind and body, we find him here
ascribing to mind not only a power over itself and its
own internal activities, which the body does not possess, but also a power, extending beyond the sphere of
thought, to control and regulate the affections of the
body.

III. The essence of the mind, as we have seen, is intelligence.   It is idea, the idea of the body, and in
being the idea of the body it is the idea of itself.   Its
characteristic attitude towards both the outward and the
inward world is that of *knowledge*.   But if we go on to
ask, What is the nature and value of its knowledge?
Spinoza's answer is, that in the first exercise of our intelligence, its knowledge is "inadequate" — or, more
definitely, it is neither a complete nor a distinct, but
only a fragmentary and confused knowledge of things.
Its point of view is purely individual; it is that of a
being who is only a part of the world, and as such apprehends only the part with which he stands in immediate connection, and even that only partially and
indistinctly; and as the mind's knowledge of itself is
relative to its knowledge of the body—as it knows itself
only in knowing, and in the measure in which it knows,
outward things—its self-consciousness is as inadequate as
its consciousness of outward objects.

[1] Eth. v. 10.

The proof of the inadequacy of that knowledge which pertains to the mind as the idea of the body, is based on the proposition that the mind knows the body *only by means of ideas of bodily affections—i.e.,* of the modifications which the body experiences in its relations to outward objects.[1] It has been shown[2] that an individual finite thing can exist only as determined by another finite thing, and that as determined by another finite thing, &c., *ad infinitum;* and as the knowledge of an effect depends on the knowledge of its cause and includes it,[3] an adequate knowledge of any individual thing would imply a knowledge of the whole endless series of causes and effects — in other words, would imply a knowledge which pertains only to the infinite intellect of God. But the human mind is only a part of that infinite intellect. Its knowledge is God's knowledge of the body, not in so far as He is infinite, but in so far as He is regarded as affected by another idea of a particular thing actually existing, or by many such ideas.[4] In other words, the idea or knowledge of the body is not the idea of the body in itself, but only of the body as determined or affected by other bodies; or the mind knows the body only by means of the ideas of the affections it experiences. Now, if we consider what is the value of the knowledge so defined, it is obvious that it must be both partial and confused. It is partial; it apprehends its objects not in the totality of their nature and relations. Its knowledge of the body, of outward bodies, and of itself, is a knowledge which excludes or conceals all but a fragment of what would

---

[1] Eth. ii. 19.  [2] Eth. i. 28.
[3] Eth. i., ax. 4.  [4] Eth. ii. 19, dem.

be necessary to true or perfect knowledge. Knowing its own body only as it affects and is affected by outward objects, it knows both only in *one* relation,—the external objects only in so far as they influence the human body, but not in their innumerable other relations;[1] the human body only in that relation in which it has been affected in a particular way, but not as it is capable of being affected in a multiplicity of other ways.[2] Further, the human body is a highly compōsite individual thing, the parts of which belong to its essence only in so far as they participate in its movements in definite reciprocal relations; but in so far as they exist in other relations, or in action and reaction with other bodies, the knowledge of their existence and activity is not included in the idea of the body which constitutes the human mind. Thus the knowledge that comes through the affections of the body is the knowledge of outward objects, of the body itself, and of its constituent parts, only in certain particular relations, and is therefore imperfect or partial. It is also, even so far as it goes, indistinct or confused. Each affection of which the mind is conscious is the result of two factors—the action of the outward object and the susceptibility of its own body—and it is incapable of determining how much is merely subjective, how much due to the outward object. "These ideas and affections, therefore, in so far as they are related to the human mind alone, are like conclusions without premisses—that is, they are confused ideas."[3]

If the knowleage that comes to the mind through the affections of the body is thus inadequate, equally inade-

[1] Eth. ii. 25.    [2] Eth. ii. 27.    [3] Eth. ii. 28.

quate must be the self-consciousness that is bound up with it. The idea of the idea must partake of the imperfection and indistinctness of its object. "As the idea of an affection of the body does not involve an adequate knowledge of the body or adequately express its nature, so the idea of that idea does not adequately express the nature of the human mind or involve an adequate knowledge of it."[1] The self-consciousness, in other words, which is the consciousness of inadequate ideas, must be itself an inadequate self-consciousness.

But besides this imperfection and confusion which characterises our first consciousness of things, or that knowledge which is mediated by the affections of the body, there is a further defect which inevitably clings to it. Not only at this stage are our particular perceptions inadequate, but the same inadequacy attends our ways of connecting or combining them. A mind which knows things only through the affections of the body, or as they present themselves in individual sensible experience, can have no other notion of the relations of things than that of arbitrary or accidental association. The affections of the body, and therefore the ideas of these affections, vary in each case with the individual susceptibility. They are limited in number by the range of individual experience, and they succeed each other in no rational order, but only in the order in which the individual chances to be affected by them. "Memory," says Spinoza, "is an association of ideas which involves the nature of things outside the body, but it is an association which arises in the mind according to the order and association of the affections

[1] Eth. ii. 29, dem.

of the body," in contradistinction from the order of intelligence "whereby the mind perceives things through their primary causes, and which is the same in all men." [1] Thus, so long as our knowledge is derived from mere *external* experience, Spinoza shows (though by the help of a somewhat crude physiological explanation, on which nothing really turns) that it is possible to regard as actually present, things which are absent or even non-existent,[2] and to connect things arbitrarily "according to the manner in which the mind has been accustomed to connect and bind together the images of things." [3] Lastly, the inadequacy and arbitrariness which is the general characteristic of this kind of knowledge finds another example in the fictitious "universals," the general or abstract terms by which we attempt to give connection and unity to our particular perceptions of things. Transcendental terms, such as "being," "thing," "something"; generic terms, such as "man," "horse," "dog," &c.,—so far from expressing real relations of things, only intensify the confusion of our individual perceptions. They are expressions of the mind's weakness, not of its strength. They arise from the fact that its capacity of forming even confused images of things is limited, so that when they exceed a certain number they run into each other, and our only resource is to group them indistinctly under some general term. Instead, therefore, of giving unity to the differences of our primary perceptions, they only redouble the original indistinctness. And they are as arbitrary as they are confused. They do not supply any objective principle by which the differences of things are explained and

[1] Eth. ii. 18, schol.  [2] Ibid., 17.  [3] Ibid., 18, schol.

harmonised, but only images or subjective conceptions, varying with individual temperament, by which we attempt to bind together diversities too complicated for ordinary thought to embrace. "Those who have most frequently looked with admiration on the *stature* of men will understand by the term 'man' an animal of erect stature; while those who have been in the habit of fixing their thoughts on something else will form a different general image, as of an animal capable of laughter, a biped without feathers, a rational animal, &c., each person forming general images according to the temperament of his own body."[1]

The knowledge which is mediated by the "affections of the body"—in other words, our first empirical consciousness of things as they are given in immediate perception—is thus in many ways imperfect and unreal. The mind, regarded simply as "the idea of the body," has no adequate knowledge "either of itself or of the body, or of outward bodies." It is but an individual thing in a boundless universe, catching only indistinct glimpses of other finite things in their immediate relation to its own individuality. It is but a transitory mode of thought, which knows itself only as the reflex of a transitory mode of matter; and of all that lies beyond itself and its immediate object it knows nothing save through the dim and broken impressions of its accidental surroundings. To ask whether such a being is capable of "adequate ideas" would seem to be equivalent to asking whether the particular can comprehend the universal, or that which is merely subjec-

[1] Eth. ii. 40, schol. 1.

tive and contingent can find in itself the expression of that which is objective and necessary.

Spinoza's answer to this question is contained in his theory of the development of knowledge. The individual point of view which constitutes the mind's first attitude towards the world, is only the beginning of knowledge. It is possible for man to rise above himself and the conditions of his finitude. The human mind has in it, by its essential nature, an element in virtue of which it can escape from the narrowness and confusion, the arbitrariness and contingency of its own subjective feelings or affections, or of that knowledge which is merely generated from them. It is possible for it, in the process of knowledge, to eliminate its own individuality, and to attain to a view of things which is untroubled by the peculiarities of individual temperament or the accidents of individual experience. From conceptions which represent only the relations of its own body to outward bodies it can rise to the apprehension of the laws or principles which are common to all bodies, and which determine, not their accidental, but their necessary relation to each other. And finally, beyond even that emancipation from itself which is implied in the knowledge of things as determined by universal laws and rules (*per leges et regulas universales*),[1] the mind is capable of attaining that supreme elevation in which all finite things and all laws and principles of finite things are referred to the ultimate unity which is their immanent principle and origin. In the light of this highest universality, it contemplates all things as they really are, and not as they seem to be,

---

[1] Eth. iii., Præf.

from the point of view of the whole, and not in partial, fragmentary aspects, in their essential relations, and not in accidental combinations, under the "form of eternity," and not under the conditions of time. In a word, the human mind, when it has realised its inherent capacity of intelligence, is no longer "the idea of the body," but the idea or intuitive apprehension of God, and of all things in God.

In the ascending scale of intelligence thus generally indicated, Spinoza specifies two stages, which he designates respectively "reason" (*ratio*) and "intuitive knowledge" (*scientia intuitiva*). In the earlier sketch of the theory which is given in the treatise on 'The Improvement of the Understanding,' these two kinds or stages of knowledge are defined as that "in which the essence of a thing is inferred from another thing," and that "in which a thing is perceived solely from its own essence, or by the knowledge of its proximate cause." In the 'Ethics' the distinction is presented in a somewhat modified form. "Reason" is that knowledge which arises "from our possessing common notions and adequate ideas of the properties of things,"[1]—"ideas which are common to all men," of those "things in which all bodies agree,"[2] "which exist equally in the human body and in external bodies, and equally in the part and in the whole of each external body."[3] "Intuitive knowledge," again, is "that kind of knowing which proceeds from an adequate idea of the formal essence of certain attributes of God to the adequate knowledge of the essence of things."[4] And this last kind of

[1] Eth. ii. 40, schol. 2.
[2] Eth. ii. 38, cor.
[3] Eth. ii. 39, dem.
[4] Eth. ii. 40, schol. 2.

knowledge he further describes as the knowledge of "the existence of individual things in so far as they are in God ; for although," he adds, "each individual thing is determined by another individual thing to exist in a certain way, nevertheless the force by which each thing perseveres in its existence follows from the eternal necessity of the nature of God."[1]

1. The kind of knowledge which is designated "reason," is, as we have just said, in the earlier form of the theory distinguished from the third or highest kind of knowledge simply as mediate from immediate, that which is reached by ratiocination from that which we obtain by intuitive perception. "Reason," in other words, denotes that knowledge of which the object is not apprehended directly and immediately, but only inferentially, by deduction according to logical principles. Of this inferential or deductive knowledge Spinoza adduces as examples the conclusion from effect to cause, or from any universal to "a property which always accompanies it." In the 'Ethics' the explanation of the matter, though varied in form, is substantially the same. There are certain common notions or fundamental principles of reason which enable us to rise above the merely individual and subjective view of things, and which form the basis of a real knowledge. Behind the phenomena of sense, which vary with the individual subject, there are certain elements or laws which are common to all things and all parts of things—a universal nature which each thing has in common with other things, and in virtue of which it is a member of the system or order of nature. Of these universal elements

[1] Eth. ii. 45, schol.

the mind can form adequate ideas; it can apprehend them in their simplicity and purity underlying the confusion of the sensible world, and so perceive in that world, not the accidental play of circumstances, but a real or rational order. These adequate ideas enable us to see things in their real agreements, differences, and oppositions. They form the basis of reason (*fundamenta rationis*)[1] or of ratiocination (*fundamenta ratiocinii*),[2] inasmuch as "whatever ideas in the mind follow from adequate ideas are also themselves adequate,"[3] and "the things we clearly and distinctly understand are either the common properties of things, or things which are deduced from those."[4] "Reason," in short, is the mind's power to form clear and distinct ideas, and deductions from such ideas.[5] This kind of knowledge, he further points out, though it raises us above our first crude perceptions of things, inasmuch as it liberates us from accidental associations, yet falls short of the highest knowledge, and partakes in some measure of the defects of ordinary knowledge. It only incompletely redeems us from that partial or abstract way of looking at things which is the radical defect of the latter. In our ordinary unscientific attitude of mind we proceed from part to part: setting out from ourselves and our immediate surroundings, we pass from object to object, regarding them as isolated, self-identical things, or only vaguely connecting them with each other by accidental associations of time and place. Reason so far corrects this abstract, disintegrated view of things, that it connects and separates them as genera and species

---

[1] Eth. ii. 44, cor. dem.    [2] Eth. ii. 40, schol. 1.
[3] Eth. ii. 40.    [4] Eth. v. 12, dem.
[5] Eth. v. 10, dem.

according to their likenesses and dissimilarities, or links them together by necessary laws, such as that of cause and effect. But in so doing reason only partially overcomes the crude abstractions of ordinary thought. When, *e.g.*, we reason from effect to cause, we still contemplate things as separate, self-identical substances connected with each other only by an external link; and however far we carry out the series of causes and effects, we can never arrive at any real principle of unity. The utmost we get by any such method is only an endless or indefinite succession of objects externally determining and determined. If the real unity of the world is to be discerned, it must be by some higher principle of knowledge—some principle which will not leave the manifold objects of the finite world lying still in disintegration, or explain one finite thing by another which is still outside of it, or by an infinite which is only the endless repetition of the finite. What we want and what "reason" cannot give us, is a first or highest principle which will at once transcend and explain all differences of the finite world, which will be seen in its own light, and in the light of which the reality and unity of all finite things will be seen.

2. "As all things are in God, and are conceived through God, we can . . . form that third kind of knowledge of which I have spoken, and of the excellence and utility of which I shall in the fifth part (of the 'Ethics') have occasion to speak."[1] It is thus that Spinoza describes that *scientia intuitiva* which forms the culminating stage of human intelligence, the attitude of mind which is furthest removed from the purely in-

[1] Eth. ii. 47, schol.

dividual point of view, and in which it apprehends all things in the light of that first principle in relation to which alone they truly are and can be known. " Reason," as we have seen, so far corrects the arbitrary abstractions of sense and imagination, but its point of view is still abstract. The link of necessity which connects things with each other is something other than and external to the things themselves. That which gives them unity is foreign to, not immanent in them. By means of such general principles as that of causality we can *infer* or conclude from one thing to another, but we do not *see* the unity that runs through them. We perceive the differences of things *and* that which unites them, but not unity in difference and difference in unity.

Now it is this highest apprehension of things which, in "intuitive knowledge," the mind attains. What Spinoza means by this phrase is a kind of knowledge in which it no longer proceeds from part to part, from difference to unity, but is determined by the idea of the whole, and proceeds from the whole to the parts, from unity to difference. It is the realisation of what, elsewhere, he had laid down as the ideal of true knowledge —viz., that the mind must grasp the idea which represents the origin and sum of nature, and see in that idea the source of all other ideas." Moreover, this knowledge is not mediate, but immediate or intuitive. In it the unity is prior to diversity, and the process from unity to difference is not one which first apprehends the principle or origin of things as an independent, self-contained reality, and then advances to the manifold existences of the finite world ; but one in which, as by a single intuitive glance of intelligence, it sees all finite things as genetically involved in their first principle. It sees the differences as the differences *of* unity, the unity as immanent in the differences. It sees God in all things, and all things in God.

That the human mind is capable of this highest kind of knowledge Spinoza rests on the consideration that all knowledge virtually involves the idea of God, and that we have only to evolve its content to bring our knowledge into correlation with its first principle or immanent source. " The idea," says he,[1] of every individual thing actually existing, necessarily involves the eternal and infinite essence of God." As all spaces must be known as in one space, or through the conception of an all-comprehending space, so all individual ideas can be known only through the all-embracing idea of God. " Inasmuch as individual things have God for their cause, in so far as He is regarded under the attribute of which they are modes, their ideas must necessarily involve the conception of the attribute of these ideas—that is, the eternal and infinite essence of God." [2] The knowledge of God is implicated with our knowledge of all things, and without that knowledge we could know nothing else. It is true that in our ordinary thinking we do not clearly apprehend that which is really the fundamental element of our consciousness ; but the reason of this is, that the unreflective mind confounds thought with imagination, and conceives itself to be incapable of thinking what it cannot represent to itself by an outward picture or image. " Men have been accustomed to associate the name of God with images of things they have been in

[1] Eth. ii. 45.        [2] Ibid., dem.

the habit of seeing," and the absence of the image is mistaken for unconsciousness of the thing. If they "could see into their own minds, they would no longer make this mistake," any more than the man who makes an error in calculation would ascribe it to an incapacity in the human mind to apprehend the idea of number, rather than to its unconscious substitution of false numbers for true. When we thus "see into our minds," or bring, by reflection, their content to clear consciousness, we discern that our ideas of all things—of ourselves, of our own bodies, and of external bodies as actually existing—presuppose and are based on an adequate knowledge of "the eternal and infinite essence of God." [1] Intuitive knowledge, therefore, is that which interprets us to ourselves, and enables us to transform our consciousness of the finite by bringing it into relation with the infinite. It not only liberates us from the arbitrary abstractions of sense and imagination, but it frees us from the abstractness that still clings to the general notions of ratiocinative thought. When we "proceed from the absolute knowledge of the essence of God to the adequate knowledge of the essence of things," from the idea of an absolute unity, which is immanent in all diversity, to particular things as only the expression of that unity in a certain definite manner, the dualism which is involved in the notion of causality vanishes. The higher universality dissolves the difference still left by the lower. The view of the world, as a succession of finite things conditioned by and conditioning each other in endless series, yields to the view in which everything is seen in the light of the infinite unity which is immanent in all. "For, al-

[1] Eth. ii. 47, schol.

though each particular thing be conditioned by another particular thing to exist in a given way, yet the force by which each particular thing perseveres in existing" (*i.e.*, its inmost essence) "follows" (not from other particular things, but) "from the eternal necessity of the nature of God."[1] The intuition of reason is possible only when diversity is seen through unity, for till then the special existence of things and their mediating link are independent. We cannot properly see the whole *at once.* Mediacy thus can become immediacy only at the highest point; and this explains the difficulty that is involved in asserting at the same time an intuitive knowledge and a deduction of ideas from the highest idea. The perfect collapse into unity is possible for reason only at the highest point where it returns, so to speak, to the directness of sense. Finally, we cannot speak of intuitive knowledge as a knowledge which is determined by time, but only as knowledge "under the form of eternity." Even ratiocinative knowledge, in so far as it lifts its objects out of their contingency into a system of unalterable relations, may be said to be knowledge of things "under *a certain* form of eternity" (*sub* quadam *specie æternitatis*). But it is only intuitive knowledge to which, in the fullest sense of the words, this description can be applied. For here our consciousness of things is a consciousness which is no longer subjected to finite limitations, but one "which proceeds from the eternal necessity of the divine nature," or which identifies itself with the principle which transcends the sphere of time and of temporal relations. "Things are conceived by us as actual in two ways—either as existing in relation

[1] Eth. ii. 45, schol.

to a given time and place, or as contained in God and following from the necessity of the divine nature."[1] Time and number are only forms of the imagination, pertaining to the phenomenal unreal aspect of things. It is only individual things, or things regarded as isolated individuals, that arise and pass away—in their inner essence they neither begin nor cease to be. When we contemplate them from a universal point of view, we enter into a region in which duration and succession have no place, where one thing is no more prior in time to another than are the different properties of a circle or a triangle. As he who grasps the idea of a circle or triangle sees all its properties to be simultaneously present in it, so he who intuitively apprehends the nature of things sees all finite existences as eternally involved in the idea of God—sees them "under the form of eternity." "Here," says Spinoza, "by existence I do not understand duration—that is, existence abstractly conceived, and as a certain form of quantity. I speak of the very nature of existence which is ascribed to individual things because of this, that from the eternal necessity of the nature of God an infinitude of things follow in infinite ways."[2]

It is unnecessary at present to enter into any detailed examination of Spinoza's theory of knowledge. What we may here point out is, that the ideal at which it aims it fails to fulfil. Setting out from the purely individual point of view of the ordinary consciousness, it traces the rise of the mind through the higher but still imperfect universality of reason, to that highest or absolute universality which is involved in the apprehension of all

---

[1] Eth. v. 29, schol.        [2] Eth. ii. 45, schol.

things in their relation to the idea of God. Expressed in modern language, the gradual evolution of thought is that in which the mind, beginning with ordinary unsophisticated experience, advances, first to the scientific attitude, and finally to that of philosophy or speculation. But whatever may be said as to the transition from the first to the second stage, the fatal defect of Spinoza's scheme of knowledge is, that the final step is, not from a lower universality to a higher, from a plurality of principles or categories to one highest principle which embraces and explains them, but simply from the diversity of the former to a mere abstract identity which lies beyond them. The principle the intuitive apprehension of which is to constitute the ultimate explanation of all the differences of the finite world is, when we examine what it means, nothing more than the common element which we reach when these differences are left out of sight. The implicit universality of intelligence, as we may express it, asserts itself, first, in raising us above the partial, accidental, confused aspect of things as they are regarded from a merely individual or subjective point of view, and in apprehending them as related to each other by universal principles or laws. But the rational or scientific point of view, though it so far corrects that of ordinary experience, leaves the impulse towards universality still unsatisfied. The claim of philosophy to be a higher explanation of the world than that of science is based on the fact, not only that science employs categories, such as substance and qualities, cause and effect, &c., which it does not explain, but that these categories give us only a provisional explanation of the world conceived of as a manifold of existences outside of each other, and

apart from their relation to the intelligence that knows
them. They connect things indeed by real and objective, instead of accidental and subjective relations, but
the highest view they reach is that of an aggregate of
finite substances acting and reacting externally on each
other, and contemplated in abstraction from the intelligence for which alone they exist. What philosophy, if
it is to justify its pretensions, must do, is to furnish us
with a higher principle to which the categories of science
may be carried back as *their* principle, and at the same
time as the principle of the mind that apprehends them
—an idea, in other words, which will be the reason at
once of the differences of things from each other, and
of the supreme difference of things from the mind that
knows them. Whether modern philosophy has achieved
this result we need not here inquire. But this much
at least is obvious, that the ultimate unity of knowing
and being cannot be found in a principle which abstracts
from their difference. If what we are in search of is a
key to the meaning of nature and man, of mind and
matter, of the manifold differences of the finite world, it
is not supplied by an idea which destroys these differences, or is itself destroyed when brought into contact
with them.

# CHAPTER XII.

### THE MORAL NATURE OF MAN.

THE ethical part of Spinoza's philosophy is based on
the metaphysical, and partakes of the merits and defects of the latter. A thorough-going pantheism knows
nothing of moral distinctions. As it admits of no qualitative difference between finite things, so it admits of no
better and worse, higher and lower, in man's nature.
God is not more revealed in what we call the noblest
than in the meanest of finite existences. Each is but a
mode of the infinite, and none can be more. Nor can
there be any part or element of any individual nature
which is more or less divine than another, or by the
triumph or subjugation of which that nature can elevate
itself to a higher or degenerate to a lower stage of being.
In such a system the terms "good" and "evil" must be
meaningless, or at most, expressions of facts of the same
order with the terms heat and cold, motion and rest, or
(in the case of sensitive beings) pleasure and pain. Finally, as in such a system the independent existence of
finite things is an illusion, and their only distinction
from the infinite a distinction which vanishes with the
false abstraction which gave it birth, any such notion as

that of aspiration, self-devotion, union with God—any such notions as form the basis of the religious life are equally excluded with those of freedom, responsibility, duty, &c., which form the basis of the moral.

But whilst, in one point of view, the metaphysic of Spinozism, as of all pantheistic systems, is subversive of what we commonly understand by "ethics," it is not the less true that the ethical in Spinoza's aim and intention was the goal to which the metaphysical part of his philosophy pointed. And even in his metaphysic itself there are ideas and principles which are incongruous with its pantheistic side, and of which his elaborate ethical theory is the logical result. The origin and explanation of all moral activity he finds in a certain self-maintaining or self-realising impulse, which is identical with the very essence of each finite individual —"the effort by which it endeavours to persevere in its own being." [1] Feeling or emotion (*affectus*) is the expression of this impulse, and modifications of feeling arise from its satisfaction or repression. When the self-maintaining impulse is satisfied, or when the mind is conscious of an increase of power, the feeling is that of pleasure or some modification of pleasure ; in the opposite case the feeling is that of pain or a modification of pain. When the individual is himself the adequate cause of such increased power, the emotion is termed an "activity" ; when the diminution or increase of power follows from something external, and of which the individual is only the partial cause, the emotion is termed a "passion," or passive state. From this account of the nature and origin of human emotion we

[1] Eth. iii. 6 and 7.

are enabled to understand the relation of the intellectual to the ethical part of Spinoza's philosophy, and the close correspondence which he traces between the successive stages of knowledge and the successive stages of man's moral life. Through all the stages of knowledge runs the self-realising impulse, taking its complexion and content from each in succession, expanding and enlarging itself with the widening sphere of intelligence, and expressing itself in emotions coloured by the intellectual atmosphere in which it breathes. At the lowest stage, corresponding to that of "vague experience," where intelligence is governed by accidental and subjective associations, the self which seeks realisation is the purely individual self, varying with individual temperament and the accidental relations of time and place. Its good and evil are nothing absolute, but only that in which a purely individual nature can experience the feeling of enlargement or repression—viz., pleasure and pain ; and as its whole experience, all that moves or affects it, arises not from the mind's own activity, but from that which is external or foreign to it —as, in other words, it is at best only the partial cause of its own emotions, and " the force whereby it perseveres in its being is infinitely surpassed by the power of external causes "—at this stage of the moral life man is simply " a part of nature," and the general condition of human nature can only be described as that of impotence or " bondage."

But whilst, regarded simply as an individual amongst other individuals, man is not, and never can be, free, human nature contains in itself the secret of its own emancipation. The bondage lies in this, that the true self is repressed by what is foreign to it. The fundamental impulse of self-maintenance, which is our very essence, has here not free play; it is in contradiction with the conditions under which it exists, and the effort to rise above these conditions is the expression of our deepest nature. All the force of that nature goes with the effort to throw off the yoke of imagination and passion, and to rise to rational freedom. Corresponding, therefore, to the stage of intelligence which Spinoza designates "reason," in which the mind passes from the sphere of inadequate to that of adequate ideas, there is a stage of moral activity, in which the universal element in man's nature asserts itself, and the mind ceasing to be the slave of external and accidental impulse, its experience becomes the expression of its own self-originated energy. On the intellectual side of our nature, reason, as we have seen, is the sphere of freedom; it liberates from the confusion and contingency of the senses and the imagination, and is itself the pure activity of the mind, all the operations of which can be "understood from our own nature as their adequate cause." But it is the sphere of freedom also as regards the moral life. To live according to reason is to live according to ourselves, to make our life the expression of our true nature. We cannot, indeed, cease to be creatures of sense and imagination, or, so long as the body exists, to have a consciousness which consists of ideas of bodily affections. But reason, though it cannot annul the conditions from which desires and passions arise, can, to a great extent, elevate us above their control. It can make us independent of passion; for "to all actions to which we are determined by passion, where the mind is passive, we can be determined by reason without passion." [1]  And it has in it, by its very nature, a power to abate the control of passion; for, in one sense, the activity of thought kills passion; by *thinking* a passion, we make it cease to be a passion.  The particular objects of our desire or aversion, love or hatred, lose their power over us when the bodily affections we ascribed to them are referred to their true origin—viz., the whole order and complex of things, and the universal laws by which they are regulated.  Seen in this light, the vehemence of passion becomes as foolish as the child's anger against the stone that hurts it, or the infuriated man's indignation against the messenger of evil tidings.  Moreover, reason quells passion by revealing the vain imagination of liberty on which passion is based.  "The mind has greater power over the passions, and is less subject to them, in so far as it understands all things as necessary." [2]  We gain true freedom by the detection of false freedom.  The feverish restlessness of hope and fear, disappointment and regret, pity and resentment, is allayed or cured when we see in our affections of body and mind the expression of a necessary and unalterable order.  Reason can no more be pleased or pained, be moved by love or hate, desire or aversion, towards the beings or events that often give rise to such emotions, than it can love or hate a triangle for its properties, or a law of nature for its inevitable results.  Finally, the fluctuations of feeling which depend on the succession of things in time are subdued or quelled, the more we learn to see in them those eternal relations which are the objects of rational

[1] Eth. iv. 59.　　　　　　[2] Eth. v. 6.

observation. Joy or sorrow come and go with the transitory relations of the imagination, but the true order of things which reason reveals is not transitory. It lifts us into a sphere in which neither the things themselves nor our ideas of them are things of time. Not the latter, for our knowledge even of things in time is not itself a thing of time; not the former, for that in the things themselves of which reason takes cognisance is not accidental and arbitrary successions, but relations which never change. Thus the mind that is guided by reason is elevated above the ebb and flow of passion, is no longer tossed to and fro on the ever-changing tides of feeling, and its only emotion is the profounder joy of acquiescence in that changeless order with which it identifies itself when it contemplates all things " under a form of eternity."

But the knowledge of things " under the form of eternity " is, in the full sense of the words, as we have seen, only attained when the mind rises to the highest stage of knowledge, which Spinoza designates *scientia intuitiva ;* and to this corresponds the culminating stage of the moral life. As knowledge is still imperfect which proceeds from finite to finite even by the link of necessary and unchanging relation, so the activity and freedom of the spiritual life are still imperfect when they are determined by affections which spring from finite relations of things. Joy in an invariable order is still a joy in which the mind regards itself and other minds, its body and other bodies, under the limits of the finite. Though the links are golden, the chain is still there. The alloy of finite passion is still possible when the mind and the objects of its contemplation lie outside of

each other, and are not referred to the ultimate unity
from which all differences spring, when it does not yet
live and breathe in unison with the universal heart and
life of the world.   But intuitive knowledge, as we have
seen, not only annuls the arbitrary abstractions of sense
and imagination, but evaporates even that residuum
of abstraction which reason or ratiocination involves.
Raised to this point of view, the mind no longer contemplates the world and itself as a system of finite
things conditioned by each other, but by the glance of
immediate intelligence sees them in the light of that
absolute unity of which they are only the infinitely
varied expression.   And this supreme attitude of intelligence reflects itself in that "intellectual love" which
is the goal and consummation of the moral life.   Intellectual love is the joy or blessedness of the mind in the
consciousness of its own perfect activity, combined with
the idea of God as its cause.   It is a joy into which no
element of passion enters, for the mind has here completely emerged from that passivity to which passion
is due.   Its consciousness is the consciousness of pure
activity, because it is determined by no other finite consciousness, but only by that infinite intelligence with
which its own inmost nature is identified.   Yet, though
absolutely unimpassioned, this joy is the highest of
which human nature is capable ; for all joy is in the
consciousness of elevation to a higher measure of power,
and here, where its consciousness of self is one with
its consciousness of God, it has reached the summit of
human perfection.   And as this joy in the consciousness
of perfection is at the same time joy in the knowledge
of God, or which is combined with the idea of God, it

is another name for the love of God. Further, as this "intellectual love" is the love to God of a mind which is itself a mode of God, and which, in all its activities, is the expression of the divine nature, it may be said that the mind's love to God is part of the infinite love wherewith God loves Himself. Yet in so describing it Spinoza does not imply that, in attaining to this its highest perfection, human nature loses its individuality, and is absorbed in indistinguishable identity with the divine. For whilst there is an idea or consciousness of self which is implicated with the affections of the body, and which therefore perishes with it, the idea or consciousness of self which intuitive knowledge involves is not implicated with the body or with temporal and spatial conditions. As knowing God and all things in God, the mind is not determined by time, it is itself eternal. Taken up into the infinite, it still knows itself in and through the infinite. Its negation of self is the negation, not of all consciousness, but only of that illusory consciousness which belongs to the imagination— the negation, *i.e.*, of that which is itself a negation, leaving to it still the affirmation of that truer self which lives now and for ever in the knowledge and love of God, and of all things in God. In other words, the negation of the finite as finite is not the negation, but the realisation of that affirmative essence of humanity which is the eternal object of the love of God.

Such, then, is an outline of the train of thought by which Spinoza reaches, in the ethical part of his work, that which, we know, was the implicit aim of all his speculation—the inquiry, "whether there may not be some real good, the discovery and attainment of which will enable the mind to enjoy constant, supreme, and perfect happiness," "which, as a thing infinite and eternal, will feed the mind wholly with joy, and be itself unmingled with sorrow." It must now be our business to trace somewhat more in detail the steps by which this conclusion is reached.

# CHAPTER XIII.

## DOCTRINE OF THE EMOTIONS—THE SELF-MAINTAINING IMPULSE.

IN Spinoza's doctrine of the emotions, we seem at first sight to find a complete reversal of the principle of his philosophy as it has been unfolded in the preceding pages. For a pantheistic there is now substituted what is apparently a purely individualistic principle. Instead of deriving all from infinite substance, he seems to make everything a deduction from a special impulse, which is identified with the particular nature of each individual thing. Whereas, hitherto, reality and modality had been opposed to each other, and to modes or individual finite things had been denied any other than a fugitive, contingent, or merely negative existence, now he seems to ascribe to each finite thing an original, indestructible individuality, an independent self-centred being which determines its relations to all other beings, is capable of asserting itself against them, and can never be swamped by them. In particular, the spiritual nature of man, of which, alike with all other modes, only a negative existence had been predicated, Spinoza now endows with a positive or affirmative essence. It is possessed of a power

" to persevere in its own being," a capacity of resisting its own suppression, and of perpetually seeking its own enlargement ; and not only so, but this inmost essence of man's individual being can survive the disintegration of the body, and instead of vanishing when brought into immediate relation to God, only then realises itself and attains to its ideal perfection.

The fundamental principle of the emotions and of the whole active and moral life of man, in Spinoza's view, is, as I have said, a certain self-asserting, self-maintaining impulse which he ascribes to every individual existence, and which is only another name for its nature or essence. " Everything, so far as it is in itself, endeavours to persist in its own being." [1] " The endeavour wherewith everything endeavours to persist in its own being is nothing else than the actual essence of the thing itself." [2] " The mind, whether as it has clear and distinct or as it has confused ideas, endeavours to persist in its own being for an indefinite time, and is conscious of this endeavour." [3] As Spinoza deals with it, this fundamental principle is an impulse in the individual, not only to self-preservation, but also to self-expansion or enlargement. It is that in virtue of which the individual nature consciously or unconsciously aspires to its own perfection, seeks after everything that contributes to that perfection, shuns everything that hinders it. [4] Though the proof which he gives of this principle— viz., that a thing cannot without contradiction " be supposed to contain anything which would destroy itself," [5] —is merely negative, and makes the self-maintaining im-

---

[1] Eth. iii. 6.     [2] Eth. iii. 7.     [3] Eth. iii. 9.
[4] Eth. iii. 12.     [5] Eth. iii. 4, dem.

pulse nothing more than self-identity or the formal agreement of each thing with itself, yet in his hands it assumes the character of a positive, active principle, reacting on its environment, rejecting all that would limit it, assimilating all that furthers or expands it. The particular form of consciousness by which this principle expresses itself is that of feeling or emotion (*affectus*), which he defines as "those affections of the body, and the ideas of them, by which its active power is increased or diminished, furthered or hindered." Emotion arises in the transition from less to greater, or from greater to less activity and power. When we "pass from a less to a greater perfection," the emotion takes the particular form of "pleasure" (*lætitia*); when the transition is of the opposite kind, the emotion is "pain" (*tristitia*). The term "desire" (*cupiditas*) is simply the self-maintaining impulse particularised, or filled with a definite content. "Desire is the very essence of man in so far as it is conceived as determined to any action by a given affection of itself." [1] These three, desire, pleasure, pain, constitute the primary emotions, of which all other emotions are only modifications or derivations. From these primary elements Spinoza, by a process, so to speak, of logical combination and permutation, aided by the principle of association, works out an elaborate scheme of the emotions, which, however ingenious as a feat of psychological analysis, adds nothing to the development of his system, and is, in that point of view, of slighter value than the other parts of the 'Ethics.'

In basing all human feeling and action on "the impulse to persist in one's being," does Spinoza reduce all

[1] Eth. iii., def. 1.

morality to self-seeking? Is his whole ethical system to be regarded as the development of a purely subjective, egoistic principle, to the exclusion of any objective or absolute standard of good and evil? There is much in his language that would appear at first sight to sanction this construction of his teaching. To this effect the following passages may be quoted :—

"By virtue and power I understand the same thing." [1] " The effort or self-preservation is the first and only foundation of virtue." [2] " To act absolutely in obedience to virtue is in us the same thing as to act, to live, to preserve one's being under the guidance of reason, on the ground of seeking what is useful to one's self." [3] " The knowledge of good and evil is nothing but the emotion of pleasure and pain in so far as we are conscious of it." [4] " The more every man endeavours and is able to seek what is useful to him—that is, to preserve his being—the more is he endowed with virtue." [5] "By good I mean that which we certainly know to be useful to us, by evil that which we certainly know to be a hindrance to us in the attainment of any good." [6]

Self-assertion would thus seem to be the only foundation, self-enlargement or increase of individual power the only measure, of virtue. As consciousness of self-enlargement is pleasure, "all things which bring pleasure are good," [7] all things which bring pain evil. By their utility or their tendency to increase our individual being, and the pleasurable emotion inplicated therewith, are our relations to other things and beings to be determined. Love is pleasure associated with the idea of another as its cause. When we rejoice in the happiness of others,

[1] Eth. iv., def. 8.   [2] Eth. iv. 22, cor.   [3] Eth. iv. 24.
[4] Eth. iv. 8.   [5] Eth. iv. 20.   [6] Eth. iv., def. 1, 2.
[7] Eth. iv., App. c. 30.

our seemingly disinterested delight is to be traced to the fact that the contemplation of another's happiness contributes to our own increase of being.[1]  Our desire that others should lead a rational or virtuous life is accounted for by the reflection that "there is no individual thing in nature which is more useful to man than a man who lives under the guidance of reason."[2]  And even the supreme virtue, the knowledge and love of God, appears to be regarded as the climax of moral perfection, because "the mind's highest utility or good is the knowledge of God."[3]

Yet, however conclusively such passages seem to point to a purely egoistic or selfish basis of morality, the conclusion is one which a closer examination may serve to modify, if it do not even lead us to see in Spinoza's ethical theory what some of the profoundest minds have discerned in it—the expression of the purest intellectual and moral disinterestedness.

1. It is to be observed, for one thing, that, in Spinoza's intention at least, the self-maintaining impulse is no new departure, no deviation from that which in the metaphysical part of his system had been set forth as the first principle of thought and being.  Though, as above defined, the impulse to persist in one's being seems to be the expression for a hard, logical self-identity, an atomic isolation or independence excluding from the individual nature all reference to other natures, finite or infinite, yet Spinoza expressly asserts that the affirmation of self, which constitutes this impulse, is, rightly understood, the affirmation of God in us.  "The force by which each individual perseveres in existence follows from the eter-

[1] Eth. iii. 21.    [2] Eth. iv. 35, cor.    [3] Eth. iv. 28, dem.

nal necessity of the nature of God."[1] "The power whereby each individual thing, and therefore man, preserves his being, is the power of God or nature. . . . Thus the power of man, in so far as it is explained through his own actual essence, is part of the infinite power of God—that is, part of His essence."[2] If, indeed, we ask how Spinoza reconciled these two things, —a God who is the immanent source and centre of all things, and an individual finite nature which is its own centre, infinite substance which is the negation of the finite, and finite things to which a real self-affirmative essence is ascribed; or again, how finite individualities can be at once contingent, evanescent modes, to which only an illusory being belongs, and things which have, through God, a real and permanent being,—to these questions Spinoza's dialectic furnishes no answer. Nevertheless, the fact remains that the affirmative element, which in the self-maintaining impulse is ascribed to the nature of man, is neither obliterated when referred to God, nor is left, on the other hand, a purely independent, self-centred thing, but is, according to Spinoza, a thing in and through which God realises Himself.

2. The impulse to persevere in one's being, as Spinoza explains it, is not the affirmation but the negation of the individual self as such. The " self " of selfishness is not maintained but destroyed by the self-affirmation of reason. In other words, the impure element vanishes from self-seeking when the self we seek is that whose essence is reason and the knowledge and love of God. Rationality cannot be too selfish, cannot seek its own satisfaction too eagerly or crave with culpable excess for the enlargement

[1] Eth. ii. 45, schol.　　　　　　[2] Eth. iv. 4, dem.

of its own being. All things that bring pleasure to it
are good, all things that bring pain to it evil; pleasure,
that is, becomes a term of moral significance and honour
when the subject of feeling is identified with reason.
That reason or a purely rational nature should love
others for its own sake rather than for theirs, means that
we cannot truly love another if we do not " love honour
more." Even to say that "man's highest utility is the
knowledge of God," or that we seek to know God because the knowledge of God is of all things the most
useful to us, is a formula which ceases to shock pious
sensibilities when translated into this equivalent, that
infinite intelligence is the supreme good of finite intelligence, or that it is in the knowledge of God that a rational
nature finds its own perfection and blessedness. Now it
is the identification of the true nature of man with reason or the divine element in him which furnishes the
key to much in Spinoza's ethical teaching that sounds
harsh and repulsive. The self which is affirmed in the
" self-maintaining impulse," and of which the satisfaction and enlargement is identified with " virtue," is not
the individual self as such, not the self of appetite and
passion, but rather that which is repressed and limited
thereby, which finds its freedom in rising above the selfish desires and its proper sphere in " the life according
to reason." " The human mind consists of adequate
and inadequate ideas." [1] The essence of man, in other
words, is the power to think. Even in the lower stage
of imagination and inadequate ideas this its true essence
manifests itself in the pain of repression or limitation by
what is foreign to itself. In the stage of " reason " the

[1] Eth. iii. 9, dem.

true self has shaken off the bondage of the non-rational and emerged into the sphere of pure self-activity. Here it knows nothing of pains and pleasures that refer only to the narrow individual self. Its " good " is no longer subjective or determined only by varying individual temperament, but a good that is common to all rational natures and determined by an objective standard. Finally, in the stage of "intuitive knowledge " the self has reached the point of enlargement at which all finite limits are left behind, and it sees and feels all things in the light of that which is universal and absolute. And here that impure self-reference to which the stigma of selfishness can be applied, has so completely vanished that even love ceases to seek a personal response. Though in the knowledge and love of God self-consciousness and self-affirmation still survive, yet the taint of subjectivity is so absolutely obliterated, that " he who loves God cannot seek that God should love him in return." [1]

3. Lastly, it is to be considered that there is an obvious distinction between selfishness and *self-realisation*, between unselfishness and self-extinction. Moral disinterestedness does not mean, even at the highest, the cessation of self-consciousness or self-satisfaction. Moral action implies in the agent the idea of a self which realises itself in that which is done, which seeks and finds satisfaction in the act. The " good " of a conscious agent, whether it be sensual pleasure or the purest intellectual and spiritual enjoyment, whether it be low or high, must be a good *for him*. No purer philanthropy can be conceived than finding *one's own* satisfaction in the welfare of others. Even in self-

[1] Eth. v. 19.

sacrifice for another there is present a reference to self, an idea of an object to be attained in which the agent seeks self-satisfaction. Without such reference even the purest self-denial is a conception that swims in the air. Though in unselfish acts the end sought is not one's own pleasure or gratification, yet we do find ourselves and our own satisfaction therein. Moreover, the self-affirmation, self-realisation, is increased, not diminished, with the unselfishness of the act. If in every benevolent feeling there must be a consciousness of self as well as of the object loved, in every benevolent act a consciousness of self as well as of the object attained, then the wider the range of benevolence, the more numerous the objects embraced in it, so much the fuller, richer, more complete becomes the self-consciousness or self-realisation of the subject. Even the knowledge and love of an infinite object is still *my* knowledge, *my* love, and the infinitude of the object implies a kindred elevation of the subject. Let slip the "my," and you sink into the spurious rapture of the mystic, or the self-annihilation of the pantheist. Whatever may be said of Spinoza's philosophy in general, in this part of it at least he knows nothing of such false self-abnegation ; yet as little does the doctrine of self-affirmation as the basis of morality introduce into his ethics a principle inconsistent with the purest moral disinterestedness. In other points of view, indeed, that principle is by no means unexceptionable, as will be seen when we examine in detail the manner in which Spinoza applies it to the elaboration of his ethical system.

# CHAPTER XIV.

### INTELLIGENCE AND WILL.

WE have seen that Spinoza finds the origin and explanation of the active or moral life in the " self-maintaining impulse," of which pleasure and pain, desire, and the innumerable varieties of feeling which spring from these fundamental emotions, are only different expressions or modifications. We have pointed out, further, that it is this self-maintaining impulse which constitutes the link between the intellectual and the emotional and active sides of man's nature, and which explains the close correspondence that can be traced between the successive stages of knowledge and the successive stages of the moral life.

There is, however, in Spinoza's account of the nature of human knowledge one doctrine to which we have not yet adverted, and which seems to imply, not simply the correspondence, but the absolute identification of the intellectual and the moral life. Knowledge and will are not elements of man's spiritual nature which, though closely related and constantly acting and reacting on each other, are yet different in nature and function. Spinoza's assertion would seem to be that, when closely examined, the active merges in the contemplative or theoretical life, and that feeling, passion, desire, volition, are only various phases of knowledge or intelligence. "There is in the mind," says he,[1] "no volition save that which an idea as idea involves." "Will and understanding are one and the same. . . . A particular volition and a particular idea are one and the same."[2] If we examine the reasons why men think otherwise, and ascribe to themselves a faculty of will different from and of wider range than that of understanding, we shall find that they are all alike futile. For one thing, popular thought, while it supposes intelligence to be purely passive, and ideas to be merely "images formed in us by contact with external bodies,"[3] regards all beyond such images as the product of the mind's own voluntary activity; whereas, if we reflect on the nature of knowledge, we shall see that ideas are not mere images like "dumb pictures on a tablet," but that every idea involves in it an element of activity, a principle of self-affirmation; in other words, that intelligence contains in it that free, voluntary activity which we commonly regard as the exclusive function of will. Common thought, again, distinguishes between truths to which we necessarily assent, which carry with them the assurance of their own reality, and arbitrary or obscure conceptions with respect to which we have the power to suspend our judgment, ascribing the former to the understanding and the latter to "the will or faculty of assent, which is free and different from the understanding."[4] Closer examination, however, teaches us

---

[1] Eth. ii. 49.  [2] Ibid., cor. and dem.
[3] Eth. ii. 49, schol.  [4] Ibid.

that the real activity of the mind is common to both processes. The difference between them is simply the difference between " adequate " and " inadequate " ideas, and the suspense of judgment which is ascribed to a faculty of volition is nothing more than the consciousness of a confused and imperfect as distinguished from a clear and distinct idea. The conception of a winged horse implies mental activity as much as that of a horse without wings, only the latter includes the affirmation of existence or reality, which the former does not. If, again, there be no faculty of will different from that of understanding, then it seems to the unreflecting mind that it would be justified in concluding that assent to what is false and evil is not essentially different from assent to what is true and good; to which Spinoza's answer is, that the idea of what is false and evil is really the idea of that which has in it no positive reality, and the distinction in question is not between two equally affirmative acts, but between the affirmation of being and the affirmation of non-entity—not between understanding and will, but between a sound and a diseased or disordered understanding. Finally, to the popular objection that it is the prerogative of will to decide between conflicting motives, and that without such a faculty, where there is an equilibrium of motives (as in the famous example of "Buridan's ass "), action would be absolutely suspended, Spinoza's reply virtually is, that the supposed conflict of motives is, when we examine what we mean, only a conflict of ideas, and that ideas never really conflict save when one idea is adequate and another confused and imperfect; that in the latter case reason is the true umpire, and that suspense or inaction would prove, not that reason fails to decide, but that the non-deciding agent is a fool or a madman.

From these and other considerations the conclusion which Spinoza reaches is, that the element of activity which is commonly regarded as peculiar to the will is one which belongs essentially to the understanding, or that "there is in the mind no volition save that which an idea as idea involves." On the other hand, if intelligence is thus held to be active, all activity, it is maintained, is intelligent, all the supposed elements of man's active life seem, when closely examined, to be only modes of thought. Thought or intelligence is not one among many co-ordinate "faculties," but it is that which constitutes the very essence of the mind, and the underlying principle of all our mental experiences and activities. "Love, desire, or the affections of the mind, by whatever name they are designated," are essentially "modes of thought." [1] To all these modes of thought "the idea is prior in nature, and when the idea exists the other modes must exist in the same individual." [2] Spinoza would thus seem to reduce the whole content of man's spiritual life to thought or intelligence and its modifications; and though he treats of other elements which pertain to the active in contradistinction from the intellectual part of man's nature—of an impulse or endeavour in the mind to persist in its own being, of pleasure and pain, desire and aversion, and of particular emotions in elaborate detail to which this impulse gives birth—yet when we examine the real significance of his teaching, these seemingly non-intel-

---

[1] Eth. ii. ax. 3.　　　　　[2] Eth. ii. 11, dem.

lectual elements, it has been held, lose their independence, and resolve themselves into the one all-absorbing principle of the theoretical intelligence. As "the essence of the mind consists of adequate and inadequate ideas," [1] so the self-maintaining impulse is nothing more than the self-affirmation by the mind of its own power of thinking.[2] Will itself is only another name for this impulse, "when referred solely to the mind;" [3] desire (*cupiditas*) is the same intellectual impulse, "in so far as it is conceived as determined to any action by some affection of itself;" [4] emotions (*affectus*) are "ideas of affections of the body by which its power of acting is increased or diminished," [5] or again, "emotion which is called a passion (or passivity of the mind) is a *confused idea* by which the mind affirms of its body, or any part of it, a power of existing greater or less than before." [6] "Pleasure (*lætitia*) is a passion by which the mind passes to a greater, pain a passion by which it passes to a less, perfection;" [7] pleasure and pain, in other words, of which all the other emotions are only specifications, are not a new element different from anything in our purely intellectual nature, but are simply "the transition from a less to a greater or from a greater to a less perfection." [8] The process by which moral progress is achieved is in the same way reduced to a purely intellectual activity. If there are any outward causes which help or hinder the activity of the body, and therefore the mind's power of thinking, the mind, in seeking to affirm or

[1] Eth. iii. 9, dem.
[2] Eth. iii. 9.
[3] Eth. iii. 9, schol.
[4] Eth. iii., aff. def. 1.
[5] Eth. iii., def. 3.
[6] Eth. iii., aff. gen. def.
[7] Eth. iii. 11, dem.
[8] Eth. iii., aff. def. 2, 3.

realise itself, endeavours to conceive or recollect the former, and, as far as possible, to exclude and forget the latter.[1] The stages of the moral life, by which it advances to its goal, and that goal itself, seem not merely to correspond but to be identified with its intellectual progress and perfection. As the dominion of the passions is that of inadequate ideas, so emancipation from their power is simply the formation of clear and distinct ideas.[2] "The power of the mind is defined solely by knowledge, its weakness or passivity by the privation of knowledge."[3] We are in moral bondage when the content of our consciousness is determined by that which is external or foreign to the mind, free when it is wholly due to the mind's own activity ; but the pure inner activity of the mind is that which it possesses when it apprehends it self, the bodily affections, and all outward things, no longer in the confused and imperfect way in which sense and imagination present them, but from a universal point of view, as part of a universal order or concatenation of things,—in other words, when it understands or thinks them according to the order of intelligence."[4] "The effort to understand is the first and sole basis of virtue."[5] "Good" and "evil" are simply equivalent to "that which helps or hinders our power to think or understand."[6] "In life it is of supreme importance to us to perfect the understanding or reason, and in this one thing consists man's highest happiness or blessedness."[7] Finally, the culmination of the moral life is attained when the understanding, by

[1] Eth. iii. 12, 13.   [2] Eth. v. 3.   [3] Eth. v. 20, schol.
[4] Eth. v. 10.   [5] Eth. iv. 26, dem.   [6] Eth. iv. 27.
[7] Eth. iv., App. 4.

the intuition of reason, grasps all the differences of finite things in their unity, discerns all ideas in their relation to the highest idea, the idea of God. "The absolute virtue of the mind is to understand; its highest virtue, therefore, to understand or know God."[1] "Blessedness is the contentment of spirit which arises from the intuitive knowledge of God."

From what has now been said it will be seen that Spinoza's identification of intelligence and will is a principle which runs through the whole of his ethical system, and there appears to be substantial ground for the assertion which has often been made, that the moral life resolves itself, in his hands, into a purely intellectual or theoretical process. If this construction of his philosophy were the whole truth, his doctrine would seem to be, not merely that ignorance is the cause and knowledge the cure of moral imperfection, but that ignorance is itself the only moral disease, and knowledge itself the true moral health and perfection of our being.

Plausible, however, as this view of Spinoza's teaching seems to be, a careful study of the 'Ethics' will, I think, lead us to regard it as one-sided and exaggerated. It is possible to maintain the essential unity of intelligence and will without obliterating all distinction between them. Spinoza's apparent identification of the practical with the theoretical side of man's nature is not inconsistent with the recognition of the distinctive character and functions of the former; and when we examine his doctrine more closely, many of the criticisms to which it has been subjected are seen to be irrelevant.

[1] Eth. iv. 28, dem.

1. It is to be considered that objections to the doctrine of the unity of knowledge and will, in order to be relevant, must contemplate knowledge and will *as employed about the same objects.* Popular thought rightly distinguishes between knowledge and goodness, between intellectual and moral power. Great moral excellence is not incompatible with a feeble and uncultured intelligence, nor intellectual elevation with a low moral life. Spinoza does not maintain, nor could any one be so absurd as to maintain, that piety and virtue are inseparable from and commensurate with literary and scientific ability, or that the qualities which constitute the mathematician, the philosopher, the artist, are necessarily and in equal measure combined with those which go to make the good citizen, the philanthropist, the saint. All that this proves, however, is only that intelligence in one province does not imply practical activity in another. To render the objection valid, what would need to be proved is, that within the same province, and when employed about the same objects, there is no necessary conjunction of knowledge and will. Now, so limited, Spinoza's doctrine, as we shall immediately see, is by no means indefensible. It may be possible to show that, within the province of the moral and spiritual, as well as within the province of what we call the secular life, knowledge and will are, if not identical, at least coexistent and commensurate — that, *e.g.*, practical goodness or piety implies in every case a measure of spiritual insight which, though not speculative or scientific, is of the nature of knowledge, and is proportionate to the purity and elevation of the life; and, on the other hand, that the man of science, the philosopher, the man of letters,

exerts in every act of his intellectual life a force and energy of will commensurate with the degree of intelligence that is called forth.

2. But even when we thus narrow the ground to which Spinoza's doctrine applies, is there not much which seems to justify ordinary thought in denying the supposed coincidence or even invariable conjunction of knowledge and will? Within the sphere of man's moral life are not knowing and willing not only distinguishable in thought, but in actual experience notoriously separable? Is it not a moral commonplace that our actions often fall short of our convictions? There are ideas which are purely contemplative and theoretical, projects which never go beyond themselves, opinions about virtue and goodness, which, through indolence or irresolution or pravity of will, are never realised in action. Thought and will are not only not invariably coincident, but in individual actions, and even through the whole course of life, are not seldom in glaring contrast with each other. Nowhere, indeed, has this incongruity been more forcibly expressed than in Spinoza's own language :—

" The powerlessness of man," says he,[1] " to govern and restrain his emotions, I call servitude. For a man who is controlled by his emotions is not his own master, but is mastered by fortune, under whose power he is often compelled, though he sees the better, to follow the worse." "I have shown why the true knowledge of good and evil awakens disturbances in the mind, and often yields to every kind of lust ; whence the saying of the poet, ' Video meliora proboque, deteriora sequor ; ' and Ecclesiastes seems to have

---

[1] Eth. iv., Pref.

had the same thought in his mind when he said, ' He that increaseth knowledge increaseth sorrow.' And this I say, . . . that we may determine what reason can and what it cannot do in governing the emotions." [1]

Spinoza's doctrine of the unity of knowledge and will is, however, not really affected by this recognition of the notorious inconsistency between human thoughts and actions. What that doctrine really means is that, within the same limits, or when employed about the same objects, intelligence and will are in our conscious experience inseparably interwoven. Every act of intelligence is at the same time an act of will, every act of will also an act of intelligence. And his answer to the above objection virtually is, that the thought or intelligence which we can conceive of as separate from or in conflict with will is not true thought, but thought falsely so called, or, in his own phraseology, thought which consists of " inadequate "—*i.e.*, " confused and imperfect—ideas."

All thought is essentially active, all will essentially intelligent. On the one hand, to represent thought as devoid of the element of activity or as a merely passive thing, is to reduce its content to " images or inanimate pictures formed in us by contact with external bodies." But mind does not become possessed of ideas as wax receives the impression of a seal, or blank paper the stamp of the printer's types. Every idea or process of thought is essentially an act or a series of acts of affirmation and negation. In the simplest perception there is something more than the passive reception of impressions from without. " Affections of the body " do not become the content of thought by a mere mechanical

[1] Eth. iv. 17, schol.

transference. To elevate them into ideas or objects of rational thought implies a spontaneous activity of the mind, stripping them of the contingency and confusion of sense and imagination, fastening on "those properties in them which are common to all things," infusing into them its own universality. Every act of judgment or process of reasoning involves in it a reaction of the mind on the objects with which it deals, connecting them in relations other than those of immediate perception, "arranging and associating them (not according to the natural but) according to the intellectual order." The idea of a triangle is, so to speak, the self-affirmation of its own content. "The idea of a triangle must involve that its three angles are equal to two right angles," and "this affirmation can neither be nor be conceived without the idea of a triangle." [1] To prove the proposition that "there is in the mind no volition save that which an idea as idea involves," Spinoza here selects his example from what ordinary thought regards as specially the province of contemplation or theoretic intelligence ; and the implied conclusion is, that if here, in what we deem its proper sphere, intelligence is shown to be essentially active, *a fortiori* the element of activity must pertain to it in what we account as more peculiarly the sphere of practical activity. If inherent activity is the characteristic of the idea when it is the idea of a geometrical figure, much more must it be the characteristic of the idea when it is that of a moral act. If it cannot be or be conceived within the domain of science save as self-realising, much less can it be or be conceived save as self-realising when it pertains to man's moral life.

[1] Eth. ii. 49, dem.

On the other hand, all will or practical activity is essentially intelligent. " Will," says Spinoza, "is the endeavour to persist in one's being when that endeavour is referred solely to the mind." [1] Will, in other words, presupposes thought. It is the conscious endeavour of the mind to realise itself and its own inherent power. Devoid of the element of intelligence, will ceases to be will, and becomes mere blind impulse or passion. "We act when anything takes place in us of which we (or that intelligence which is our essence) are the adequate cause—that is, when anything follows in us from our nature which that nature taken by itself makes clearly and distinctly intelligible. We are passive when anything takes place in us or follows from our nature, of which we are not the cause, save partially." [2] In modern language, will is distinguished from animal impulse by this, that in the former and not in the latter there is present the element of self-consciousness and self-determination. The merely animal nature is lost in the feeling of the moment. Its experience is a succession of feelings or impulses, each of which expires with its immediate satisfaction; it contains no constant element of self-consciousness to which the successive feelings are referred, no permanent self which realises itself in them. Its impulses and actions are not self-originated, but forced upon it from without. They are not woven into a continuous experience by reference to any universal centre of thought, and are connected together at most only by the general life-feeling that pervades them. In a rational or intelligent being, on the other hand, there is present throughout all its feelings the uniting element

[1] Eth. iii. 9, schol.        [2] Eth. iii., def. 2.

of reference to one self-conscious subject, and through all its volitions the uniting element of self-determination. In willing, it knows that it wills and what it wills; it is conscious at once of the object willed and of itself as willing it. It is conscious of a self which is distinguished from, yet realised in, all its particular volitions and actions, and in each particular case as realised in this action and not another. Thought or self-consciousness, in short, is the common element of all voluntary acts, and that which gives them their special character and complexion as the acts of a moral agent. Now, though in Spinoza's philosophy individual minds are only modes of the Divine Substance, and as such are necessarily destitute of all independence or capacity of self-determination, yet he attributes to them a self-maintaining impulse which is identical with their very essence, and to this principle he assigns all the functions of a self-conscious, self-determining individuality. It is in virtue of this principle that he can maintain the distinction between the blindness of the passive impulses and emotions, and the self-conscious, intelligent activity of all human volitions.

From what has now been said it is clear that Spinoza's doctrine of the unity of knowledge and will is to be understood as implying, not that these elements coexist side by side or in mechanical conjunction, but that they are inseparably interwoven with each other in our conscious experience. He does not mean that our spiritual life, or any part of it, is *made up* of these two elements —of an element of will added to an element of thought —so that what we first think, we then will; his doctrine is that no thought would be what it is if an element of will did not enter into it, no volition what it is if it were not essentially intelligent. We can see, therefore, how, from Spinoza's point of view, the popular objection above noticed is to be met. If it be said that experience disproves the inseparableness of thinking and willing, that we are conscious of thoughts, opinions, convictions which are never realised in action, of actions which conflict with our ideas and convictions—the answer is, that in all such cases there is no real separation of knowledge from will, for the knowledge which is divorced from will is not true knowledge, the will that is divorced from knowledge not really will. Knowledge that is inert or inactive is not real knowledge; it does not consist of "adequate," but only of "confused and imperfect ideas." When we see the right without willing it, our seeing is not the same seeing with that of the mind which *both* sees and wills.[1] We sometimes express this to ourselves by saying that there are things we cannot know unless we love them; that there is no real perception of beauty or goodness into which the element of feeling — of love, admiration, self-devotion — does not enter; that it is only the pure in heart who can see God. The object that is before the mind which only inertly contemplates a moral and spiritual act, is something essentially different from the object that is before the mind in which contemplation immediately and necessarily passes into action. In the former case, the mind is looking at an object as outside of and foreign to itself, the form of which may engage the powers of observation, comparison, reflection, or which it may classify under some general head or category, such as

[1] Cf. Green's Prolegomena to Ethics, p. 152 ff.

"good," or "just," or "pious"; in the latter, at an object which is regarded not merely as good, but as *my* good, that in which I discern the fulfilment and realisation of my own inmost nature. When this discernment is present, when the object of thought is apprehended as not foreign or external, but one in which I find myself, with which I identify myself, which is the medium of my own self-realisation—there is no possible separation between the act of knowing and the act of willing. The object known is known as that the affirmation of which is indissolubly bound up with my self-affirmation. I cannot know it without willing it, for not to will it, or to deny it, would be equivalent to self-negation. I cannot will it without knowing it, for to will it is to become conscious of myself as realised in it.

Lastly, it is to be observed that Spinoza's doctrine of the unity of thought and will does not imply the denial of all distinction between the contemplative and the active life. Thought and will are present in all our mental employments alike, whether they be those which have for their end simply the acquisition of knowledge, or those which have for their end the performance of some outward act. It does not follow, however, that the relation of these two factors is precisely the same in both cases, or that we cannot distinguish between thought and will as they are manifested in the theoretic, and thought and will as they are manifested in the practical life—between, *e.g.*, the attitude of the mind in the solution of a mathematical problem and the attitude of the mind in the performance of a moral act. Spinoza's philosophy is couched in too abstract a form to admit of any speculative treatment of the dis-

tinction between the theoretic or scientific and the active
life, yet in the ethical part of his system the distinction,
though not formally, is virtually recognised. As modern
thought represents it, the theoretic and the practical
life are only different sides or aspects of the same process. In both there is a reconciliation between the ideal
and the actual, between consciousness and its object,
between thought and things. But the difference lies in
this, that in the one case we begin with the actual, the
objective, the particular, and end with the ideal, the
subjective, the universal; in the other the process is
reversed. In both, the same elements are present—a
universal, undetermined yet determining element, and a
particular or determined element—and in both there is
an effort to overcome the opposition between them. But
in the theoretic life, or that of knowledge in the limited
sense, the universal element is present at first only implicitly or potentially. In the endeavour to overcome
the opposition between itself and the world, thought
takes up at first a purely objective attitude. The manifold objects with which it deals present themselves as
something external or foreign to the conscious subject.
But the latent presupposition under which it acts is that
the objects it contemplates are not really foreign to itself, that the principle which constitutes its own essence
is that which also constitutes the essence of things without, and that it is possible for reason or intelligence to
find itself at home in the world. The whole process of
knowledge, therefore, is a bringing back of the world
into thought. Underlying the particularity, the diversity, the contingency of the phenomenal world, consciousness silently discerns the presence of that unity

universality, and necessity which are its own essential
characteristics. And every step in this process is a
step towards the complete transformation of the particular into the universal, the actual into the ideal, the
manifold and accidental objects of thought into the
unity and necessity of self-consciousness. In the practical life, on the other hand, the reconciliation between
consciousness and the objective world begins from the
opposite pole. That life may be described as the continuous effort of the self-conscious subject to realise
itself in the outward world. It starts where the theoretical life ends. To that which is already a realised
content of thought it seeks to give further realisation in
some outward act. Whether it be an æsthetic or moral
or religious ideal, the mind is conscious of a conception
which involves in it the possibility, the desire, and the
effort for its embodiment in some particular concrete
form and under the conditions of the phenomenal
world. The vision of beauty which exists in the creative imagination of the artist, he seeks to infuse into the
rudeness and unconsciousness of matter and material
forms and colours. To the conception of righteous-
ness, goodness, holiness, which dwells in the mind
of the good or pious man, he seeks to give outward
actuality or realisation, and so to make the mere
physical relations of things and the functions of the
animal life instinct with the life of spirit—to make the
outward world the expression of the inner world of
thought. Thus, in both the theoretical and the practical life, it is the same general result which is accomplished—viz., the reconciliation between the actual and
ideal; and in both cases alike the process is permeated

by the presence and activity of the inseparable elements of thought and will. Yet this unity of the two is still consistent with their distinction as different aspects of the same process, inasmuch as the reconciliation is that which proceeds, on the one hand, from the object to the subject, from the particular to the universal; on the other, from the subject to the object, from the universal to the particular. In Spinoza's philosophy there is not to be found any formal analysis of the process into its opposite yet related movements; yet we should err in concluding that he ignores the distinction between them, or that his principle of the unity of thought and will implies the resolution of the moral life into a purely theoretical process. His account of the emotions and passions, his theory of the bondage of the human mind and of its freedom, and of the method by which that freedom is achieved—the whole specially ethical part of his system, in short, constitutes an elaborate exposition of the active as distinguished from the purely intellectual life. And if, as we have seen, there is much in his treatment of ethical problems which seems to imply the identification of virtue with knowledge, of moral evil with ignorance, the true explanation is, that while he describes the moral life in terms of knowledge, knowledge with him is that highest kind of knowledge above referred to, which includes or "connotes" will, or which is instinct with the element of activity. All other knowledge is not really knowledge, but only "confused and imperfect ideas." Such ideas may be, nay, must be, inert. They not merely do not lead to moral action, but the mind that is the subject of them is the passive slave of its own "bodily affections," and the ex-

ternal influences with which these affections are implicated. But "adequate ideas" are not dead or passive
but living things. They are self-realising. To think
them is to live them, to be quick with spiritual activity,
to be master of one's self and the world. So far from
man's moral life being reduced to a merely contemplative
process, a thing of ideas without volitions, Spinoza's
view is that no such ideas exist, or if they can be said
to exist, that they belong not to the realm of true knowledge, but to that of illusion and ignorance. An idea
which is "adequate," or which alone deserves the name,
is one which by its very essence asserts itself against
all that is foreign and hostile to the mind; it cannot
coexist with confusion and error and the passions that
are bred of them, any more than light can coexist with
darkness. When the mind, or the self-maintaining impulse which is one with its essence, identifies itself with
such an idea, it is *ipso facto* possessed of moral vitality
and power. And when it rises to the highest kind of
knowledge, the intuitive apprehension of that idea which
comprehends and transcends all other ideas—in other
words, when the self-affirming impulse realises its true
significance as not the affirmation of the individual self,
but the self-affirmation of God in us—then does it attain
to the perfection of virtue and power.[1] The goal of the
intellectual life is thus, at one and the same time, the
culmination of the moral life, and the best expression
for both is that "intellectual love" which consists in
the consciousness of the mind's own perfect activity
"combined with the idea of God as its cause."

[1] Eth. v. 27.

# CHAPTER XV.

### THE BONDAGE AND FREEDOM OF MAN.

In the latter portion of his work Spinoza, as we have seen, contemplates the course of man's moral life as a movement from bondage to freedom, from the stage of passivity in which he is not, to that of activity or the "life according to reason," in which he is "the adequate cause of his own actions." Regarded as an individual mode amidst the infinite series of finite modes, he is only "a part of nature," a link in the endless concatenation of causes and effects; his self-activity is infinitely surpassed by the power of external causes, and the freedom he ascribes to himself is only an illusory freedom, due to the fact that he is conscious of his own thoughts and actions, but not of the causes that determine them. Yet though thus, by the very essence of his finite nature, man is under a law of external necessity, the possibility of freedom is not thereby precluded. It is possible for him to elevate himself, through reason, above all encroachment of outward influences on his own self-determination. Accordingly, the last Book of the 'Ethics' is devoted to the development of the idea of freedom, or of that state of moral perfection in which

man has become at once the source of his own spiritual
life and sharer in the life of God.

The difficulty which meets us in this part of Spinoza's
speculations is not simply that of his apparent reassertion of a doctrine he had formerly denied.  For necessity and freedom are not predicated of the same subject
at one and the same time, but are viewed as different
stages in man's moral life.  But though a transition
from the bondage of natural necessity to spiritual freedom is not inconceivable, the question arises whether it is
conceivable under the conditions here laid down, or in
the manner here described.  If we start from the idea
of man as but a unit amidst the infinite multiplicity of
other finite units, a single force encompassed and determined by the endless series of natural forces, is not
freedom excluded by the very conditions of the problem ?
To make freedom a possible achievement, there must be
at least some fulcrum on which it can be made to rest,
some qualitative distinction between the one force which
is destined to triumph and the many forces which are to
be overcome.   If each finite mode, each member of the
series of causes and effects, has precisely the same value
as another, is not the possibility of freedom simply in
the ratio of one to infinity ?  If individuality be only
the "force by which each individual persists in his
own existence," and that is infinitely surpassed by the
multiplicity of similar external forces, is not individual
freedom reduced to a numerical contradiction ?  Must
not man be something more than "a part of nature" to
begin with, in order to the possibility of escape from its
bondage ?

But even if we concede the possibility of freedom,

can the transition be accomplished in the way in which
Spinoza describes it? The problem is that which arises
from the conflict between the positive or self-asserting
and the negative or passive elements of man's nature ;
and Spinoza's manner of solving it is, as we shall see,
simply by the elimination of the latter. The negative
element disappears, leaving only the purely affirmative
to hold the field. But as in the idea of God, so in that
of man, pure affirmation, apart from negation, is an
impossible conception. In the struggle with passion,
according to Spinoza, reason prevails, but it prevails, not
by overcoming and subordinating passion, but simply
by abstracting from or excluding it. Yet if it is not
shown that in some way the natural desires and passions
can be rationalised, they are simply left behind as an
unresolved element. As organic life does not maintain
itself by the exclusion, but by the transformation, of
mechanical and chemical elements, so the ideal of the
rational life is that not of a passionless life, but of a
life in which passion is transcended and transformed.
In one sense man can never cease to be " a part of
nature," but in the higher life nature has itself become
a part of reason.

The force of these and other criticisms of the concluding part of the ' Ethics ' will be seen by considering a
little more in detail (1) Spinoza's conception of human
bondage, and (2) his theory of the transition from bondage to freedom.

### THE BONDAGE OF MAN.

When we examine what Spinoza means by " the
bondage of man," we find that it ultimately resolves

itself into that conditioned or determined nature which pertains to all individual finite things. Freedom is self-activity or self-determination, bondage is subjection to external causation. We act or are active " when anything takes place in us of which we are the adequate cause, or which can be deduced solely from the laws of our own nature ; " " we are passive, therefore, in so far as we are a part of nature—a part, that is, which cannot be conceived by itself and without the other parts." [1] But as " no individual finite thing can exist or be determined to act unless it be determined to exist and act by another which is also finite and has a determined exist· ence, as that also by a third, &c.," [2] it follows that " it is impossible that man should not be a part of nature or should be capable of undergoing only changes which can be understood through his own nature, and of which it is the adequate cause." [3]

It is true, as we have seen, that Spinoza introduces into his account of the individual nature an element which seems to modify the law of absolute external causation, a self-maintaining impulse or capacity to re-act on outward influences, and to " persevere in its own being." But inasmuch as this element of apparent independence belongs to all finite things alike, it does not in the least modify the preponderance of the whole or of the infinite multiplicity of external causes over each individual thing, or affect man's bondage as a part of nature. " The force by which a man persists in existing is limited and infinitely surpassed by the power of external causes." [4] Moreover, when we consider the special case of man as an intelligent and moral

[1] Eth. iv. 2, dem.    [2] Eth. i. 28.    [3] Eth. iv. 4.    [4] Eth. iv. 2.

being, this all-dominating power of nature over the individual loses nothing of its force. The medium by which nature exerts its power over him is the influence of the passions; the struggle of the individual with the determining power of external causes becomes, in the case of man, the struggle of the mind or the idea of the body with the passive emotions. But the passive emotions are simply various modifications of the feelings of pleasure and pain, which reflect the affections of the body, or necessarily arise when the body is affected by external causes; and the mind in the unequal struggle has no more power to resist the emotions than the body, as an individual mode of extension, to resist its affections by external nature. " By pleasure," says Spinoza, " I mean a *passive* state by which the mind passes to a greater, by pain a *passive* state by which it passes to a lesser, perfection." " Emotion, which is called a passivity of the soul, is a confused idea by which the mind affirms of its body a force of existence greater or less than before, and by which it is determined to think one thing rather than another." [1] Thus the whole content of the mind's experience, all that moves or affects it, is due, not to its own activity, but to something that is external and foreign to it. If, under the sway of passion, it has sometimes a feeling of increased as well as of diminished power, the former, alike with the latter, as being determined from without, is only the witness to its bondage. The strength of passion is only a spurious strength, an activity that is produced by passivity, and which, like the increased power produced by wine, is in reality a sign of weakness. Spinoza's conclusion there-

[1] Eth. iii., general def. of Emotion.

fore is, that neither in mind nor body, neither as a mode of thought nor as a mode of extension, can the individual man be the free cause of his own actions, that "in the mind there is no free will,"[1] and that if men think themselves free, it is only because "they are conscious of their volitions and desires, and never dream of the causes which have disposed them so to will and desire."[2] "It is impossible," says he, "that man should not be a part of nature; . . . hence it follows that he is necessarily always in subjection to passions, that he follows and obeys the general order of nature, and that he accommodates himself thereto as the nature of things requires."[3] "I have explained," he writes, at the conclusion of his account of the emotions, "the principal emotions and changes of mind which arise from the combination of the three primary emotions, desire, pleasure, and pain. It is evident from this that we are in many ways driven about by external causes, and like the waves of the sea driven by contending winds, we are swayed hither and thither, unconscious of the issue and of our destiny."[4]

Such, then, is Spinoza's account of the state of bondage from which man's moral history starts. That it is not a complete or exhaustive account of human nature, but only of its first or lowest stage, he himself expressly tells us. It is only the diagnosis of the disease which is necessary in order to the understanding of the cure. "It is necessary to know the infirmity of our nature "— its impotence, that is, under the sway of the passions— "before we can determine what reason can do to liberate

---

[1] Eth. ii. 48.      [2] Eth. i., App.
[3] Eth. iv. 4 and cor.      [4] Eth. iii. 59, schol.

us from their control." [1]     But before passing to what he
has to say of " the course that is prescribed to us by
reason," we may pause for a moment to consider whether
his description of what he calls " the impotence of human nature " is self-consistent, and whether that impotence has not been so defined as to place it beyond the
reach of remedy.     In other words, we may inquire, in
the first place, whether the conception of a conscious
being under a law of causation in the same sense as a
modification of matter, is a possible conception ; and
secondly, whether, if conceivable, it can be made a basis
for anything higher.     Is such a state of bondage possible for a conscious subject ?     If possible, can he ever
emerge from it ?

1. The bondage of man, as we have seen, is or arises
from that conditioned or determined nature which pertains to all individual finite things.     It is common to
body and mind—to man as a mode of extension, and to
man as a mode of thought.     In both points of view he
is determined by what is external to his own being ;
the mind is a link in the series of ideas in the same
sense in which the body is a link in the series of material
causes and effects.     The former is no more the author of
its own desires and volitions than the latter of its own
affections of motion and rest.     Both are under a law
of external, mechanical causation.     Mind is simply " a
spiritual automaton."     The order and connection of
thoughts is the same as the order and connection of
things.     But unless the two processes are absolutely
identical—in which case the distinction between thought
and extension would be a distinction without a difference

---

[1] Eth. iv. 17, schol.

—can we attach any meaning to the conception of an idea externally operated on by another idea, or of a mind externally acted on by its passions, as one material thing or body by another? Ideas, Spinoza himself tells us, "are not mere images formed in us by contact with external bodies like lifeless pictures on a panel." We can think one body or mode of extension as lying outside of and acting on another; but can we conceive of the process as exactly reflected or paralleled in the relation of *the idea* of one body to that of another? We can, of course, think or have an idea of mechanical causation, but the idea of a mechanical effect is not mechanically determined by the idea of a mechanical cause. A passion is "a confused idea, by the presence of which the mind is determined to think one thing rather than another." A passion, that is to say, is "present to the mind," and then, by its operation on the mind, thoughts and desires spring up therein. But a passion, a feeling of pleasure or pain, cannot be first present to the mind in the sense of being externally in contact with it, and then begin to operate upon it. Being present to the mind means that the mind is conscious of it, that it is already, in a sense, *in* the mind, and therefore the subsequent mental changes —thoughts, desires, volitions—are not the result of a merely external causation. The change in the mind is not determined by the passion, as one physical event is determined by an antecedent event, but the mind is determined by a condition of which it is itself the source. The earliest or lowest stage at which we can date the beginning of man's mental history is one in which he is not "a part of nature," in the sense of being subjected to appetites, impulses, passions which are out-

side of the nature that is to be determined by them. It
may, indeed, be possible to conceive of a lower stage than
this—of sensitive creatures that are under the control of
blind impulse, and therefore absolutely determined from
without. But if the lower animals be such creatures,
self-conscious beings from the very outset of their conscious life belong to a different order. If there is a
stage at which man can be regarded as a being of merely
animal impulses and passions, so long as it lasts his
moral history has not begun. A conscious impulse is
not the same as a merely natural or animal impulse.
The infusion of the element of consciousness changes
its nature. In becoming a motive of human action,
an appetite or passion undergoes a radical transformation. It is no longer an external motor acting on the
mind; it has already been taken out of the sphere of
externality, and in its character of motor become a
thing, in a sense, of the mind's own creation. In so
far, therefore, as the passions are natural forces, and
man can be regarded as a part of nature under the
bondage of external causation, he is not yet a thinking, conscious being; and the moment you conceive
of him as such, it ceases to be possible for you to
account for his actions by a law of external causation
—an element of self-determination enters into all
that determines him. Unmotived volition and action
is indeed an absurd and impossible notion, but equally
absurd is that of a conscious being impelled by
purely external causes. "Human bondage," therefore,
in Spinoza's sense of the words, is not thinkable,
and could only be made to seem thinkable by a
false separation between motives and volition — be-

tween passions acting on the mind, and the mind on which they act.

2. It may be urged as a further objection to Spinoza's doctrine, that if man *were* under such a bondage he could never escape from it. Spinoza proceeds to show how reason liberates man from the slavery of passion and elevates him into participation in the freedom and blessedness of God. But his conception of human freedom, however true in itself, is not legitimately reached. His "free man" is not the man with whom he started, and it is only by an unconscious modification of his original conception that he contrives to rear upon it his doctrine of freedom. To make freedom a possible attainment, there must be some germ of it to begin with. Imagination may picture to itself the transformation of a stone or plant or animal into a rational nature, but for thought there can be no such transformation. The stone or organism does not become a man, but the idea of the former is dropped and that of the latter substituted for it. In the same way Spinoza's bondsman may be represented as becoming a free man; but from his definition of the former the transformation is for imagination only, not for thought. If the agencies that constitute nature or the system of being lie outside of the individual mind, and dominate it from without, they can never cease to do so. Mind can only become free in the presence of what is external to it, by supposing it from the outset capable of finding itself therein—that is, by supposing in it that which has virtually annulled the externality. Limiting conditions can never cease to limit a nature that is not from the first potentially beyond the limits. A slave could never become a free citizen of the State unless he

were capable of finding himself in the constitution and laws of the State. If animal passions rule man from without, an animal he must remain. Reason indeed may, as Spinoza shows, attain the supremacy in man's life; but it is only because man is from the beginning something different from the being of whom Spinoza speaks, for only that being which, in some sense, creates the forces that act on it, can have in it the latent capacity to control them. It is, in short, the presence in mind of something which is not subject to the bondage of externality, that constitutes the fulcrum by which its freedom can be achieved.

### TRANSITION FROM BONDAGE TO FREEDOM.

Spinoza's conception of human bondage is, as we have seen, self-contradictory. A being who is subject to a law of purely external causation is incapable of freedom, and therefore incapable of bondage. To be a part of nature would be no bondage to man if he *could* be a part of it. The very term " bondage " implies that essentially and from the first he is something more. One mode of matter is not in bondage to another, a physical effect is not in bondage to its cause; to be so related is simply the expression of its very nature. Subjection to the passions would be no slavery; the vicious man would be as innocent as an animal, if like the animal he were blindly determined by his appetites. Spinoza's "bondage," as interpreted by the proof he gives of it, is simply modality or finitude, and it applies to man as a mode of thought precisely as it applies to him as a mode of extension. It implies no more reaction in the individual mind than in a stone, against the determining power of the infinite series of external causes. But, in order to lend to "bondage" the deeper signification which the term implies, and to make it the basis of a theory of freedom, Spinoza unconsciously shifts the definition of the subject of bondage. What he wants in mind is a self which can be the source of its own activity, and which, in so far as it is not so, is in bondage. Man must be something more than an individual in a world of individuals, a larger universal nature must be ascribed to him, if the limits of individuality are to be dealt with as hindrances to freedom. A life controlled by passion can be stamped as "impotence," only if reason be assumed to be the essence, and a rational life the proper destiny of the being so controlled. To make this assumption possible, Spinoza changes and deepens the significance of that which constitutes the essence of mind. The self-maintaining impulse in mind, which is identical with its essence, in order to be "infinitely surpassed" by that of all other finite natures, is at first nothing more and deeper in the former than in the latter. As endowed with it, the individual mind is, at most, only quantitatively distinguished from the infinite multiplicity of other individuals, one force amidst the infinitude of forces, to which it necessarily succumbs. But to make it at once capable of the bondage of nature and of rising above it, it has to be invested with the functions and to play the part of a self-conscious, self-determining subject. Its essence is understanding or reason, its essential function is knowledge or the capacity of adequate ideas—that knowledge which, as we have seen, is not inert or merely theoretical knowledge, but knowledge which is instinct with the activity of will; and the goal of which is "the consciousness of the mind's own perfect activity combined with the idea of God."

"The effort of self-maintenance," Spinoza writes,[1] "is nothing but the essence of a thing itself, . . . its power of doing those things which follow necessarily from its nature. But the essence of reason is nothing but our mind in so far as it clearly and distinctly understands. . . . The effort of the mind by which it endeavours to persevere in its own being is nothing else than understanding, and this effort at understanding is the first and sole basis of virtue,"—the source, that is, of its moral and spiritual life. "The essence of the mind consists in knowledge, which involves the knowledge of God, and without it, it can neither be nor be conceived."[2] "Man acts absolutely according to the laws of his own nature when he lives under the guidance of reason."[3] "To act rationally is nothing else than to do those things which follow from the necessity of our own nature considered in itself alone."[4] "We know assuredly nothing to be good save what helps, nothing to be evil save what hinders, understanding."[5]

By this tacit modification of the definition of mind, Spinoza, as we have said, infuses into it that element of self-determination which makes it a possible subject of bondage and of a process of emancipation from bondage.

(1.) As to the former: human bondage, instead of being merely another name for finitude, or the determination of a single mode by the infinite series of external modes, becomes now the subjection of reason or of a being essentially rational to the irrational. It is no longer simply the relation of one "part of nature" to

---

[1] Eth. iv. 26, dem.  [2] Ibid., 37, dem.
[3] Eth. iv. 35, cor. 1.  [4] Eth. iv. 59, dem.
[5] Eth. iv. 27.

the whole, but it is the subjection of the spiritual to the natural. Reason or intelligence is essentially active, a rational nature has in it the spring of perpetual activity. It is of its very essence to realise itself, to be the adequate cause of its own thoughts and volitions, to make its whole experience the expression of its own essence; and as pain and all painful emotions are the indications of restrained or diminished power, it is the characteristic of a rational nature to be a stranger to pain, to revel, so to speak, in the unbroken consciousness of its own energy. But, through the medium of the passions, a foreign element gains access to the mind, ideas intrude upon it which are no longer its own creation, but which reflect the involuntary affections of the body by the external world. A host of desires and emotions arise in it of which it is not itself the source; the presence of pain, and of emotions coloured by pain, betrays its repressed activity; and even its pleasurable or joyous emotions, and the sense of power that accompanies them, are not of legitimate origin, but, being due to external stimulus, are the sign of the mind's weakness, not of its strength. Again, it is of the very essence of a rational nature, not only to determine itself, but to determine itself by uniform and invariable principles of action. "Whatever the mind conceives under the guidance of reason, it conceives under the same form of eternity or necessity, and it is affected by it with the same certitude "[1]—*i.e.*, independently of all variable conditions or of the accidents of time and place. The good which is its satisfaction is an absolute good, a good which cannot be diminished by distance or lapse of time, and which

[1] Eth. iv. 62, dem.

is the same for all minds.   But it is of the very nature
of the passions to introduce into the mind an element of
fitfulness and caprice, and to determine our actions by a
good which is contingent and fluctuating.   Pleasure and
pain, reflecting as they do the affections of the body,
vary with individual temperament, with the accidental
and ever-changing relations of the individual to outward
things, with the nearness or distance in time and space
of the objects that affect us.   Hence the inroad on the
mind of a whole brood of emotions—of desire and aversion, hope and fear, pride and humility, timidity and
daring, exultation and remorse, &c.—which disturb its
equanimity, and render it the slave of accident and irra-
tionality.   Hence, too, the tyranny of warring passions,
and the disturbance of that harmony and repose which
constitute the atmosphere of reason.   For whilst the
objects of reason are the same for all minds, and they
who seek them seek a good which is common to all,
which can never be diminished by the multiplicity of
participants, and which each individual must desire that
others should seek ;[1] on the other hand, pleasure and
pain, from which the passions spring, are in their nature
purely individual.   Not only do their objects affect different men in an infinite variety of ways, so that what
one desires and loves, another may hate and shun, but
their appropriation by one implies the loss of them to
all besides.   Envy, jealousy, anger, hatred, all the malign
passions, beset those who make pleasure their good.   In
these and other ways Spinoza shows that the passions,
as the word indicates, imply the passivity or bondage of
man's true nature.   The essence of the mind is reason,

[1] Eth. iv. 18, 36, 37.

the autonomy of reason its freedom ; but in so far as the mind is under the control of passion, our actions "no longer follow from the laws of our own nature, but are determined by what is alien to it." To let passion rule is a kind of suicide, for a suicide is one "who is over-come by external causes, and those which are contrary to his own nature."[1] On the other hand, "man is free in so far as he is led by reason, for then only is he determined to act by causes which can be adequately understood by his own nature alone."[2] "We see thus the difference between a man who is led solely by emo-tion or opinion and a man who is led by reason. The former, whether he will or no, does those things of which he is utterly ignorant; the latter does those things only which he knows to be of the highest importance in life, and which therefore he desires above all. There-fore I call the former a slave, the latter a free man."[3]

(2.) The conception of human bondage which Spinoza has now reached supplies him with a basis for his doc-trine of freedom, and indicates the process by which the transition from bondage to freedom is mediated. So long as bondage is identical with determination or finitude, freedom is impossible, or possible only by the annulling of the very existence of the being to whom it pertains. But if the freedom of man be conceived, not as indetermination but as determination by the laws of his own nature, the possibility thereof resolves itself into the question whether that nature can rise above the external influences which dominate it. As the lowest stage of knowledge is that of imagination or inadequate ideas, so the lowest stage of the moral life is that of

[1] Eth. iv. 20, schol.    [2] Tract. Pol., cap. ii. 11.    [3] Eth. iv. 66, schol.

bondage to the passions, which are, if not simply another form of inadequate ideas, necessarily generated by
them. Can we rise from this state; and if so, how?
Is freedom possible; and if possible, what is the process
by which it is achieved?

As to the first of these questions, it may be said that
the answer is involved in the doctrine that the activity
of reason is essentially pleasurable, and that pain belongs
only to the passions. The pain of bondage is the pro-
phecy of freedom. Pain, in other words, is the consciousness of limitation or repressed activity, and the
mind that is conscious of its limits is already virtually
beyond them. If man could be perfectly happy under
the dominion of passion, his moral condition would be
hopeless. The fact that in the lowest stage of selfish
indulgence there is an element of unrest is the witness
to the presence in man of a nature greater than his passions, and capable of rising above them.

But granting the possibility of freedom, how is it to
be attained? In the conflict of passion what are the
weapons at the command of reason? In answer to this
question, Spinoza enumerates what he terms " the
remedies of the emotions, or what the mind, considered
in itself alone, can do against them." [1] The more important of these " remedies " we shall briefly consider.

1. " The mind's power over the emotions consists,
first, in the actual knowledge of the emotions." The
knowledge of passion destroys passion. " An emotion
which is a passion ceases to be a passion as soon as we
form a clear and distinct idea of it." [2] Spinoza's proof
of this proposition is in substance this—that a passion

[1] Eth. v. 20, schol.        [2] Eth. v. 3.

is, or rests on, " a confused idea," and that forming a
clear and distinct idea of it is equivalent to the vanishing of the confusion. Error is extinguished, and its
power over the mind ceases when we know it *as* error.
Moreover, a passion is a confused idea " of *an affection
of the body.*" But there is no affection of the body of
which we cannot form a clear and distinct idea. We
can rise above the confusion of ordinary knowledge to
the clear intelligence of reason. When, therefore, we
think a passion, what remains of it is not the passion
itself, but the true idea of it, or that is involved in it.
It is thus transferred from the sphere of our passivity to
that of our activity. Reason not only masters passion,
but receives a fresh accession of power ; it not only de-
tects the illusion, but becomes possessed of the truth
that underlies it, so that what we sought blindly from
passion we now seek intelligently or from rational
motives.

Stripped of its technical form, the drift of Spinoza's
argument seems to be this : When it is asserted that
by the knowledge of our passions we gain the mastery
over them, or " that every one has the power clearly and
distinctly to understand himself and his emotions, and
therefore, if not absolutely, yet in part, of bringing it
about that he should not be subject to them," [1] it is
obviously not meant that to have a theoretical knowledge of passion is to be exempt from its control, which
would be as absurd as to say that the diagnosis of a
disease is equivalent to its cure. Nor, again, is Spinoza's
doctrine simply the commonplace maxim, that as an
enemy we know is comparatively harmless, so by study-

[1] Eth. v. 4, schol.

ing our passions we learn how to be on our guard against them. But what he means is, that when we gain the point of view of true knowledge, passion loses its hold over us. As, in the intellectual sphere, the aspect of the world as it is for imagination, in which all things are regarded from a purely individual standpoint, is of necessity annulled when we rise to the higher standpoint of reason, in which all things are discerned in their universal and necessary relations, — so, in the ethical sphere, the attitude of purely individual feeling, in which things are good or evil only as they contribute to the satisfaction of our appetites and passions, vanishes away when we rise to that higher attitude in which we identify ourselves with the universal interests, and look on our particular pleasures and pains in the light of that universal order of which we are but an insignificant part. So viewed, our particular satisfactions lose their deceptive importance. They become no more to us, or to reason in us, than those of other individuals, and infinitely less than the interests of that universe of being to which we and they belong. Thus, regarded from the point of view of reason, the passions cease to exist for us except in so far as they are functions of the universal, or forms under which reason itself is realised.

These considerations explain to us also the sequel of Spinoza's argument, in which he maintains that in thus knowing our passions we transform them into elements of the mind's activity. "To all actions," he writes, "to which we are determined by passion, we can be determined without passion by reason."[1] "Every desire," it

[1] Eth. iv. 59.

is added, " which springs from an emotion wherein the
mind is passive, would become useless if men were guided
by reason." [1]   And again : " All appetites or desires are
passions only in so far as they spring from inadequate
ideas, and the same results are ranked as virtues when
they are aroused or generated by adequate ideas.   For
all desires by which we are determined to any action
may arise as well from adequate as from inadequate
ideas." [2]   There is, in other words, a rational meaning or
end underlying the passions, and what we seek blindly
under the influence of passion we may seek deliberately
under the guidance of reason.   When we know or form
an adequate idea of a passion, we discern this underlying end, and make it an object of conscious deliberate
pursuit.   " We must endeavour to acquire as far as
possible a clear and distinct idea of every emotion, in
order that the mind may be thus, through emotion,
determined to think of those things which it clearly and
distinctly perceives and in which it fully acquiesces, and
thus that the emotion itself may be separated from the
thought of an external cause and connected with true
thoughts ; whence it will come to pass, not only that
love, hatred, &c., will be destroyed, but also that
appetites and desires which usually arise from such
emotions will become incapable of excess." [3]   Even the
lowest appetites are capable of being thus transferred
from the sphere of passion to that of reason, from the
passive to the active side of our nature.   The wise or
free man is no longer impelled by hunger or lust, but
by the rational endeavour after that to which these
appetites point — the preservation and continuance of

[1] Eth. iv. 59, schol.        [2] Eth. v. 4, schol.        [3] Ibid.

the life of the individual and the race. Ambition and
kindred passions are based on the desire "that other
men should live after our fashion ; " but this is only an
irrational aim when it is the dictate of blind, selfish
impulse ; in a nature that is elevated to the universality
of reason it becomes simply the endeavour that all men
should lead a rational life. Animal courage or daring
purged of its impulsive character, becomes that wise
presence of mind which may express itself as much in
evading danger as in facing and overcoming it.[1] Even
those emotions, such as pity or compassion, which we
are wont to regard as good and praiseworthy, are, considered merely as emotions, bad and hurtful ;[2] but reason
or the rational man extracts the valuable element in
them, and instead of being impulsively moved by the
calamities and tears of the wretched, seeks on rational
grounds to ameliorate their condition.[3] Thus, in general,
the knowledge of passion annihilates passion, and sub-
stitutes for it the calm and deliberate activity of reason.
A perfectly wise man would be absolutely passionless,
and therefore absolutely free. He "would hate no man,
envy no man, be angry with no man," and for the same
reason, would love and pity no man, do nothing at the
mere dictate of feeling, but would order his life from
purely rational motives for the general good.[4]

2. As another and kindred "remedy for the passions,"
or means of attaining freedom, Spinoza points out that
"the mind can bring it about that all bodily affections
or images of things should be referred," (*a*) to "the
common properties of things or deductions therefrom,"

---

[1] Eth. iv. 69.       [2] Eth. iv. 50.
[3] Ibid., dem.       [4] Eth. iv. 73, dem. and schol.

or (*b*) to "the idea of God."[1] This "remedy for the passions" is only the converse or correlate of that which we have just considered. Thought or reason transforms the object as well as the subject of passion. When I think or know myself, the passion vanishes; when I think or know the world, it ceases to be that world which appeals to passion. The latter result is, indeed, already involved in the former. Even from Spinoza's peculiar point of view, thought and its outward object stand or fall with each other. The world, as it was for inadequate thought, no longer exists for that which has become adequate; thought cannot rise from the individual to the universal without implying a parallel elevation in the extended world which is its object.

But though the one transformation implies the other, it is possible, following our author, to consider them separately. The dominion of passion may be conceived of as the dominion of the world and the things of the world over a nature larger than themselves — of the world as it is for sense and imagination over a nature the essence of which is reason, of the things of the world in their fictitious reality and independence over a nature the essence of which is the idea or self-affirmation of God. The "bondage," on that supposition, would be that of an infinite nature imprisoned in the finite, of a being whose essence is light, harmony, eternal order and unity, in a world of darkness and discordancy. The deliverance from this bondage is that "remedy for the passions" to which Spinoza here points. Annihilate the world, and the passions which were related to it die a natural death. But the world on which

---

[1] Eth. v. 14 and 12.

passion fed has no real existence. Nothing really is as to imagination it seemed to be. The individual things to which the affections of the body were referred, and which, through these affections, became the objects of desire and aversion, love and hate, are purely illusory. The body and its affections, and all bodies which affect it, are nothing save as determined by universal relations of cause and effect, which link the whole order or system of things into one vast unity. The mind that is the prey of the passions is wasting itself on a vain show, fastening on that as real and permanent which is fugitive and evanescent. Thought or reason dissolves the show, and with it the passions to which it gave birth. Passion, again, in its fluctuation and variableness, is based on relations to a world which is the scene of arbitrariness and accident. But there is no such world. The "common properties," the universal laws, of things determine their relations by an absolute necessity, and when we "refer the affections of the body" to these, when the world puts off the mask of change and contingency, and the presence of eternal order and necessity confronts us, the restless alternations of satiety and discontent vanish with the illusory world they reflected. "If we remove a disturbance of the mind or an emotion from the thought of an external cause, and connect it with other thoughts, then will love or hatred towards the external cause, and also the fluctuations of the mind which arise from these emotions, be destroyed."[1] But further, in the real world which supplants the illusory world of imagination, there is something deeper even than the "common properties" which

[1] Eth. v. 2.

reason discerns. Thought, even when it has grasped the universal principles or laws which bind all finite things in the bonds of an unchangeable necessity, falls short of apprehending their deepest meaning. "The mind can bring it about that all bodily affections and images of things should be referred to the idea of God."[1] It is possible, as we have seen, for thought to rise to a point of view from which the world is contemplated, not merely as a system of things conditioning and conditioned by each other, but as a system in which all things are seen in the light of that absolute unity of which they are only the infinitely varied expression. The true "existence of things" is that which is ascribed to them because of this, that from the eternal necessity of the nature of God an infinity of things follows in infinite ways."[2] The system of the world, in other words, contains an element of unresolved diversity till the particular existence of things, and their mediating link of causation, are no longer independent, and by the glance of immediate "intellectual intuition" we can, so to speak, see the whole at once—all diversity in unity, all thinking things, all objects of thought as expressions of that "idea of God" which is their immanent principle and essence. In this highest and truest knowledge of the world lies the secret of complete emancipation from the bondage of passion, and of the attainment of perfect freedom. In the sphere of the passions that emotion is most vivid and powerful which is referred to a present rather than an absent object, or to a greater rather than a lesser number of objects, or to objects that most frequently recur; and an emotion possessing all these

[1] Eth. v. 14.　　　　　　[2] Eth. ii. 45, schol.

characteristics would prevail over every other. But if there be one object or idea which is ever present and incapable of being excluded by any other, which all things and thoughts suggest, and from which everything else derives its significance and reality—then must that idea, and the emotion to which it gives rise, dominate every other in the mind in which it dwells. Now, just such is the idea of God. It is the idea to which it is possible for the mind " to refer all bodily affections or images of things," and in the mind which has achieved this result, to which all things speak of God, or are seen only as they exist in God, all passions that relate only to things finite and transient are quelled, and every other emotion is absorbed in that " intellectual love " which is only another aspect of the intuitive knowledge of God. Finally, whilst every other emotion limits the mind's activity, this is the expression of its highest freedom. For whilst all passion "springs from pleasure or pain, accompanied with the idea of an external cause," this emotion springs from a cause which is no longer outward or foreign to the mind, but is its own inmost essence. Subjection to absolute truth is the freedom of intelligence. For the mind, the essence of which is that self-affirming impulse which is in reality the self-affirmation of God in it, and for which the world is a world in which all things are seen in God, or awaken the thought and love of God, subjection to what is external ceases; every object it contemplates, everything that stirs the fount of feeling, only contributes to its own purest activity. The mind that is one with God is free of a universe in which itself and all things live and move and have their being in God.

In reviewing this theory of the transition from bondage to freedom, it may be pointed out that its main defect seems to lie in the abstract ideal of man's highest life on which it is based. Freedom is pure self-affirmation or self-activity, all passion is negation of that activity. The ideal, therefore, of the moral life is that of an absolutely passionless life. The "life according to reason" is that in which the agent is determined "by reason without passion." Reason and passion cannot coexist. Where emotion is contrary to reason, it is noxious ; where it coincides with reason, it is useless : in either case, it is an invasion from without on that purely self-affirming activity in which the mind's freedom consists. The triumph of reason is not the subjugation but the extinction of passion. To think a passion is to kill it. Thought and passion are opposed as activity and passivity, and the positing of the former is equivalent to the annulling of the latter. Further, it follows from this that the free or rational life is one from which pain or sorrow is absolutely excluded. Pain is the indication of repressed activity ; pleasure, in the sense in which it is not of the nature of passion, of unimpeded or expanding activity. Into the spiritual life, therefore, no feeling of which pain or sorrow is an element can enter ; and judged by this criterion, humility, penitence, pity, compassion, and kindred emotions must be pronounced to be evil.[1]

But it is to be remarked that a freedom which is thus identified with passionless intelligence, or the pure self-affirmation of reason apart from negation, is either an impossible notion, or a notion which is only a moment

[1] Eth. iv. 50, 53, 54.

or factor in the true idea of freedom. It is true that the affirmation of a self which is above and beyond the passions, though not in itself spiritual freedom, is a step in the process towards it. It is of the very essence of a spiritual nature to be conscious of a self which is more than any or all particular desires and affections, which does not come and go with the succession of feelings, but underneath all their transiency and changefulness remains ever one with itself, posits or affirms itself in opposition to their negativity. But though this self-affirmation is an element of the process, it is only an element. A purely self-affirming intelligence, or, otherwise expressed, a rational will which has no materials of activity outside of itself, is a mere abstraction. It is a determiner without anything to determine, a universal without the particular, the blank form of the moral life without any filling or content. Reason can never realise itself merely by willing to be rational ; it can only do so by willing particular acts which come under the form of rationality. And this implies that the general principle or aim of reason can only fulfil itself through particular desires, impulses, passions, which have their own ends or objects. An intelligence feeding only on itself dies of inanition, or rather, never begins to live. But whilst thus the extinction of passion would be the extinction of spiritual life, or whilst an intelligence that could annihilate passion would annihilate the very materials of its own existence, yet, on the other hand, the passions, in so far as they remain an element of the spiritual life, do not remain unchanged. Reason, if it does not annul, transmutes them. In the moral strife the conquest is not that of a victor who slays his enemies, but who makes them

his own thralls. Or rather it is more than that; for in
the conflict with the passions reason achieves its own
freedom by infusing into them its own rationality. It
realises itself by elevating the natural impulses and
desires into its own universality. As the touch of art
glorifies matter, transmutes stones and pigments into the
beauty and splendour of the ideal; or as organic life,
whilst it takes up inorganic materials into itself, leaves
them not unchanged, but assimilates and transforms
them, suffuses them with its own power and energy,—so
the impulses and passions of the natural self are but the
raw material which the spiritual self transforms into the
organs of its own life. The free man, the man who has
entered into the universal life of reason, is still a creature
of flesh and blood; he hungers and thirsts, he is no
stranger to ordinary appetites and impulses, or to those
wider passions which animate the most unspiritual
natures. But in living, not for his individual pleasure,
but for the higher ends of the spirit, the passions, whether
as the mere organic basis of the spiritual life, or as controlled and denied for the sake of it, or as used up as its
resources, become, to the spirit, instinct with its own
vitality and freedom.

# CHAPTER XVI.

## IMMORTALITY AND THE BLESSED LIFE.

SPINOZA's doctrine of immortality is, in one point of view, only another form of his doctrine of freedom. It is the passions or passive emotions which hinder the mind's inherent activity and subject it to the control of a foreign element. But so long as the body exists, the passions must more or less limit the autonomy of reason. For the passions correspond to and reflect the affections which the body receives from external bodies; or, otherwise expressed, they are due to the illusory influence of the imagination, which contemplates outward objects in their accidental relations to the body and gives to them a false substantiality and independence. A passion is "a confused idea by which the mind affirms greater or less power of *its body* than before, and by the presence of which it is determined to think one thing rather than another." "Whatsoever hinders the power or activity of the body, the idea of that thing hinders that of the mind."[1] Whilst, therefore, the body endures, we must be more or less the slaves of imagination and passion. If the mind were wholly imagination it would perish with the body

[1] Eth. iii. 11.

and its affections. The illusory world and the ideas
that reflect it would vanish together. But, as we have
just seen, there is that in the mind which enables it to
rise above the slavery of passion, to emancipate itself
from the illusions that are generated by ideas of bodily
affections. The true. essence of mind is reason, which
sees things, not under the fictitious limits of time, but
under the form of eternity and in their immanent relation to the idea of God. It is this essence of the mind
which constitutes what Spinoza calls its "better part,"
and in which lies the secret at once of its freedom and its
immortality. It makes man free, for it raises him above
the desires that are related to the accidental and transient,
and brings him under the dominion of that "intellectual love" which is the expression of his own deepest
nature. It makes man immortal, for, having no relation
to the body and its affections, it has in it nothing that
can be affected by the destruction of the body. "There
is nothing in nature that is contrary to this intellectual
love or can take it away."[1] "It is possible for the.
human mind to be of such a nature that that in it which
we have shown to perish with the body is of little importance in comparison with that in it which endures."[2]
"The eternal part of the mind is the understanding,
through which alone we are said to act; the part which
we have shown to perish is the imagination, through
which alone we are said to be passive."[3]

There is, however, another and very peculiar aspect
of Spinoza's doctrine of immortality which remains to
be explained. We naturally ask how any such survival
of the mind after the destruction of the body as is here

[1] Eth. v. 37.     [2] Eth. v. 38, schol.     [3] Eth. v. 40, cor.

maintained, is consistent with the fundamental doctrine of the uniform parallelism of thought and extension, or with the principle that to all that takes place in the human mind as a mode of thought there must be something corresponding in the human body as a mode of extension. Spinoza's answer to this question turns on the distinction which, according to him, obtains between the " essence " and the " actual existence " of the body. The mind's survival does not leave us with something in the sphere of thought to which nothing in the sphere of extension corresponds. For though the particular mode of extension which we designate this actually existing body, or the body " in so far as it is explained by duration and can be defined by time," ceases to exist, there is nevertheless an " essence " of the body which can only be conceived through the essence of God or under the form of eternity, and which therefore endures when everything corporeal of which we can speak in terms of time passes away. " God," says Spinoza, " is the cause not only of the existence of this or that human body, but also of its essence." [1] " There is necessarily in God (and therefore in the human mind) an idea which expresses the essence of the human body." [2] It would therefore appear that not only the mind, but the body also, survives death. The parallelism of thought and extension is not affected by the destruction of the actually existing body. In both there is something that passes away, in both something that remains. If that particular mode of extension which we call the actually existing body passes away, so also does that mode of thought which constitutes the *idea* of the actually existing body.

[1] Eth. v. 22, dem.      [2] Eth. v. 23, dem.

On the other hand, if the immortal element in mind is the reason, which contemplates all things under the form of eternity, in like manner the immortal element in the body is that " essence of the body " which is the object of reason. The " form of eternity " belongs alike to the essence of the body and to the essence of the mind.

1. In criticising this theory, it may be remarked that in such phrases as "the duration of the mind without relation to the body," " the mind does not imagine, &c., save while the body endures," Spinoza employs language which, as addressed to the ordinary ear, is misleading, inasmuch as it suggests the notion of an incorporeal immortality, a survival of the purely spiritual element of man's nature when the material element has passed away. Such phraseology perhaps betrays an unconscious concession to the popular conception of the material as the grosser, the mental as the nobler element, and of immortality as the emancipation of the spirit from the bondage of matter. In any case, such language is obviously inconsistent with Spinoza's doctrine as above explained. Spinoza knows nothing of the false spiritualism which recoils from the supposed grossness or " pravity " of matter. To him, on the contrary, matter is as divine as mind, modes of matter are as much the expression of God as modes of mind. On his principles it would be equally true and equally false to say that the body survives the mind, and to say that the mind survives the body. To each he ascribes an " essence " which is distinct from its "actual existence "; and if the essence of the mind survives the body regarded as a particular, transient modification of matter, the essence of the body

survives the mind regarded as the idea of that modification, or the particular modification of thought which
corresponds to it.

2. It is a more important criticism of Spinoza's doctrine that it ascribes to death or the destruction of the
body what is really due to reason, as the destroyer of
the illusions of imagination. The triumph of mind is
not the destruction of the body, but the destruction of a
false view of it. It is not achieved by the cessation of
the body's existence, but by the dissipation of the illusory reality ascribed to it. The immortality which is
predicated of the mind is not continuity of existence
after death, but its capacity to rise above the category
of time and to see itself, the body and all things, under
the form of eternity. To speak of this as something
future, or as a capacity of living on after a certain date,
or of surviving a certain event, is simply to explain in
terms of time that the very nature of which is to transcend time. The immortality which is sanctioned by
Spinoza's principles is not a quantitative but a qualitative
endowment—not existence for indefinite time, but the
quality of being above time. It is an immortality, therefore, which may be attained here and now. In so far as
we rise to the stage of intuitive intelligence and intellectual love, we have an immediate experience of it, we
enter at once into the sphere of eternity, and the old
world of imagination vanishes away. And if we ask,
What is the relation of this eternal consciousness to the
life or death of the body? it might be answered that
the moral acceptance of death is the supreme act of
liberation. For the mind that sees things under the
form of eternity, the body, as a phenomenon in time,

has already vanished, the disillusioning power of reason has anticipated in a deeper way the physical disintegration of death. Spinoza knows nothing of the Platonic notion of the corporeal state as an imprisonment of the soul, from which death liberates it. The mind that knows God has already achieved its liberation, and the eternity in which it dwells is neither hindered nor helped by the destruction of the body. According to his own principles, therefore, it is an obvious inconsistency in Spinoza to speak of a subjection of the mind to imagination and passion " so long as the body endures," or of the " destruction of the body " as contributing in any measure to its emancipation. For the higher consciousness of the mind, the body has been already destroyed, and the only emancipation of which the mind is capable is one which reason, and not the destruction of the body, has accomplished.

3. Spinoza's doctrine implies a tacit ascription to the mind of a superiority over the body which is inconsistent with their parallelism as modes of thought and extension. That doctrine is, as we have seen, that there is an essence of mind and an essence of body which both alike transcend the category of time, and are part of the eternal nature of God. But whilst Spinoza's conception of the nature of mind supplies a ground for its superiority to time, its permanence through all change, he assigns no similar ground for the perpetuity of the body. Modes of thought are determined by other modes; but besides this, there is a reduplication of thought upon itself; in other words, thought thinks itself. Modes of extension are determined by other modes, but there is no similar return of each mode of extension upon itself, nor, from

the very nature of the thing, is any such return conceivable. Now, though the conception of mind as not
only idea of the body, but as the idea of that idea, does
not amount to what is involved in the modern doctrine
of self-consciousness, yet in Spinoza's speculations it
performs in some measure the functions which that
doctrine ascribes to the mind. As conscious of itself,
mind contains in its very essence a principle of continuity, a unity which remains constant through all phenomenal changes. It can abstract from all determinations,
and it is that to which all determinations are referred—
the living, indestructible point of centrality to which
the thoughts and feelings that compose our conscious
life are drawn back. But there is nothing approximat-
ing to this principle of self-centrality in Spinoza's con
ception of the body. "The human body is composed,"
he tells us,[1] "of many individual parts of diverse
nature, each one of which is extremely complex," and
"these individual parts of the body, and therefore the
body itself, are constantly being affected by external
bodies." In all this diversity and change there is no
principle of unity; the unity to which the body as a
composite thing is referred is not in itself, but in the
"idea of the body," or the mind that thinks it.

4. Spinoza's conception of immortality, or of the eternal element in mind, is, as we have seen, simply that of
a mind for which the illusion of time has disappeared.
But to drop or eliminate an illusion is not to account for
it, or to explain its relation to our mental and spiritual
life. Spinoza points out as a fact that time as well as
figure, number, measure, are only illusory forms of ima-

[1] Eth. ii., post. 1 and 3.

gination, and that reason rises above them. But even an illusion must be in some way grounded in the intelligence that experiences it. It can be explained only by tracing its origin, and by showing that it forms a necessary stage in the development of the finite mind. Time, in other words, is not explained even as an illusion, unless in the eternal there is shown to be a reason for it ; nor is the eternal which rises above time to be understood unless the negation of time is shown to be contained in it. If the aspect of things " under the form of eternity " has no necessary relation to their aspect as things in time, the latter is a mere excrescence in the system, and for any reason that appears, might have been omitted altogether. If thinking things under the form of time is not a necessary stage in the process towards true knowledge, there is no reason why the mind should not have started at once from the point of view in which nothing is illusory, and in which eternal realities are immediately apprehended. Spinoza contrasts reason and imagination, the point of view in which things are regarded as independent realities, and the point of view in which they are seen in the light of the idea of God, or under the form of eternity. But he makes no attempt to show the relation between the lower and the higher point of view. He simply pronounces the former to be false and illusory, and the latter to be an attitude of mind in which the former is dropped or left behind. But is there no way, it may be asked, in which it can be shown that the determination of things in time, not merely empirically precedes, but is a necessary presupposition of their determination under the form of eternity ? Is it not possible to discern that

the rise from imaginative to rational knowledge is not
an accident in the history of thought, but a necessary
step in the process by which a self-conscious intelligence realises itself and its own inherent wealth ?   The
answer to this question may be said to be involved in
the very nature of intelligence.   The relation of imagination to reason is simply the relation, in modern
language, of consciousness to self-consciousness.   The
consciousness of self implies relation to objects which
are opposed to self, and yet which, as related to self,
form a necessary element of its life.   It is only by the
presentation to itself of an external world—*i.e.*, of a
world conceived of under the forms of externality—that
mind or intelligence can, by the relating or reclaiming of
that world to itself, become conscious of its own latent
content.   Thought, in other words, is not a resting
identity, but a process, a life, of which the very
essence is ceaseless activity, or movement from unity
to difference and from difference to unity.   It is not
by brooding on itself in some pure, supersensuous
sphere of untroubled spirituality, but by going forth
into a world that, in the first instance, is outside of
and foreign to itself, and of which the constituent
elements in their self-externality in space and succession in time, are the contradiction of its own inherent
unity, and then by the recognition of that world as not
really foreign or independent or discordant, but in its
real or essential nature related to and finding its meaning and unity in thought—it is by this perpetual process
of differentiation and integration that self-conscious intelligence ceases to be a lifeless abstraction, and becomes
a concrete reality.   But if this be so, the differentiat-

ing movement is presupposed in the integrating, the world of imagination is no longer a mere illusion which somehow the mind outlives, a dream from which it awakes, but a necessary step in the life of spirit and in its progress to higher things. Time is not a mere subjective deception which passes away, but a form of objectivity which it is of the very essence of spirit to posit and transcend. It is only by the affirmation and negation of time that we can rise to the contemplation of things under the form of eternity. The eternal life is not that which abstracts from the temporal, but that which contains while it annuls it.

5. The most important question as to Spinoza's doctrine of immortality still remains, and that is the question, not whether the individual mind can in any way be said to survive the body, but whether in their relation to God there can be said to be any real survival of either. The view which we take of man's nature implies and must be based on a corresponding view of the nature of God. Whatever independence we ascribe to the finite involves as its correlate an idea of the infinite which admits of and is the ground of that independence. Does Spinoza's idea of God admit of and furnish a basis for his doctrine of human freedom and immortality? The peculiarity of the view of man's nature and destiny which we have now explained is that it is just at the point where the limit between the finite and infinite vanishes, and where indeed there is the strongest reassertion of the doctrine that the finite is and is conceived only through the infinite, that instead of being suppressed or indistinguishably absorbed, the finite mind is represented as attain-

ing the most complete individuality and activity. "The eternal part of the mind is the understanding through which alone we are said to act, the part which we have shown to perish is the imagination through which only we are said to be passive."[1] The state which constitutes the supreme or eternal destiny of man is not simply that of absolute unity with God, but that in which man attains to the *consciousness* of that unity, and in which the distinction between itself and God is not only not obliterated but intensified. "The mind as eternal has a knowledge of God which is necessarily adequate and is fitted to know all those things which follow from this knowledge, . . . and the more potent any one becomes in this kind of knowledge, the more completely is he conscious of himself and of God."[2] Not only is it a state in which the mind has attained the maximum of self-originated activity, and therefore its highest individual perfection, but with the consciousness of this comes also the highest joy or blessedness. For "if joy consists in the transition to a greater perfection, assuredly blessedness must consist in the mind being endowed with perfection itself."[3] "He who knows things by this kind of knowledge passes to the highest human perfection, and therefore is affected by the highest joy, and that a joy which is accompanied by the idea of himself and of his own virtue."[4] Finally, all these elements of individual perfection—freedom, activity, self - consciousness, self - determination — are summed up in that attitude of mind which Spinoza designates "intellectual love," which he defines as "joy

---

[1] Eth. v. 40, cor.   [2] Eth. v. 31, dem. and cor.
[3] Eth. v. 33, schol.   [4] Eth. v. 27, dem.

or delight accompanied by the idea of one's self, and therefore by the idea of God as its cause." [1] The perfection of human nature, in other words, is a state of blessedness in which the consciousness of self is not lost in God, but actually based on the consciousness of God.

Can we find in Spinoza's idea of the divine nature any room or ground for this conception of the nature and destiny of man? The answer must be, that the idea of God on which Spinoza's whole system is ostensibly based is one which involves the denial of any reality or independence to the finite. It is by negation of all individual finite things that that idea is reached. It is by abstracting from all distinctions material and mental, and even from the distinction of matter and mind itself, that we attain to that pure, indeterminate unity, that colourless, moveless abstraction of substance which is Spinoza's formal conception of the nature of God.

But this though formally is not really the idea of God on which Spinoza's system rests. What he sought to reach was a principle which would constitute the explanation of man and the world, from which "an infinite number of things in infinite ways must necessarily follow," and from the adequate knowledge of which the mind could proceed to the adequate knowledge of the nature of things." [2] And though the idea of God which he formulates does not constitute such a principle, yet in the course of his speculations we find that idea undergoing various modifications which, if carried out to their logical results, would have involved the complete reconstruction of his philosophy.

[1] Eth. v. 32, cor.                    [2] Eth. ii. 40, sch. 2.

(1.) His constant use of the phrase *quatenus* is really an acknowledgment of the inadequacy of the premiss it is introduced to qualify—an expedient, in other words, for surreptitiously reaching results not logically justifiable on his own principles. The infinitude which is conceived of as pure indetermination would be tampered with if any finite existence could be regarded as an expression of the essential nature of God; yet Spinoza is not content with a barren infinitude—an infinitude which leaves nature and man unaccounted for. Hence the frequent recurrence of such expressions as these : " The idea of an individual thing actually existing has God for its cause, not *in so far as* He is infinite, but *in so far as* He is regarded as affected by another idea of an individual thing, &c. ; " [1] " God has this or that idea, not *in so far as* He is infinite, but *in so far as* He is expressed by the nature of the human mind or constitutes the essence of the human mind ; " [2] " The intellectual love of the mind toward God is the very love with which He loves Himself, not *in so far as* He is infinite, but *in so far as* He can be expressed by the essence of the human mind conceived under the form of eternity." [3] The infinite can never be expressed by a nature which is nothing but the negation of the infinite. Yet this inevitable conclusion Spinoza will not let himself acknowledge. The whole moral use and value of his philosophy would vanish if man could not find the origin and end of his being in God, and so the self-contained, self-identical infinite must break through its isolation and reveal itself in the essence of the human mind. How or on what philosophical ground this rev-

[1] Eth. ii. 9.　　[2] Eth. ii. 11, cor.　　[3] Eth. v. 36.

elation is to be conceived Spinoza does not attempt
to explain; but to speak of "God in so far as He
is expressed by the human mind," or of the human
mind as surviving in its individuality "in so far as God
can be expressed by its essence under the form of
eternity," would be to employ words without meaning
if this "in so far" did not point to something positive
and real in the nature of God. To say that a thing
exists or survives *in so far* as the divine idea is expressed in it, would be absurd if Spinoza believed that the
divine idea did not express itself in it at all. The ever-
recurring phrase must have been to its author something
more than a transparent artifice or a *petitio principii*.

(2.) Whilst Spinoza rejects the anthropomorphic idea
of God as a being who acts on nature from without or
whose essence contains arbitrary elements after the
analogy of man's imperfect thought and will, he yet
constantly ascribes activity to God. An indeterminate
absolute is a dead and moveless absolute. Whilst
God's activity cannot proceed from any external cause
or constraint, but must be the expression of an internal
necessity, yet He is essentially and eternally active.
"The omnipotence of God has been from eternity actual,
and will to eternity remain in the same actuality."[1]
"From God's supreme power or infinite nature an
infinite number of things in infinite ways—that is, all
things—have necessarily flowed forth."[2]  And this conception of the essential productive activity of the divine
nature is based on the principle that the more reality a
thing has, the more properties follow therefrom, and
therefore the infinite nature "has absolutely infinite

[1] Eth. i. 17, sch.                         [2] Ibid.

attributes, of which each expresses infinite essence in its own kind." [1] The infinite which is the negation of all properties or determinations thus becomes the infinite which has an infinite number of properties or determinations.

(3.) It is true indeed, as we formerly saw, that the properties or attributes which Spinoza ascribes to God he is compelled by stress of logic to remove from the nature of God or Substance, absolutely viewed, and to regard as having an existence only relatively to finite intelligence. They are not distinctions which pertain to the divine essence as it is in itself, but only distinctions "which the understanding perceives as constituting that essence." They do not exist, in other words, for or through God's own thought, but for or through the thought of finite minds. Yet it is to be observed that there are indications that, however illogically, the attributes had for him the significance of absolute and not relative distinctions in the divine nature; and further, that it is not the human but the divine intelligence in and for which he conceived them to exist. "By God," says he,[2] "I understand a being absolutely infinite — that is, Substance consisting of infinite attributes of which each expresses eternal and infinite essence." "By attributes of God is to be understood that which expresses the essence of the divine Substance." [3] "The attributes of God which express His eternal essence, express at the same time His eternal existence." [4] Further, as we have seen, though in his formal doctrine Spinoza places thought on a level with extension and all other

[1] Eth. i. 16, dem.    [2] Eth. i., def. 6.
[3] Eth. i. 19, dem.    [4] Eth. i. 20, dem.

possible attributes, he really ascribes to the former an altogether higher and more comprehensive function. It is thought or intelligence in man for which both extension and thought exist; and as all other possible attributes exist for some intelligence, not only are the infinitude of attributes accompanied each by a parallel attribute of thought, but each and all of them exist *for* thought. In this conception of an infinite number of intelligences for which the attributes of God exist, Spinoza is hovering on the brink of the idea of an infinite intelligence as not an attribute or distinction outwardly ascribed to God, but the principle of distinction in the divine essence from which all attributes or distinctions flow. But he goes further still than this. Infinite intelligence is for him not merely the aggregate of an indefinite number of finite minds, it is infinite in a truer sense. For, as we have attempted to show, the conception of "the absolutely infinite intellect," as one of what Spinoza terms "infinite modes," is simply a device by which he is unconsciously seeking to introduce into the idea of God that element of activity which neither his abstract substance nor even its attributes contain. The gulf between the moveless infinite and the finite world is thus bridged over by an expedient which, ostensibly without affecting the indeterminateness of the absolute substance, makes it quick with the life of creative thought—introduces into it, in other words, what is virtually the principle of self-consciousness and self-determination.

## CONCLUSION.

THE last word of Spinoza's philosophy seems to be the contradiction of the first. Not only does he often fluctuate between principles radically irreconcilable, but he seems to reassert at the close of his speculations what he had denied at the beginning. The indeterminate infinite, which is the negation of the finite, becomes the infinite, which necessarily expresses itself in the finite, and which contains in it, as an essential element, the idea of the human mind under the form of eternity. The all-absorbing, lifeless substance becomes the God who knows and loves Himself and man with an infinite "intellectual love." On the other hand, the conception of the human mind as but an evanescent mode of the infinite substance, whose independent existence is an illusion, and which can become one with God only by ceasing to be distinguishable from God, yields to that of a nature endowed with indestructible individuality, capable of knowing both itself and God, and which, in becoming one with God, attains to its own conscious perfection and blessedness. The freedom of man, which is at first rejected as but the illusion of a being who is unconscious of the conditions under which, in body and mind, he is fast bound in the toils of an inevitable necessity, is reasserted as the essential prerogative of a nature which, as knowing itself through the infinite, is no longer subjected to finite limitations. The doctrine of a final cause or ideal end of existence, which was excluded as impossible in a world in which all that is, and as it is, is given along with the necessary existence of God, is restored in the conception of the human mind as having in it, in its rudest experience, the implicit consciousness of an infinite ideal, which, through reason and intuitive knowledge, it is capable of realising, and of the realisation of which its actual life is the process. At the outset, in one word, we seem to have a pantheistic unity in which nature and man, all the manifold existences of the finite world, are swallowed up; at the close, an infinite self-conscious mind, in which all finite thought and being find their reality and explanation.

Is it possible to harmonise these opposite aspects of Spinoza's system, and to free it from the inherent weakness which they seem to involve? Can we make him self-consistent, as many of his interpreters have done, only by emphasising one side or aspect of his teaching, and ignoring or explaining away all that seems to conflict with it—by clearing it of all individualistic elements, so as to reduce it to an uncompromising pantheism, or by eliminating the pantheistic element as mere scholastic surplusage, in order to find in it an anticipation of modern individualism and empiricism?

The answer is, that though Spinoza's philosophy cannot, in the form in which he presents it, be freed from inconsistency, yet much of that inconsistency is due to the limitations of an imperfect logic, and that the philosophy of a later time has taught us how it is possible to embrace in one system ideas which in him seem to be antagonistic. There is a point of view which he at most only vaguely foreshadowed, in which it is possible to maintain (1) at once the nothingness of the finite world before God and its reality in and through God, and (2) the idea of an infinite unity transcending all differences, which nevertheless expresses itself in nature and man, in all the manifold differences of finite thought and being.

1. The negation of the finite by which Spinoza rises to the idea of God is, in one sense, an element which enters into the essence of all spiritual life. But when we consider the twofold aspect in which Spinoza himself represents this negative movement,—that, on the one hand, which is involved in the principle that all determination is negation; and that, on the other hand, which is involved in the rise of the human mind from the lower to the higher stages of knowledge,—we can discern in his teaching an approximation to the idea of a negation which is only a step to a higher affirmation—in other words, of that *self*-negation or self-renunciation which is the condition of self-realisation in the intellectual, the moral, and the religious life. It is the condition of the intellectual life. Scientific knowledge is the revelation to or in my consciousness of a system of unalterable relations, a world of objective realities which I can neither make nor unmake, and which only he who abnegates his individual fancies and opinions can apprehend; and all knowledge rests on the tacit presupposition of an absolute truth or reason, which is the measure of individual opinion, which cannot be questioned without self-contradiction,

which in our very doubts and uncertainties we assume, and to which in its every movement the finite intelligence must surrender itself. The intellectual life is one which I can live only by ceasing to assert myself or to think my own thoughts, by quelling and suppressing all thought that pertains to me as this particular self, and identifying myself with an intelligence that is universal and absolute. Yet the negation of which we thus speak is not an absolute negation. The finite intelligence is not absorbed or lost in the infinite to which it surrenders itself. Surrender or subjection to absolute truth is not the extinction of the finite mind, but the realisation of its true life. The life of absolute truth or reason is not a life that is foreign to us, but one in which we come to our own. The annulling of any life that is separate from or opposed to it, is the quickening, the liberation, the reassertion of our own intelligence.

And the same thing is true of the moral life. Here, too, it is possible to reconcile Spinoza's denial of any reality to the finite in the face of the infinite, with his reassertion of its reality in and through the infinite. For in the moral life of man negation is ever a necessary step to affirmation, it is only through the renunciation of the natural life that we rise into the spiritual. The natural life is that of the individual regarded as a being of natural tendencies, of impulses, instincts, appetites which look to nothing beyond their immediate satisfaction. They pertain to him as this particular self, and they seem to point to no other end than his own private pleasure. But man never *is* a mere individual, or, in this sense, a particular self, and his passions are always so far transformed by self-consciousness that the

attainment of their immediate objects is never their
complete satisfaction. He has, so to speak, not only
to satisfy *them*, but to satisfy himself ; and the self
he has thus to satisfy is not his own individuality as a
being separate from others, but a self which is developed
in him, just in proportion as he makes himself an instru-
ment to the life of others. Hence it is of the very
essence of a moral being that to be himself he must
be more than himself. Shut up within the limits of
purely isolated satisfactions, infinitely the larger part of
his nature remains undeveloped. To realise the capacities of his own being he must take up into it the life of
the other members of the social organism. It is in proportion to the deepening and widening of his sympathies
that his life grows richer and fuller ; and its ideal purity
and perfection are conceivable only as the identification
of himself with a life which is universal and infinite.
But if this be so, then the higher or spiritual life implies
the negation of the lower or natural life. It is impossible to lead at the same time a life that is merely particular and a life that is universal, to be at once bounded
by individual impulses, and giving free play to capacities
that are virtually limitless. In the very act of living
for others we die to self. And as the intellectual life
involves the abandonment of all thought that is merely
our own, so the moral life involves the abnegation of
all desire, volition, action that begins and ends with the
will of the individual self.

Lastly, the religious life is, above all, that which con-
forms to the idea of self-realisation through self-negation.
For if true religion is not the appeasing of an alien
power, or the propitiating of it for the attainment of our

own ends, neither can it be the mere prostration of the finite before the infinite. With Spinoza we can discern that it involves the negation of all that pertains to the individual as " a part of nature " ; and yet admit the justice of his condemnation of asceticism as a *tristis et torva superstitio,* and of his assertion that joy is itself a progress to a greater perfection. We can see a meaning in the doctrine that finite beings have no existence save as vanishing modes of the divine substance, and at the same time in the seemingly contradictory doctrine that the self-affirming impulse, which is the very essence of the finite, reaches its highest activity in absolute union with God. We can perceive, in one word, how the negation of the finite before God, may be the beginning of a process which ends with the reaffirmation of the finite in and through God.

2. Finally, this negation and reaffirmation of the finite through the infinite involves a correlative conception of the divine nature which harmonises elements that in Spinoza appear to be irreconcilable. The unity which transcends and the unity which comprehends all the differences of the finite world ; the God who is at once absolutely undetermined and infinitely determined, beyond whom is no reality, yet from whom an infinite number of things in infinite ways necessarily proceeds, who must be conceived of as the negation of finite thought and being, yet who expresses or reveals Himself in nature and in the human mind,—is there any point of view from which ideas so discordant can be harmonised ? Can thought compass a conception which will read a meaning at once into the featureless, moveless infinite whose eternal repose no breath of living

thought or feeling can disturb, and into the infinite, who knows and loves Himself in His creatures with an infinite "intellectual love"? The answer is, that what Spinoza was feeling after through all these contradictory expressions, is to be found in the conception of God as absolute Spirit. For when we examine what this conception means, we shall find that it includes at once what Spinoza sought in the unity which lies beyond all determinations and in the unity which is itself the source of all the determinations of the finite world. All philosophy must rest on the presupposition of the ultimate unity of knowing and being—on the principle, in other words, that there is in the intelligible universe no absolute or irreconcilable division, no element which in its hard, irreducible independence is incapable of being embraced in the intelligible totality or system of things. All the manifold distinctions of things and thoughts must be so conceived of as to be capable of being comprehended in one organic whole—capable, that is, in the utmost diversity that can be ascribed to them, of being brought back to unity. All philosophy, moreover, which is not atheistic, must find that ultimate unity in the idea of God. Without rending the universe and falling into dualism, whatever reality and independence are ascribed to nature and man, that reality and independence must not only have its source in God, but must not be pressed beyond the point at which it is still consistent with the relation of all things to God. To say that God is absolutely infinite, is to say that in His nature must be contained a reason for the existence of the finite world, and also that nothing in the finite world can have or retain any existence or reality that is outside of God.

What this implies is an idea of the nature of God as a unity which reveals, yet maintains and realises, itself in all the distinctions of the finite world. Now the one idea which perfectly fulfils this condition is that of God as infinite, self-conscious Spirit. For only in thought or self-consciousness have we a unity whose nature it is to be infinitely determined, yet which in all its determinations never goes beyond itself, but in all this multiplicity and variety is only and ever realising itself. Of this unity we find the type, though only the imperfect type, in our own minds. The philosophic interpretation of the world may be said to be the application to nature and man of a principle with whose action we are conversant in our own intelligence. It is of the very nature of thought to reveal itself, to give itself objectivity, to discover to itself its own inherent wealth by going forth to objects that are opposed to, and in one sense external and foreign to itself. Mind or intelligence is no abstract, self-contained identity, having its whole reality in its own self-included being. A consciousness that is conscious of nothing, a thinking subject which opposes to itself no external object, is a mere blank, an abstraction which has no reality. Without a world of objects in time and space, without other kindred intelligences, without society and history, without the ever-moving mirror of the external world, consciousness could never exist, mind could never awaken from the slumber of unconsciousness and become aware of itself. But it is also of the very nature of mind in all this endless objectivity to maintain itself. The self that thinks is never borne away from or lost to itself and its own oneness in the

objects of its thought. It is the one constant in their
ever-changing succession, the indivisible unity whose presence to them reclaims them from chaos. But further,
it not only maintains but realises itself in and through
the objects it contemplates. They are *its own* objects.
If it begins by opposing the world to itself, its next
movement is to retract the opposition, to annul the
seeming foreignness, to find itself therein. Knowledge
is a revelation, not simply of the world to the observing mind, but of the observing mind to itself. Those
unchangeable relations which we call laws of nature are
nothing foreign to thought; they are rational or intelligible relations, discoveries to the intelligence that
grasps them of a realm that is its own, of which in the
very act of apprehending them it comes into possession.
And still more do our social relations in the family, the
community, the state, become to us a revelation of ourselves, a revelation of a life which, though in one sense
other and larger than our own, is still our own. Thus
the whole process of knowledge is a gradual annulling
by the mind of that self-externality which is thought's
first attitude towards the outward world, and a gradual
self-creation or realisation of its own content. Consciousness, in other words, through the mediation of
externality realises itself or becomes self-consciousness.

Now the principle with whose action in our own
consciousness we are thus conversant is one which is
applicable, not simply to our intelligence, but to all
intelligence, and above all to that intelligence of which
our own is the highest finite expression. It is the
essential characteristic of spirit as spirit to be object to
itself, to go forth into objectivity and return upon itself.

To conceive of God as an abstract, self-identical infinite
would be to make Him not greater but less than finite
intelligence—less by all that spiritual wealth which is
involved in our relations to nature and man.    The
abstract or merely quantitative infinite excludes the
consciousness of any existence other than itself.    It
can remain "secure of itself" only by the reduction of
all finite thought and being to unreality and illusion.
But the infinitude which is preserved only by the absolute negation of the finite world is a barren infinitude.
Its greatness is the greatness of a metaphysical figment,
the greatness which is attained by leaving out from it
all those elements of life and thought and love which
constitute the wealth of a spiritual nature.    On the
other hand, an infinite whose essence is intelligence or
self-consciousness, whilst it contains in it the necessity of
relation to a finite world, is not limited by that necessity.
For in so conceiving of it, as we have seen, the limitation
we ascribe to it is a limitation which is the medium of
its own self-realisation—a going forth from itself which
is no lessening or loss, but only a step in the process by
which it returns upon itself in a complete fulness of
being.    Viewed in the light of this conception, nature
and man are neither severed from God nor lost in God,
but have all their significance as expressing or manifesting God.    The external world, instead of being deprived
of reality, is endowed with that highest reality which
arises from this, that from the lowest inorganic matter
to the highest forms of organic life, reason or thought
underlies it; and that ideal unity of nature which
science partially discloses, which art, by its imaginative
creations, foreshadows, is only then clearly apprehended

when we recognise it as the unity of one spiritual principle, one infinite self-consciousness which goes forth to
the utmost verge of self-externality in a world that exists
under the conditions of space and time, yet in all this
manifold objectivity remains ever one with itself. Above
all, in the light of this idea of God as infinite Spirit we
can see how man has a being and reality of his own,
which yet is no limit to the nature of God, but the only
medium of its complete manifestation. For only in the
communication of its own life to kindred intelligence is
there what can be termed, in the full sense of the word,
a *revelation* of the Being whose nature is thought and
love. Only in its relation to finite intelligence do we
see the veil removed from that twofold movement—that
going forth from itself and return upon itself which is
the very life of infinite Spirit. Only in man does the
divine Spirit go forth from itself; for what God gives
to man is nothing less than Himself, a reproduction of
His own nature, a participation in His own life and
being. Thought, indeed, in us is limited in this sense,
that the knowable world exists independently of our
knowledge of it, and that there are boundless possibilities
of knowledge which for us have not become actual; but
in the very fact that thought or self-consciousness can be
limited by nothing which lies outside of itself, that every
conceivable advance in knowledge is only a realisation of
ourselves, and that the very consciousness of our limits
implies that there is that in us which transcends them—
in this lies the proof that it is of the essence of finite
spirit to share in the infinitude from which it springs.
Yet in this communication of Himself to man there is no
outflow from the infinite source which does not return

upon itself. Without life in the life of others spirit
would not be truly spirit. In spiritual life, giving and
receiving, loss and gain, self-surrender and self-enrich-
ment are ideas which implicate and pass into each other.
Infinite intelligence is not limited but fulfilled by the
existence of finite, for, as we have seen, it is the characteristic of the latter that to realise itself it must abnegate
itself. To renounce every thought and volition that is
merely its own, to become the transparent medium of
the infinite mind and will, to be conscious of its distinction from God only that it may return into indivisible
unity with God—this is its only possible way to self-
realisation. For this self-abnegation, rightly interpreted,
is not the subjugation of the finite intelligence to an outward and absolute authority, but it reaches its perfection
when the thought and will to which it surrenders itself
is recognised as its own—in it as well as above it ; when
it is not two concurrent voices that speak in its thought,
but the one voice of infinite reason; when duty has ceased
to be self-denial, and the dictates of the absolute will
blend indivisibly with the affirmation of its own. In so
far as this ideal is realised it may be said that in the
utmost activity of the spiritual life in man God never
breaks through the charmed circle of His own infinitude.
It is His own knowledge that is reflected in the human
mind, His own love that comes back upon Him through
the channel of human hearts. It is not the finite as
finite which God knows and loves, nor the finite as
finite which seeks to be known and loved, but the
finite which is transfigured with an infinite element, the
finite that is not a thing of time, but that is and knows
itself under the form of eternity. We have here a point

of view in which the contradictions under which Spinoza's thought seems ever to labour can be regarded as the accidents of an unconscious struggle after a deeper principle in which they are solved and harmonised. In the light of that principle we can speak with him of an indeterminate and infinite unity in which all finite distinctions lose themselves, and with him we can see that there is no paradox in the assertion that "he who loves God does not desire that God should love him in return." We can discern at the same time a profound meaning in those apparently mystical utterances in which he seems to gather up the final result of his speculation—"God loves Himself with an infinite intellectual love;" "God in so far as He loves Himself loves man;" "the intellectual love of the mind to God is part of the infinite love wherewith God loves Himself;" "the love of God to man and the intellectual love of man to God are one and the same."

END OF SPINOZA.